Introduction to United States Public Documents

LIBRARY SCIENCE TEXT SERIES

Introduction to Public Services for Library Technicians. By Marty Bloomberg.

Introduction to Technical Services for Library Technicians. 2nd ed. By Marty Bloomberg and G. Edward Evans.

A Guide to the Library of Congress Classification. 2nd ed. By J. Phillip Immroth.

Science and Engineering Reference Sources: A Guide for Students and Librarians. By Harold Robert Malinowsky.

The Vertical File and Its Satellites: A Handbook of Acquisition, Processing and Organization. By Shirley Miller.

The School Library Media Center. By Emanuel T. Prostano and Joyce S. Prostano.

The Humanities: A Selective Guide to Information Sources. By A. Robert Rogers.

The School Library and Educational Change. By Martin Rossoff.

Introduction to Cataloging and Classification. 4th rev. ed. By Bohdan S. Wynar.

Joe Morehead

INTRODUCTION TO

United States Public Documents

1975

LIBRARIES UNLIMITED, INC.   Littleton, Colo.

LIBRARIES UNLIMITED, INC.
P.O. Box 263
Littleton, Colorado 80120

Library of Congress Cataloging in Publication Data

Morehead, Joe, 1931–
    Introduction to United States public documents.

    (Library science text series)
    Includes bibliographical references and index.
    1.   United States–Government publications.
2.   United States.   Government Printing Office.
I.   Title.
Z1223.Z7M67   015'.73   74-23628
ISBN 0-87287-106-1 lib. bdg.

PREFACE

The need for a contemporary treatise on federal publications has long been felt and acknowledged. A number of sources have dealt with aspects of public documents; this work attempts to delineate the relationship between the production and distribution of government materials and their control, access, and management in libraries and information centers. The signal assumption in this presentation is that the records of government activity are intended for the education of the citizen in our society. Accordingly, the purpose of this work is to set forth an introductory account of public documents, their locus, diffusion, habitation, and use.

Every effort has been made to suggest the ubiquity of federal government materials as basic sources of information. Because virtually all libraries acquire some public documents, any category of library, regardless of its size or mission, can use the text as a guide. It provides the beginning librarian with an introduction and the experienced practitioner with a source of new or forgotten information. Finally, the organization and content are designed to serve as a basic text for the library school student and as a guide for the student in other academic disciplines.

The organization of the text reflects the problems of government documents with regard to issuance and public utility. The early chapters focus on the control of documents in an institutional setting; the later chapters emphasize the production and dissemination of materials administered through the complex instrumentalities of government. The conceptual design for the chapters that deal with specific titles and series is based upon the principle of provenance—the responsible issuing unit within the structure and hierarchy of the federal edifice. It is hoped that the perspective thus afforded will illumine the bibliographic, research, and reference enterprise.

A project of this kind is, in a genuine sense, a joint effort; I am profoundly indebted to all those individuals with whom I have worked, corresponded, and spoken, and from whom I have sought knowledge and advice over the last decade.

Several persons have been of considerable assistance to me in the preparation of this treatise: James Bennett Childs, emeritus bibliographer in government publications at the Library of Congress; LeRoy C. Schwarzkopf, documents librarian at the University of Maryland's McKeldin Library; and John L. Andriot, whose works are universally known and appreciated in the documents world. Their many kindnesses and wise suggestions made my task significantly less difficult.

Grateful appreciation is due the following individuals in the various stages of preparation and completion of this work: John Courtney, my graduate assistant, for his research help during the writing; Marilyn Cohan for her nonpareil typing of the manuscript; Professor Dorothy Cole, School of Library and Information Science, SUNY at Albany, for her assistance in the preparation of the index; Sally Wynkoop, esteemed editor, for her direction and redoubtable editorial skills; Ann Harwell, whose copy-editing has proved most salutary, and Judy Caraghar, through whose careful typesetting and skillful artwork a typescript became a book.

Shortcomings in the design and content of the work are, of course, my responsibility alone.

Joe Morehead

TABLE OF CONTENTS

1—GOVERNMENT PRINTING OFFICE, 1

2—SUPERINTENDENT OF DOCUMENTS, 12

3–DEPOSITORY LIBRARY SYSTEM, 29

4—ADMINISTERING DOCUMENTS COLLECTIONS, 49

5—GENERAL GUIDES TO FEDERAL PUBLICATIONS, 75

6—LEGISLATIVE BRANCH MATERIALS, 91

7—PUBLICATIONS OF THE PRESIDENCY, 148

8–DEPARTMENT AND AGENCY PUBLICATIONS, 169

9–DOCUMENTS OF INDEPENDENT AND REGULATORY AGENCIES, 211

10–REPORTS OF ADVISORY COMMITTEES AND COMMISSIONS, 229

11—PUBLICATIONS OF THE JUDICIARY, 240

LIST OF ILLUSTRATIONS

for Bebe and Adam
and
for my parents

INTRODUCTION

Governments must be seen to exist. They publish numerous records of their activities as a way of establishing and validating their existence. Presumably the documents they issue are meant to be read, at least by those for whom they are intended. Certainly they are meant to be retained, and implicit in their preservation is the act of retrieval. Whether written for the few or the many, whether issued in small or in large quantity, and whether deposited in one place or in a number of locations, publications of governments are putatively a matter of public record. But access to this record is often more a theoretical ideal than a matter of easy right.

As governments are impelled to publish and obliged to disseminate symbolic evidence of their claim to legitimacy, institutions such as libraries are required, by regulation and by professional mandate, to house their publications and to make them available to all who have a need to know. But the manner by which the former is accomplished affects significantly the means of executing the latter. Librarians may have a small voice in changing the odd and often inscrutable way in which governments choose to reveal their actions through their published records, but they are pledged to employ all necessary measures to insure reasonable control and access.

Yet governments have a penchant for concealing their activities from public scrutiny. Indeed, the central paradox that informs government publishing is the need at once to reveal and to conceal. Librarians thus have a dual task, that of mastering the apparatus of control over what is revealed while seeking diligently to ferret out what has been withheld. The principles that animate the efforts of the Government Documents Round Table of the American Library Association are worthy testimony to this dual obligation.

It is not enough to complain that governments fail to produce and distribute documents for the benefit of libraries and their public, nor is it profitable to decry the absence of logic in the processes of production and dissemination. For principalities will never effect an easy congruence of their recorded conduct to the satisfaction of their recipients, while the idea of a wholly rational decision-making process in governments is an intellectual fiction. That the world of documents is not Panglossian suggests neither reason for despair nor cause for apathy. While there are no sure solutions to the control and access processes, there are bibliographic instruments that can be learned. Documents librarianship is that most exasperating and rewarding of all tasks, for the peculiar challenge that one faces in this discipline is the need to be a "generalist" in areas that encompass the whole of recorded information. The knowledgeable documents librarian is a necessity, the highly skilled practitioner an exemplar of virtuosity in the profession.

Of the universe of documents printed and issued by governments, federal publications enjoy the greatest control and access. Compared to the publications of states and municipalities, the bibliographic apparatus of United States public documents is relatively sophisticated and largely amenable to mastery. Consider, first, some definitions of a government publication, offered in the attempt to encompass the scope of federal documents and to distinguish them from other written records:

> "Government Publications" as used in this chapter, means informational matter which is published as an individual document at Government expense, or as required by law.[1]

*

> Any publication printed at Government expense or published by authority of Congress or any Government publishing office, or of which an edition has been bought by Congress or any Government office for division among Members of Congress or distribution to Government officials or the public, shall be considered a public document.[2]

*

> A government publication is a publication: (1) bearing the imprint of the Government Printing Office or printed at the Government Printing Office for the use of a government agency; (2) or a publication bearing the name, imprint or seal of a government agency and recognized and used by such an agency in its operations or distributed officially in the course of government business; the aforementioned criteria shall apply regardless of whether it was printed at the Government Printing Office or whether the cost of the printing was charged to government or private funds; (3) or a publication which is issued by a commercial establishment, organization, journal, or individual and of which an edition or reprint is

obtained by a government unit, provided the reprint or official edition bears the printed name, imprint, or seal of the agency concerned; it shall not include reprints which are purchased by the government, but which do not contain the printed name, imprint, or seal of the agency distributing it; the fact that a government officer or employee is the author of the article shall not operate to make the article a government publication.[3]

To the word "printed" as used in the above definitions must be added the term "processed." In the early 1930s this word began to appear in both the *Monthly Catalog* and the biennial *Document Catalog* to indicate those documents produced by duplicating methods other than printing—mimeographing, multigraphing, multilithing and the like. The growth of processed publications in recent years has been dramatic. Moreover, advances in technology further modify and refine the definitions; government materials represent an unstable, ever-changing mass that appears and reappears in new guises, peripheral associations, and quasi-official forms. The uninitiated may view attempts to define a government publication as an exercise in academic punctilio, but these attempts become necessary in decisions of record-keeping, storage, and general library policy.

Another problem central to government publications is that of bibliographic control, which involves "the constant and never-ending need to determine when and by what act the agencies were and are being established, and which are currently instrumentalities of the federal government."[4] The dynamics of change have a profound effect upon the proper assignment of government materials, for even when a publication has been adequately defined its provenance must be accurately ascertained. Government reorganization often plays havoc with the appropriate control of materials. Because the government seems almost willfully to ignore the librarian's need for precision and specificity, efforts must be made to devise and refine an apparatus that yields access and retrieval.

Considerations of organization, administration, control, access and reference capabilities are ineluctably one. Although the parts of this work will perforce be presented discretely, it is hoped that the organization will provide the reader with a conceptual overview in which the function and place of public documents can be made manifest. Throughout, the words and phrases "government publications," "materials," "reports," and "public documents" are used synonymously save where specificity requires otherwise, as in the Serial Set. This is consciously done as a stylistic device to minimize the monotony of repetition. The author prefers the phrase "public documents" as a more realistic connotation of records that are available to individuals and institutions; publications of government that are physically or otherwise inaccessible are of no value to the public.

Since this is an introductory text, the author seeks to do no more than present the contours of documents and their distinctive characteristics; the cited materials are exemplary rather than definitive. Chapters 1 through 4 attempt to describe the administrative machinery by which both government and libraries manage and execute the transfer of government information. Chapter 5 introduces the reader to some of the general guides in the process of control. The remaining chapters consider the major public documents that issue from the five acknowledged arms of the federal establishment.

No one can gain mastery of federal documents by perusing a text; skills that the documents librarian must possess require the day-to-day practice that comes only with professional service. The rewards of working with public documents far outweigh the frustrations; it is hoped that this prologue to the working situation will better acquaint the reader with the structure of the entities whence these unfailingly interesting and variegated materials issue.

REFERENCES

1. 44 *U.S.C.* 1901.
2. *Checklist of United States Public Documents, 1789-1909* (3d ed., rev. & enl.; Washington: Govt. Print. Off., 1911).
3. L. F. Schmeckebier, "Some Problems of Government Publications," in A.L.A. Committee on Public Documents, *Public Documents* (Chicago: American Library Assn., 1936), pp. 28-29.
4. J. B. Childs, "Bibliographic Control of Federal, State and Local Documents," *Library Trends* 15: 6 (July 1966).

1

GOVERNMENT PRINTING OFFICE

If you stand on Capitol Hill, at the top of the high flight of stairs leading into the Senate, and look straight north, you will see the Government Printing Office. It is in dreary contrast to the pure whiteness of the Capitol. A long rectangle of sooty brick, domineered by a scorched cupola, from whose apparent ashes rises the Phoenix of a gilt eagle. . . . Making a straight way from Capitol Hill across Tiber Creek, which you will cross by stepping-stones deposited in its basin, and taking a footpath across lots where geese and pigs browse upon plentiful barrenness, you will reach the printing-house in 10 or 15 minutes, and hear the hum of its machinery.

The near exterior view is no better than the remote one. A huge factory of red brick, about 350 feet long, with the gables and one side facing separate streets, and the other side fenced up to enclose boiler houses, paper storehouses, wagon-sheds, wastepaper barracks, and an accessory wing for stereotyping and for a machine shop—this is all that a passing pedestrian knows of the GPO.

—John B. Ellis, *Sights and Secrets of the National Capital*
(New York: U.S. Publishing Company, 1869)

INTRODUCTION

For sundry reasons pure and impure, significant and trivial, apposite and impertinent, the effects of government action or decision are made manifest through the visible symbols of documents. The publications of the federal establishment "probably exceed those of any other government or of any commercial publisher."[1] But their production, a ceaseless, worldwide activity, takes place in the thousands of agencies and other administrative entities with

1

printing plants and duplicating or mimeographing capabilities. Accordingly, when we speak of the Government Printing Office (GPO) as the major publisher of federal documents, we are considering an enterprise that, by the best estimates, accounts for less than one-half of all government printing.[2]

Indeed, the word *publisher* should perhaps be avoided in discussions of the generation and distribution of government publications. To the recipient of government documents, institutional or individual, the GPO in Washington, D.C., personifies the locus of production and distribution, but that is a convenient oversimplification. A myriad of government units prints and disseminates documents wholly outside the control and confines of the GPO. The GPO itself is responsible for certain important field printing and contract printing activities, including commercially procured work, so that the term "government printing" is less a geographical distinction than an administrative one.

As the aegis of GPO responsibility and control has become more confusing with the proliferation of documents, so too has the definition of a "government publication" become more difficult to fix with precision. Nevertheless, the GPO's main printing plant and headquarters are in the nation's capital, the directives for printing issue from those offices, and the Washington, D.C., complex houses the *single* largest facility for the production of government materials. Moreover, this locus is also the seat of the Public Documents Department, where the Superintendent of Documents manages the sales program and the depository library program. For librarians, the GPO in this sense is identified most conspicuously, and this is where any discussion of the world of federal documents must begin.

BACKGROUND

During the eighteenth century, printing was still an infant art; an expert printer, working hard, could hope to accomplish but two or three pages of composition a day. Printing for the early Congresses was handled entirely by private firms. Among these, the firm of Gales and Seaton dominated the printing of congressional proceedings from 1789 to 1818, but the imprint of several other establishments was carried on congressional documents for this period. In 1818 a congressional committee recommended the creation of a government printing office, in order "to produce promptitude, uniformity, accuracy and elegance in the execution of the public printing" for "the work of Congress . . . and that of the various departments." The current system of low bidder, the committee reported, created delays and a product "executed in such an inelegant and incorrect manner, as must bring disgrace and ridicule on the literature, and the press of our country."[3] But nothing came of the proposal, and "half a century would pass before these words would be implemented by action."[4]

Despite a number of acts that Congress passed during the first half of the nineteenth century in an attempt to bring some integrity into the commercial printing of government documents, the system was increasingly beset with corruption and patronage. Profiteering, waste, and egregious inefficiency flourished until Congress passed and President Buchanan signed into law the Printing Act of 1860. The act created a Superintendent of Public Printing to manage the official printing and binding "authorized by the Senate and House of Representatives, the executive and judicial departments, and the Court of Claims." The officers of this new agency were enjoined not to "have any interest, direct or indirect, in the publication of any newspaper or periodical" or other binding, engraving, or procurement activities that would suggest a conflict of interest. If the new Superintendent were to "corruptly collude" with private publishers, a fine and penitentiary sentence awaited him.[5] With these sober warnings, the doors of the GPO were officially opened on March 4, 1861, the same day Abraham Lincoln was inaugurated, on the eve of the Civil War.

In the years following the end of the civil conflict, a number of amendments to the 1860 act attempted to effect firmer control over public printing. Congress in 1876 changed the title of the chief officer to that of Public Printer, the position to be filled by presidential appointment with the advice and consent of the Senate. By 1890, over 1,800 people were employed at the GPO, which was now being bruited in periodical accounts as "the largest printing office in the world." And in 1895 Congress passed a comprehensive act codifying the public printing laws in force and creating the office of Superintendent of Documents.

The Printing Act of 1895 represented the second significant piece of legislation on public printing. In addition to its landmark provisions of the creation of the Public Documents office and the beginnings of a formal depository library system, it consolidated the control and power of the Public Printer as the principal agent for the production of documents. Despite the fact that the 1860 act vested the GPO with the authority to handle "all government printing," a number of agencies were still securing private firms for their publications. Since 1860, however, some units within the federal executive branch had been discovering that the GPO produced a better product at a lower cost, and they began to divert their printing to the young office. The new act placed all federal printing offices under the control of the Public Printer—"those then in operation and any that might be put in operation later." Certain agencies were excepted from this regulation, but the Printer was now empowered to abolish any other printing operations when in his judgment—with the approval of the Joint Committee on Printing—"the economy of the public service would be thereby advanced." With the act of 1895 the primacy of the GPO as printer and publisher for all congressional and much agency printing was clearly intended, and it was thought that the centralization of printing was accomplished.[6]

Over the years, the centralization and control which the Printing Act mandated rapidly deteriorated. Nevertheless, the act of 1895, with the usual amendments refining this and that procedure or introducing a nuance for expediency, served as the basic legal instrument for the activities of the Public Printer until 1962, when major changes in sections of the earlier act were effected. But these changes had more impact upon the depository library program than upon the functions of the Printer. With the passage of time, the GPO has undergone important, even crucial, changes that affect libraries apart from the role of the Public Documents Department within the GPO's organizational structure. It is to these recent developments that our attention will be directed. In perspective, this brief sketch of GPO history does scant justice to the interesting and often colorful record of "the largest printing office in the world." Two authoritative accounts of the GPO are found in the authorized version, *100 GPO Years, 1861-1961: A History of United States Public Printing* (Washington: Govt. Print. Off., 1961), and in a work by Robert E. Kling, Jr., *The Government Printing Office* (New York: Praeger, 1970). The former is a chronological report of GPO activities, with numerous citations from the laws enacted over that period, plus accounts from newspapers and other secondary sources that described the unfolding drama. The latter, written by a former Superintendent of Documents, draws heavily upon *100 GPO Years* and carries the story up to 1970.

THE GPO TODAY

Functions

The mission of the GPO is to provide the printing and binding services required by the Congress and the various government departments in accordance with law and with the Government Printing and Binding Regulations. That law has been codified in Title 44 of the *United States Code*, Public Printing and Documents. In order to accomplish this mission, the Public Printer is required to have sufficient equipment and an adequate complement of trained graphic arts employees to meet the peak-load requirements for the Congress and the urgent needs of the departments. These services, which include the furnishing of blank paper, inks, and similar supplies to all governmental activities on order, cover specifically all congressional work, the bulk of which is produced on very close schedules in order to meet "must" delivery dates.[7] Within the organization of the GPO, the Public Documents Department functions as a unit with its own separate appropriation, but the Public Printer is responsible for its operation.

The GPO is the child of Congress. As early as 1875, Chief Justice Morrison R. Waite, ruling on the GPO's true position in relation to the federal establishment, declared:

> In short, the GPO superintendent seems to have a department of his own, in which he is in a sense supreme. Certainly he is not under control of any of the executive departments. Apparently he is more responsible to Congress than to any other authority.[8]

In 1932, a Comptroller General's decision stated that the GPO was indeed a part of the legislative branch not subject to legislation applicable only to the executive departments and independent establishments of the government. Without doubt the GPO is an anomaly in the federal administrative system—while the Public Printer is a presidential appointee, the President does not exercise direct or delegated control of the GPO's management.[9]

The Congressional Joint Committee on Printing (JCP) acts as the supervisory body for the GPO, its "board of directors." The JCP "not only has statutory authority over the classes of work done outside of the GPO, as well as full authority over the establishment of printing capabilities elsewhere in government, but contracts between the GPO and commercial contractors also must be approved by JCP." Moreover, the JCP is charged by law with employing "any measure it considers necessary to remedy neglect, delay, duplication, or waste in the public printing and binding and the distribution of Government publications."[10]

Obeisance to the Congress is reinforced annually when the Public Printer and the Superintendent of Documents go, hat in hand, to testify before House and Senate subcommittees on legislative branch appropriations and defend their budgetary requests for the forthcoming fiscal year. The published hearings of this testimony provide the best single source of information about the activities and plans of the GPO and are available to depository libraries. Hearings before the House subcommittee carry a Superintendent of Documents classification of Y4.Ap 6/1: L 52/year and are sent to depository libraries under Item 101i. The counterpart hearings in the Senate (Y4.Ap 6/2: L 51/year; Item 1033) cover much the same ground, but the House hearings are usually more detailed.

Operations

A small number of field printing facilities, located on federal property, handles minor requests, primarily of a local nature, that can be carried out more efficiently and with less cost than either commercial procurement or the main Washington plant could do. Most field printing work consists of overnight or daily jobs in small quantities. Usually these documents are for local or even internal consumption, but there are notable exceptions. The valuable periodical *Commerce Business Daily* is printed at the Chicago field service facility but enjoys nationwide distribution. Similarly, GPO's Denver facility has for several years been printing civil service examinations. In each case the dictates of expediency and inexpensive operation loom paramount.

Regional printing procurement offices are operational in ten regions throughout the country. They act as brokerage houses; their officials are authorized to advertise for bids or set up an "open-end" contract with commercial printers in the region. Contracts for commercially procured printing have increased, and the trend has been justified as good fiscal policy and good politics. Since the regional procurement system was initiated in 1968, Public Printers have testified that the operation is both efficient and cheap. An estimated 90 percent of commercial printers are categorized as "small businesses" and the GPO works in concert with the Small Business Administration to insure the viability of the arrangement.[11]

A superficial glance at a roomful of government publications shows that documents come in a bewildering assortment of shapes and sizes. Each printing order becomes a "separate custom-made job," and the flexibility of commercial procurement combined with GPO field printing insures a good product. If materials are of an unclassified nature, are not required by an agency in a hurry, and are to be printed in an amount that secures the printer a margin of profit, they are let out on a competitive bid basis. In 1961, the percentage of commercially procured printing was 42.5 of the total GPO production; now it is well over 50 percent. Indeed, the JCP is committed to the continuing expansion of commercially procured government printing. In his first official appearance as Public Printer, Thomas F. McCormick addressed a conference sponsored by Printing Industries of America; he struck a responsive chord with his audience when he affirmed his support of the JCP mandate. "Much of my personal attention will be directed toward improving and enlarging the GPO regional printing procurement program through which millions of dollars in printing contracts flow annually to commercial printing and publishing industries. It appears to be just good business sense to insure a successful relationship between government and the commercial printing industry. I intend to foster this program."[12] There is a historical irony in this increasing reliance upon commercial printers; the GPO was conceived to thwart the rapacious inefficiency of commercial profiteering.

Documents produced for the government by commercial means still carry the GPO imprint. They are *not* to be confused with the large class of "non-GPO" publications produced by the facilities of agencies independent of the GPO. The nature and significance of non-GPO documents in the overall publishing role of the federal establishment will be discussed in Chapter 3.

Computer Technology

The GPO today is regarded as a leader in the graphic arts industry. Indeed, it is obliged to evince leadership in this area, for it has been the single largest contributor to the "print explosion." Although the GPO is consistently underfunded by Congress, it yet has the money to pioneer in printing techniques not available to commercial printing houses. But the devouring appetite of the government's publishing ventures threatens continually to stretch existing technologies to the limit of their capabilities.

The chief time-consumer in the printing process is composition—the conversion of manuscript copy to some finished graphic form. A book page can be set into type in about fifteen minutes by a competent linotype operator, but the composing process, including proofreading, correction, and verification, is lengthy and complex. Accordingly, technological emphasis has concentrated upon shortening and simplifying this process. In 1962 the Public Printer convened a committee to study and recommend a solution to the problems that stem from the reproduction of material produced by high-speed printers on automatic data processing equipment. The committee proposed "a high-speed electronic phototypesetting device operating from magnetic tapes which would produce a fully-formatted page of hard copy," and bids were invited. An award was made to the Mergenthaler Linotype Company, which teamed with CBS Laboratories on the project, and in 1967 the "Linotron" was born.[13]

The Linotron is the fastest, largest, and most expensive photocomposing machine in the printing industry. It is a custom-made electronic photo-typesetting machine that can almost effortlessly link the modern high-speed computer to the old art of printing. The material to be printed arrives at the machine in the form of encoded magnetic tape from other departmental computers. On instruction from the computer tape, the Linotron finds the character and typeface desired and at computer speed sets the document a page at a time. Each one thousand characters can be set electronically in any of eight print sizes in a second. What emerges is a film strip that is ready to be developed and turned into hard copy.

A second Linotron system was placed in operation in 1969. By 1970, a former Public Printer was able to state that the systems had saved enough money in two years of operation to be self-sustaining. The acceleration of the printing process by computerized composition has been dramatic. In 1974 the Superintendent of Documents noted that "a page of the Chicago Telephone Directory consisting of approximately 22,000 characters would be completed in about 20 seconds, or at the rate of three pages per minute." Moreover, the system permits reduction of the number of printed pages by almost 40 percent; this translates into fewer negatives, fewer plates, less presswork, less paper and, ultimately, lower costs. In fiscal year 1974 the GPO composed over three-quarters of a million pages on the two Linotron systems.[14]

Micropublishing

In 1970 the Public Printer secured permission from the Joint Committee on Printing to study the feasibility of making GPO publications available in microform. The advisory committee that was formed, which included representatives from the Library of Congress and the American Library Association, recommended to the GPO that a dual micrographic system incorporating the standard 98-frame, 105 x 148.75mm microfiche and roll microfilm be considered. Moreover, the committee suggested that distribution of the microforms be made optional to depository libraries.

Commercial firms in the micropublishing business view any move by the GPO to supply libraries with free or cheap copies of documents on micro-facsimile as a threat to their survival. As late as October 1973, the problem of where to proceed in this venture remained unresolved. Part II of the 1973 *Biennial Report of Depository Libraries* was a questionnaire designed to determine the interest of the library community in receiving certain categories of documents in microform. Solutions to this problem need to be arrived at with care, for a full-scale micropublishing program by the GPO has momentous and probably irreversible consequences for libraries and information centers.

While clarification of the larger issues continues, in late 1972 the Superintendent of Documents offered for sale its first microfilm publication— *Postal Rate and Fee Increases, 1971*, the complete record of the Postal Rate Commission's hearings on the subject. The proceedings were made available in sets of three microfilm reels at $12.00 per set (Y3.P84/4:2 Un3/micro.; S/N 5262-0002). The announcement that carried the sales notice promised more documents in *microfilm* in the future. The Public Printer, however, leans toward a standardized fiche.

Facilities

Worrying about and fighting for adequate physical facilities has informed much of the GPO's history. When Cornelius Wendell was elected printer for the House of Representatives in 1857, he "erected at a very great expense, and doubtless with much risk as to the future productiveness of the investment of capital, the most complete and extensive printing establishment on this continent."[15] Located at North Capitol and H Streets in Washington, it was purchased by the government through authorization of the 1860 printing act and became the first GPO. At the time its facilities were considered ample to execute all work required by both Houses of Congress "and also to perform any work which might be obtained from private sources." Two years later Public Printer John D. Defrees was making a plea for more space.

The Civil War brought a large increase in printing and binding requirements. Moreover, other agencies were sending more and more of their work to the GPO because of its superior product. In 1869 the GPO took over a U.S. Treasury printing plant and in the process acquired both electrotype and stereotype equipment; the following year the plant at the Navy Department and that of the Paymaster General were placed under GPO control. Despite these additions, the clamor for a larger main plant grew. Congress in 1871 appropriated funds for enlarging the present site by one-third, at a cost of $45,000. Not enough, cried the Public Printer the following year, but this time "Congress turned a deaf ear to his complaints."[16]

During the last three decades of the nineteenth century, minor alterations were made to the existing structure while the several Public Printers agitated for a new building. In 1898 the Congress appropriated $225,000 for the purchase of land for an additional building and an amount "not exceeding $2 million" was voted for construction. The Chief of Engineers of the Army designed the structure, construction began in 1899, and the building was occupied in 1903.[17] Situated on North Capitol and G Streets, it solved only momentarily the critical space problem. In 1930 a new eight-story building was erected on G Street west of the 1903 structure. By this time, the need to replace the original GPO building, now an old dilapidated storehouse and fire hazard, was urgent. In 1936 the JCP approved an initial appropriation for a new, fireproof building, including money for a warehouse. In 1939 the Public Printer laid the cornerstone of the new edifice in appropriate ceremonies. A sealed copper box placed in the cornerstone contained a Bible, a flag, photographs of President Roosevelt and Public Printer Augustus E. Giegengack, annual reports of the Public Printer, a roster of employees, the *Congressional Directory* for the 76th Congress, 1st session, a copy of the *Congressional Record* for February 20, 1939, the *Official Register*, copies of all Washington newspapers, and "sundry other publications." The warehouse and the new main building were completed in 1938 and 1940, respectively.[18]

If space was a recurrent theme in the history of the GPO, it reached major proportions as an issue during the decade of the 1960s. During the last decade, the Public Printer viewed the annexation of existing facilities as a short-range solution of dubious merit. The desired solution, relocation, was judged favorably by the JCP, who established criteria: a new site should be no more than 30 minutes from the Capitol; the tract was to be served by rail; and sufficient acreage to satisfy a one-production-level concept was needed. Because both the Public Printer and the JCP agreed that the new site should be government-owned rather than leased, the bureaucratic maze mandated that the coordination to effect this plan should involve the General Services Administration's Public Buildings Service, the Public Works committees of both houses of Congress, and, of course, the Appropriations committees. As the planning progressed, these were joined by the National Capital Planning Commission, the Defense Department, the Justice Department's Bureau of Prisons, the House Armed Services Committee and the Penn Central Railroad.[19]

In 1969 the JCP approved a site in Prince Georges County, but the expense involved and the problem of transporting "a large number of our low-paid employees" to work and back were deemed formidable. Alternate plans involved finding a site in the District of Columbia for a new facility or expanding the present location. By 1971 the Public Printer was able to report to the congressional subcommittee on legislative branch appropriations that a decision had been made to stay at North Capitol and H. As Public Printer Spence noted, "We can best serve the Congress by being four blocks away rather than some 14 miles, that our physical buildings are good, sound structures, but that they should be expanded so that we can better aline our equipment and put in more modern equipment."[20]

Before the 93d Congress, the most recently appointed Public Printer requested $4.6 million to acquire land adjacent to the GPO and an additional $3.2 million for a design and review study for expanded warehousing facilities. This would consolidate warehousing and permit a smoother flow of work and materials.

The best solution is relocation of the plant. In the 1860s the area around the GPO was known as "Swampoodle," a picturesque sobriquet (probably a corruption of "swamp-puddle") used by early Irish settlers. Near the site a tributary of old Tiber Creek flowed southwest through swampland toward the Capitol, and in the spring the creek overflowed its banks on its upper reaches. It was a dismal area, with its profusion of shanties, grime, geese, and goats. Today barnyard creatures no longer browse and the roads are paved, but the site is a high crime area.

The combination of personnel problems and space difficulties has created an issue that seems to elude satisfactory resolution. The Superintendent of Documents nicely summarized the physical shortcomings by noting that

> We have four buildings ranging in age from 35 years to 70 years. The three main buildings have eight floors with a basement and there are 33 entrances and 37 elevators. Suffice it to say, our physical setup is hardly conducive to the free flow of production.[21]

At the same time, there is a long-standing commitment to keep the activity located in the inner city. "About half the GPO's workers are black, and they have resisted earlier plans to move the operation beyond the Beltway into either Maryland or Virginia." In 1974 GPO officials were looking favorably upon a site in the Brentwood section of the city to the east of New York Avenue and North

Capitol Street. The Government-Industry Advisory Board recommended that Congress allocate up to $16 million to be used for a relocation feasibility study. If approved, such a move would consolidate GPO's 8,500 employees under one roof. Planners say that the new building ideally would have only two or three stories, "and that all printing operations would be located in a football field-sized first floor." Whatever the solution, all parties agree that the present situation is intolerable.[22]

Reports

By authority of 44 *U.S.C.* 309(c) the Public Printer is required to submit to the Congress an annual budget. Pursuant to 44 *U.S.C.* 508 he is required to submit to the Joint Committee on Printing estimates of the quantity of paper of all descriptions needed for the public printing and binding for the ensuing year. The *Annual Report of the Public Printer* is submitted at the beginning of each session, but under authority of 44 *U.S.C.* 1117, the GPO discontinued printing the annual reports in 1947. Consequently, they are not available for distribution to depository libraries. Typewritten copies are available at the GPO for public inspection, and photocopies can be made available to interested persons for a fee.[23]

REFERENCES

1. Laurence F. Schmeckebier and Roy B. Eastin, *Government Publications and Their Use* (2d rev. ed.; Washington: Brookings, 1969), p. 1.

2. U.S. Congress, House, Committee on Appropriations, Subcommittee on Legislative Branch Appropriations, *Legislative Branch Appropriations for 1971*, Hearing, 91st Cong., 2d Sess., March 6, 1970 (Washington: Govt. Print. Off., 1970), p. 558.

3. *100 GPO Years, 1861-1961: A History of United States Public Printing* (Washington: Govt. Print. Off., 1961), p. 15.

4. Robert E. Kling, Jr., *The Government Printing Office* (New York: Praeger, 1970), p. 12.

5. *100 GPO Years*, pp. 31-33.

6. Kling, pp. 33-34.

7. *How to Do Business with the GPO* (rev. October 1970; Washington: Govt. Print. Off., 1970), p. 1.

8. *100 GPO Years*, p. 162.

9. Ibid., p. 163.

10. Kling, p. 136.

11. *Legislative Branch Appropriations for 1971*, pp. 554-57.

12. *Printing News* XC: 4 (March 3, 1973).

13. Kling, pp. 197-200.

14. W. H. Lewis, "Superintendent of Documents on the GPO and Its Plans," *Illinois Libraries* 56: 262 (April 1974).

15. *100 GPO Years*, p. 24.

16.   Kling, pp. 25-26.

17.   Ibid., p. 35.

18.   *100 GPO Years*, pp. 120, 128, 130.

19.   Kling, pp. 187-96.

20.   *Legislative Branch Appropriations for 1972* (House), p. 94.

21.   W. H. Lewis, "Superintendent of Documents on the GPO and Its Plans," p. 260.

22.   Mike Causey, "The Federal Diary," *The Washington Post*, April 2, 1974.

23.   44 *U.S.C.* 1117 permits agencies the option of discontinuing the printing of annual or special reports under their respective jurisdictions "in order to keep expenditures for printing and binding within appropriations." When this potentially mischievous option is exercised, "the original copy shall be kept on file in the office of the heads of the respective departments, independent offices or establishments for public inspection." The *Annual Report of the Public Printer* for FY 1973 was available in photocopy form for $6.

2

SUPERINTENDENT OF DOCUMENTS

One studying today the mechanism and administration of the Federal government . . . cannot but be struck with the enormous development of what are called the non-essential functions of government. The power of the government is used in a thousand ways to accomplish ends not in themselves necessary to the maintenance of law and order, but solely to do certain things that are believed to be for the advantage of the people and which cannot be done as well under private auspices.

To the student, the most interesting portion of this work is that undertaken for the purpose of making contributions to human knowledge. Within comparative recent years the government has established numerous scientific and educational bureaus whose sole or chief function is the collection of special information and its publication and distribution among the people. . . .

Unfortunately, the system of issuing and distributing government publications in the past has been such that it would seem that, if deliberate design had been exercised, this task of the student could not have been made a more difficult one. There has been an utter lack of system in the methods employed by the government. Starting from a small beginning, public printing has grown here and there as demands have arisen, until the present enormous output has been reached. Each branch of the government has looked out for its own interests, and the present confused and complicated system has been the outcome. The result of this condition of affairs is that to the majority of persons these publications are closed books. Not only are they in many cases unobtainable, but their very existence is unknown. Most librarians have given up in despair their attempts to obtain complete sets of government documents or to catalog those that they have.

—William Franklin Willoughby, "Government Publications," *Yale Review* (August 1896)

BACKGROUND

The Printing Act of 1895 created the Office of Superintendent of Documents to effect "a more intelligent distribution of Government publications," because the procedures in force at the time were hopelessly chaotic. The first Superintendent, F. A. Crandall, registered dismay at the "bewildering congeries of volumes, numbers, and parts . . . of Congressional documents," and of the overall operation stated:

> Of course the present system was not devised by anybody. There was never anybody who could have devised it. Like Topsy, it "jist growed."[1]

Topsy's haphazard growth generated abuse in the dispersal of documents; the Congress was chiefly to blame for the distribution of its quota of publications in a manner "too promiscuous among persons who did not appreciate their true value." Documents had been turning up in secondhand book stores for sale, "thus abusing the generosity of the Government." Some libraries "were overwhelmed by mountains of government publications, while others received no regular distribution at all." Moreover, "no standard system for titling government documents existed" rendering "practical cataloging . . . virtually impossible."[2] Little wonder that comments like Mr. Willoughby's had been appearing in the press and journals.

While the act of 1860 had endeavored to correct the several problems in the printing of documents, the act of 1895 sought to remedy the defects in distribution. It directed the Superintendent to

> receive and care for all surplus documents in the possession of Government offices; assort and catalog them; supervise their distribution and sale; catalog and index monthly and annually all documents published; in fine, to render accessible to librarian and the public generally the vast store of Government publications.[3]

To carry out this mission, a Public Documents Division was established within the GPO; the Superintendent was subordinate to the Public Printer but "was to exercise full authority over the tangled government documents situation."[4] Established in leased quarters on the sixth floor of the Union Building on G Street NW, near Seventh, accompanied by the usual lamentations of inadequate space, the Division began "the giant task of taking over 134,000 publications accumulated by the departments, hundreds of boxes from the House and Senate document rooms, and over 21,000 publications in the GPO."[5] Distribution to depository libraries was systematized, the enormous job of cataloging was begun, and the sales program was initiated. Thus 106 years after George Washington took the oath of office of President of the United States, a semblance of management was introduced into the dissemination of the publications of the federal establishment.

FUNCTIONS

A description of duties is found in every annual volume of hearings before the House and Senate subcommittees on legislative branch appropriations. The Superintendent of Documents is charged with four functions: the sale of government publications; the compilation of catalogs and indexes of publications; mailing of certain publications for members of Congress and other government agencies; and the distribution of publications to designated depository libraries.

The 1895 act enjoined the Superintendent to build a library of government documents so that the cataloging function could be more effectively managed. By the assiduous efforts of the early Superintendents, a library was collected that housed the most nearly complete set of federal publications in existence. Although no copies could be found of a number of publications issued prior to 1895, the acquisitions policy was remarkably successful, for the library's early stock was "obtained from overages returned by libraries or extra material given irregularly by Government Printing Office customers."[6]

However, the library of the Public Documents Department, housed in the oldest of the GPO's four buildings on North Capitol Street, did not have proper facilities for reference service and afforded only limited access for other government agencies when the materials needed could not be located elsewhere. In the summer of 1972, the General Services Administration announced the transfer of the collection to the National Archives. The initial move of nearly two million publications and some 76,000 maps was completed by the end of the year. Future transfers are scheduled in biennial increments, so that all that remains of the old Public Documents Department collection are documents of two-year recency for cataloging purposes. Researcher complaints were given as the principal reason for the transfer. The National Archives has extensive research facilities, whereas the GPO never succeeded in conquering its old *bête noire*, space. Moreover, the collection was not open to the public.[7]

The materials are still accessioned as records of the GPO, the transfer having been effected as an archival unit retaining its SUDOCS classification scheme; those with a need to know are now able to use the collection in its more commodious environs and may order photocopies. Public use of the collection is available as prescribed for the other materials in the National Archives under Title 41 of the *Code of Federal Regulations*, Part 105-61.[8]

The Sales Program

The primary mission of the Superintendent of Documents is to serve as sales agent for government publications, and the sales program is that unique phenomenon in government, a self-sustaining operation. In 1895 the Superintendent was empowered "to sell at cost any public document in its charge, the distribution of which is not specifically directed by law."[9] His stock for the first years was acquired from extra copies that libraries had been sent or departments had received. Reprint authority for departmental publications was granted in 1904 and for congressional documents in 1922. Far from relying on the leftover largesse of libraries and agencies, the Superintendent today obtains sales publications from the GPO by submitting printing orders for the number of copies he estimates he will need to meet the public demand.

Prices

Government publications were originally sold at cost. But by 1874 the price was legislated at cost plus 10 percent. Recent regulations permit prices of most documents to be based on costs as determined by the Public Printer plus a 50 percent markup.

Government materials had long enjoyed a price structure well below commercially produced publications of similar quality and length. This is no longer the case. A dramatic increase in prices in 1973 required a warning notice from the Office of the Superintendent, which was included in mail-order shipments:

> Prices of Government publications are subject to change without prior notice. Substantial increases in costs have made it necessary for the Superintendent of Documents to increase the selling prices of most publications offered. As it is infeasible to manually correct the prices in all of the publications now in stock, the prices charged on your order may differ from the prices printed in the publications.

While a GPO spokesman announced that prices of publications "in general will be boosted 80 percent," many publications in 1973 and 1974 doubled or tripled in cost. New postal rates, printing, labor, and paper costs were blamed for the increases, which some felt to be outrageous. Officials justified the increases on the ground that prices of government documents had been too low. Since the sale of documents to the public at low cost purports to inform with minimal financial discomfort, high prices are an effective form of censorship.[10]

In its first year of operation, the Office of Superintendent of Documents reported sales of about 3,000 publications for $889.[11] In fiscal year 1973 SUDOCS sold 78 million publications in the amount of over 23 million dollars. The current cost-plus factor enables the Public Documents Department to realize a net profit on sales, which is calculated as the difference between appropriations and income. Profits, generally within the range of $1 million or more, are returned to the Treasury. Most significantly, profits warm the hearts of the members of the House and Senate Appropriations committees.

Branch Bookstores

On March 21, 1967, the first retail bookstore for the sale of government publications outside the Washington, D.C., area was opened in the Everett McKinley Dirksen federal building in Chicago.[12] All bookstores have proved to be self-sustaining operations; their financial health has exceeded GPO expectations. Located primarily in federal office buildings, property owned by the government, they stock approximately one thousand of SUDOC's most popular titles. Since the bookstores are run along the lines of a commercial bookstore, customers can browse and purchase what is available. If the item is not in stock, order forms are conveniently located and one may secure the document from GPO's central office. The customer may request that the order be mailed either to the bookstore where he can pick it up, or to his home or office. Thus the bookstores take the pressure off the Washington, D.C., operation and, in theory, "provide a faster, more efficient and more economical service to the buying public."[13]

Area Distribution Centers

In 1971 a separate processing facility was opened in Philadelphia and the following year the western part of the country was represented by a center in Pueblo, Colorado. Unlike the bookstores, these facilities were established primarily to distribute GPO publications. Smaller replicas of the processing unit at the Central Office in Washington, D.C., the area distribution centers reduce the workload of the main processing section. In 1971, the acting Superintendent testified that "we are presently occupying the same space for processing of orders that we were some 25 years ago. During this span of time the volume of sales orders has increased by some 398 percent. Consequently the walls are beginning to bulge. . . ."[14] Because the equipment is not fully automated, the time lag for processing documents has become unconscionably lengthy; regional distribution, like regional bookstores, is seen as speeding the ordering process.

The Washington, D.C., operation still remains the largest mail order processing unit, but the storage problem has been somewhat alleviated. The *Selected U.S. Government Publications* directs potential customers to one or the other of the centers on its order forms, and both centers attempt to stock for six months all publications listed in this monthly compilation. At first the presumption of geographical location was to serve a defined body of customers. However, SUDOCS found it easier to depart from this procedure in certain special categories. All customers in the United States that wanted the June 1972 edition of the *National Drug Code Directory* were given a form that had to be mailed to Philadelphia. Conversely, individuals and non-depository libraries wishing to secure a copy of *Marihuana: A Signal of Misunderstanding* or the 1973 edition of *Your Federal Income Tax* sent their orders to Pueblo, regardless of residence. But the area distribution center concept is in single pursuit of SUDOC's gravest problem: a reduction of the delay in filling orders.

Other Agencies

Sales of government publications printed by the GPO are handled by other departments and bureaus, such as Interior, Commerce, Labor, the IRS and the Small Business Administration. Section 72a of Title 44 of the *United States Code* empowers SUDOCS to designate "any Government office his agent for the sale of Government publications under such regulations as shall be agreed upon by the Superintendent of Documents and the head of the respective department or establishment of the Government."[15] Often the same document is available from an agency and from the Superintendent, an unnecessary and sometimes confusing division. Nevertheless, the Superintendent remains the chief sales agent for GPO publications.

Commercial Sellers

Booksellers are reluctant to become involved in the business of selling documents because of the low discount percent. The trade discount schedule for all authorized bookdealers is 25 percent regardless of quantity. In 1972 a gentleman named Martin Nizny opened a retail outlet in a Dayton, Ohio, department store. For this historic occasion, the Superintendent of Documents attended opening ceremonies. The proprietor, who reported initial favorable response, said that his decision to enter this area where no one had dared to venture before was based on the healthy balance sheet of the GPO's San Francisco retail outlet.[16]

Libraries

The Superintendent is permitted by law to allow a 25 percent discount to anyone else who purchases 100 or more copies of a single publication going to one address, on condition that they adhere to the public sales price set by the Superintendent and that publications not be overprinted with any advertising matter. Some libraries have taken advantage of this opportunity, for there appear to be no drawbacks to participation, and the promotional gains are potentially strong. Expectedly, the popular titles such as *Infant Care*, *Your Federal Income Tax*, and the publications of the Small Business Administration's Starting and Managing Series lend themselves to this sort of project. Librarians who have been involved in this sales venture report favorable patron response; the service is most useful in communities that are far removed from a branch bookstore.[17]

Out-of-print documents are a perennial problem, abetted by the Superintendent's penchant for conservative ordering. If enough interest is shown in a specific publication that is not in print, SUDOCS will order copies printed, but this occurs only in cases of extraordinary demand. Like any commercial sales agent, the Superintendent must have knowledge of his potential audience and an intuitive sense of publishing realities, but he cannot reprint to accommodate a relatively small market.

Order Processing

The Office of the Superintendent has been caught between the Scylla of rising demand from the public for government materials and the Charybdis of antiquated manual processing operations. Like the GPO itself, the Public

Documents Department complains of space, staffing difficulties, and inadequate funding. Indeed, there is a question whether the Superintendent's operations would not be better performed geographically separate from the GPO. An attempt was made in 1973 to process mail order requests for documents within a 21-workday cycle. Maximum effort has been devoted to modernization of the order processing system. The goal is fully automated mailing and processing methods.

High prices and inept distribution of materials through the mail have been the two most vocally criticized areas of the Superintendent's operations. GPO officials are aware of their shortcomings. As a former Superintendent gamely said, "It's all too vast to say that next week I'll be able to take care of all the problems. After all, how do you eat an elephant? A bite at a time."[18]

Catalogs and Indexes

In 1902 the Documents Division handled "the enormous number of 1,645,000 documents, including depository library distribution," and the Superintendent noted that "the task of cataloging public documents was being done by eleven catalogers." He found that this "specialized field of cataloging was a most difficult problem" and hoped that "library schools would give the subject ... more attention in the future, as there will always be a demand for experts in that branch of the profession."[19]

Over seventy years later, another Superintendent of Documents pointed out that the Library Section of the Public Documents Department "employs about a dozen professional librarians, and a complement of technicians, library assistants, and clerk-typists," and added that "much of this staff's available time is spent cataloging documents for inclusion in the Documents library."[20] Although that library, as we noted, was moved to the National Archives, the compilation of catalogs and indexes has remained the responsibility of the Office of the Superintendent. And, as was true at the turn of the century, the business of cataloging documents and providing an adequate index for access continues to beget problems.

All agencies issue catalogs, or "lists," of their documents at specified or irregular times, but the Public Documents Department, as issuing agency, is charged with publishing reference tools that are indispensable to libraries large and small. In addition to general monographs and miscellaneous lists, it is required by law to issue the *Numerical Lists and Schedule of Volumes* for libraries with congressional holdings, plus three items that virtually all libraries must receive: the *Monthly Catalog of United States Government Publications*, *Selected U.S. Government Publications*, and *Price Lists*. Together these comprise the bibliographic apparatus of GPO public documents; librarians must be familiar with them.

The Monthly Catalog

First issued in 1895, it has endured six name changes. From January 1951 it has been issued under its current title, and all librarians know it simply as the *Monthly Catalog* (MC). Although it has been called the *Cumulative Book Index* for government documents, the analogy does not hold sufficiently to be useful. Let us consider the *Monthly Catalog sui generis* and discuss some of its salient features; after one has become accustomed to its peculiarities, the *Monthly Catalog* is not difficult to use.

- The MC is arranged alphabetically by issuing agency.[21] Prior to September 1947, arrangement was by departments and independent agencies with the subordinate units subsumed; the current order is less clumsy.
- Beginning with the September 1947 issue the index refers to entry numbers, located in the left-hand column of each page. Before that, index entries referred to page numbers; the present arrangement reduces the time spent in locating the citation.
- At the bottom of every page of the MC, five symbols indicate the sale and distribution pattern of all documents cited. The bibliographical information accompanying each citation includes the appropriate symbol.
- The monthly and annual indexes to the MC used to be arranged in an interfiled author-title-subject format. Beginning in 1974, the indexes consist of three separate parts: a regular subject index, a personal author index, and a title index (Figures 1, 2, 3, 4).
- Three issues are of special significance. The February MC contains an appendix that lists periodicals and subscription publications alphabetically by title. Unannotated, the entries give basic bibliographic data and ordering information. The appendix should be used in conjunction with the most recent edition of *Price List* 36, *Government Periodicals and Subscription Services.*

The September MC includes in a separate section a list of designated depository libraries, arranged alphabetically by state and by city within each state. The name of the library and the date it became a depository are given. This list may be used in conjunction with an annual publication issued as a committee print by the Joint Committee on Printing: titled *Government Depository Libraries*, it is arranged by congressional district, including senatorial designation. The publication also includes a brief explanation of the depository library system and an extract of laws in force pertaining to depository libraries.

The December MC includes a cumulative index to cover all entries for the calendar year.

- Additional useful features in the MC include a section that previews publications in the process of being printed, in order to permit advance sales orders; a section on new classification numbers; corrections for previous issues; general information; and a list of GPO bookstores.
- The MC does *not* list individual bills by number,[22] individual patent specifications, Supreme Court decisions, federal specifications and standards, DSA regulations, Army regulations, and individual maps and charts issued by the Geological Survey and other map-making agencies. Only those technical reports that are considered government publications are entered in the MC. Because this

Figure 1

MONTHLY CATALOG: MAIN ENTRY

03870   1070. Cleaning metal furniture; [adapted by Glenda Pifer]. [Oct. 1973.] [2] p. il. 4° (Extension Service.) [From How to clean metal furniture, B2313, by Cooperative Extension Service, University of Wisconsin. Issued with perforations.] * Paper, $7.00 per 100 ● Item 14–A
A 1.68 : 1070

03871   1071. Have a sparkling clean kitchen sink; [adapted by Glenda Pifer]. [Oct. 1973.] [2] p. il. 4° (Extension Service.) [From How to have sparkling clean kitchen sink, Special circular 161, by Cooperative Extension Service, University of Wisconsin. Issued with perforations.] * Paper, $7.00 per 100 ● Item 14–A
A 1.68 : 1071

Figure 2

MONTHLY CATALOG: SUBJECT INDEX

Furnaces, furnaces and space heaters, Federal item identification guide, 04275
Furnishing (apparel), see Clothing.
Furniture:
    cleaning metal furniture, 03870
    cleaning wood furniture, 03866
    used furniture can be good buy, 03862
Fuseholders, Federal item identification guide, 04276

Figure 3

MONTHLY CATALOG: AUTHOR INDEX

Phillips, Douglas R., American woods, 04426
Pifer Glenda :
    Cleaning kitchen ranges, 03872
    Cleaning metal furniture, 03870
    Cleaning windows, mirrors, other glass, 03865
    Cleaning wood furniture, 03866
    Have sparkling clean kitchen sink, 03871
    How to clean and defrost refrigerator, 03874

Figure 4

MONTHLY CATALOG: TITLE INDEX

China, tableware, 04419
Chronological schedule, air pollution training courses, 04355
Classified index of National Labor Relations Board decisions and related court decisions, 04673
Cleaning kitchen ranges, 03872
Cleaning metal furniture, 03870
Cleaning windows, mirrors, other glass, 03865

constitutes a very small percentage of the total technical report literature, one must use NTIS's abstracting and indexing tools. The contents of individual issues of periodicals and press releases are not indexed.

● Two decennial cumulative indexes have been prepared covering the period 1941-1950 and 1951-1960; future cumulations are contemplated quinquennially. The monthly indexes are "title oriented," but the Public Documents Department Library maintains an authority file of subject headings to prepare the subject index. Some forms are included as subjects, a useful device that enables the librarian or patron to seek information under headings such as catalogs, bibliographies, indexes, and directories.

Commercial firms that publish aids designed to supplement the MC's author and subject indexing include Pierian Press and Carrollton Press. The former issues comprehensive personal author indexes that are especially useful for the years 1947 through 1962, when personal authors were excluded from the MC. The latter's subject index facilitates searching through its master single-alphabet sequence; moreover, the publisher has made available the full text of the MC from 1895 through 1971 on microfilm.[23]

The *Monthly Catalog* contains over 15,000 entries annually; its compilation is the primary task of the librarians at the Public Documents Department Library. Entries are numbered consecutively, but due to a clerical error the number sequence extended from January 1972 to December 1973. In January 1974, entries began again with #1. Moreover, the distinctive color scheme that began with the January 1973 MC has been adopted so that the catalog for a given year can be more easily identified on the shelves.

Although the MC has its shortcomings, it is the seminal reference aid for GPO publications. The divided index that appeared with the January 1974 issue of the MC was greeted with enthusiasm; however, a number of specific improvements have been suggested by practicing documents librarians. Recommendations have included expanding the personal author index to list joint authors, translators, directors and producers of audiovisual material, and committee chairmen. A cumulated thesaurus of terms, keywords, and subjects used in past and current issues is considered desirable. It has been suggested that popular names of monographs be included, and that there be an index by accession numbers, with cross references to both stock numbers and class numbers. A separately published cumulated monthly index has also been suggested. In 1973 an Advisory Council to the Public Printer on Depository Libraries was organized to assist the GPO in its problems, and a subcommittee on Documents Office Informational Tools exists within this structure to advise the Superintendent in ways of improving tools like the *Monthly Catalog*.[24]

Selected U.S. Government Publications

The chief promotional instrument for the Superintendent's mail order operation is the *Selected U.S. Government Publications*, known to librarians as the *Selected List*. Well over one million individuals and institutions subscribe to this free listing of documents which purport to be new, relevant, and of general interest.

First issued in 1928, it began as a weekly service, changed to semi-monthly status in 1942 and became a bi-weekly (every two weeks) in 1951. Beginning with volume 1, number 1, 1972, it changed from a leaflet format to a 12- to 15-page booklet listing approximately 100 publications available for sale by the Superintendent. With volume 3, number 3, the *Selected List* became a monthly; the first issue (March 1974) under this schedule was enlarged to include almost 200 publications. The monthly format is expected to save mailing costs while maintaining the same total number of documents listed.

Arrangement is by broad subject categories such as Business & Industry, Congress, and Education interspersed with frivolous headings such as Just for You, Odds 'N Ends, and Konsumer's Korner. A few publications in each issue are prominently cited and illustrated. The last page of each issue highlights one important government periodical, with an adequate annotation.

What constitutes a popular title is sometimes difficult to determine. Along with mention of a publication of manifest popularity (*Sport Fishing, USA*), one finds a title like *Structural and Stratigraphic Framework and Spatial Distribution of Permeability of the Atlantic Coastal Plain, North Carolina to New York*. An order form is placed in the center of the booklet; orders may be accompanied by check, money order, coupons, or may be charged to one's deposit account. The form indicates whether the order is to be placed with the Philadelphia or the Pueblo distribution center.

Perennial classics that are kept in print or reprinted are announced from time to time. The distribution center indicated on the order form can fill the order for six months after listing. Meant to be a current ordering tool, the *Selected List* affords non-depository libraries an opportunity to build a collection tailored to the clients' needs.

Price Lists

When in late 1973 the price structure underwent precipitous change, a series of subject pamphlets known as *Price Lists* (PL's) became inoperative. For a time it was thought that they would simply be reissued reflecting the new prices. In March 1974, however, the Superintendent announced that, with the exception of PL 36 (*Government Periodicals and Subscription Services*), publication of the series would be postponed indefinitely.[25]

Price Lists identified "popular" in-print publications sold by the Superintendent and in this respect complemented the *Selected List*. In recent years, about 50 lists were issued on an irregular basis. Each list was assigned a PL number, but because their titles reflected current subject interests, many have been discontinued since the series began in 1893. Their titles reveal a peculiar quasi-subject approach. For example, PL 11, *Home Economics*; PL 44, *Plants*; PL 71, *Child Development*; and PL 72, *Homes* indicate a broad classification. But a provenance organization is seen in PL 19, *Army*; PL 70, *Census*; and PL 83, *Library of Congress*. Individual lists were arranged by broad subject with some subdivisions.

PL 36, the list that apparently escaped the price debacle, is divided into two sections. Section I lists alphabetically by title most (though not all) periodicals currently available for sale by subscription from SUDOCS. Brief annotations accompany the basic bibliographic and ordering information. Section II lists alphabetically by title other publications, usually of a looseleaf service, which are issued irregularly. Like the *Selected List*, PL's were issued without cost to individuals and institutions.[26]

Classification

With the exception of documents for sale by NTIS, entries in the *Monthly Catalog* include, at the end of the citation, an alphameric notation known as the SUDOCS class number. The Superintendent of Documents classification system was established in the Library of the Public Documents Department sometime between 1895 and 1903. The first explanation of the system was given in 1903 by William Leander Post, then in charge of the Library, who gave credit for the concept to Adelaide R. Hasse. Ms. Hasse had used the system in assigning classification numbers to a Department of Agriculture List of Publications. It has expanded as the federal establishment has grown, and has changed in some details, but it has retained the principles upon which it was first based. For many years it served as the ordering notation as well as the classification of the document, but SUDOCS now has a multi-digit stock number for ordering purposes.

The system is based on the principle of *provenance*, whereby the several publications of any government author—a department, bureau, agency—are grouped together under like notation. Essentially, this sort of arrangement guarantees no inevitable grouping of similar subject matter, for a book on children's poetry and a guide to the official publications of Swaziland are documents of the same government author (in this case the Library of Congress). In the system, the classification reflects the organizational structure of the United States government, and this is at once the scheme's strength and its weakness.

The concept of provenance avoids the tortuous Procrustean problems of a scheme like the Dewey decimal classification, but it is at the mercy of any government reorganization. Since reorganization happens not infrequently, the publications of some authors are located in several places in the system. One egregious example of reorganization affecting classification occurred when the Department of Health, Education and Welfare was created in 1953 and the functions of the Federal Security Agency, which was thereby abolished, were transferred to the new Cabinet-level entity. Publications of the old agency had been designated "FS" and for several years the Superintendent carried HEW publications that way. Finally the letters were changed to "HE," reinstating the mnemonic advantage but thoroughly demoralizing documents librarians.

When changes in reorganization require changes in the classification librarians have three options. They may continue the old notations; they may assign new notations as issued and change all the notations on the older publications to conform to the new notation; or they may assign new notations as issued and leave the old letters and numbers on the earlier materials. The last strategy appears to accommodate the fewest disadvantages. Cross references have to be prepared only when change of author or classification is made; revision, corrections, and replacement of old records are unnecessary; no reshelving of materials is called for; and no pencil or ink changes need to be made on the documents. Most importantly, the value of the *Monthly Catalog* as a book catalog remains intact.

Still, the problem of reclassification remains a vexing one, and the literature of librarianship is liberally sprinkled with debate on the issue. In an open-stack documents collection, the option discussed above discourages browsing, but in a provenance system this activity is less significant than it is, for example, in Dewey. Nevertheless, some users find it annoying to have the publications of the *Index-Catalog of the Library of the Surgeon-General's Office* shelved in four places. Whatever options librarians choose, the larger factors of the place and function of documents in the overall collection will dictate the decision; in any case, rigidity in the decision-making process should be eschewed.

The Superintendent's classification scheme groups subordinate units with the parent organization; and each executive department and agency, the Judiciary, Congress, and the major independent establishments are assigned a place. The place is determined by the alphabetical designation ascribed to each, as "A" for Agriculture Department, "Ju" for Judiciary, and "FT" for Federal Trade Commission. To set off the subordinate bureaus and offices, numbers are added to the letters, the digit "1" assigned to the secretary's or administrator's office of the parent organization. Succeeding numbers are applied, in order, to the lesser agencies, these having been arranged alphabetically when the system was established. A period follows the alphameric notation representing the bureau or office, for example:

Agriculture Department (including Secretary's Office)	A 1.
Forest Service	A 13.
National Agricultural Library	A 17.
Information Office	A 21.

The second segment in the scheme provides for category designations. For the various series of publications issued by a particular agency or bureau, a number is ascribed followed by a colon:

1:     Annual reports
2:     General publications (unnumbered and of a miscellaneous nature)
3:     Bulletins
4:     Circulars
5:     Laws (administered by the agency and published by it)
6:     Regulations, rules and instructions
7:     Releases
8:     Handbooks, manuals, guides

New series closely related to already existing series are designated by use of the shilling mark after the number assigned to the existing series, followed by a digit for each related series (starting with "2"). Separates are distinguished by use of a lower case letter beginning with "a" rather than by numbers, for example:

4:      Circulars
4/a: Separates from Circulars (numbered)
4/b: Separates from Circulars (unnumbered)
4/2:   Administrative Circulars
4/3:   Technical Circulars

By combining the designations for authors and those for the series published by the authors, the class stems are obtained for the several series issued, for example:

A 43.4/2: = Extension Service (of the Department of Agriculture), Administrative Circulars

Now we are ready for the notations that follow the colon. These are simply known as book numbers. For numbered series, which constitute the majority of government documents, the digits reflect the number of the book, for example, Department of Agriculture Leaflet 381 would be A 1.35: 381. For revisions of numbered publications, the shilling mark and number corresponding to the revision are added. Thus when Leaflet 381 first appears in revised form, the notation would read A 1.35: 381/2.

General publications are usually monographs, and these unnumbered documents are given a book number based upon the principal subject word of the title, using a 2-figure Cutter table. Revisions of unnumbered publications are identified by addition of the shilling mark and the last three digits of the year of revision. If necessary, shilling marks following the original Cutter number further distinguish the individuality of the work.

The system described above governs the classification of most government authors. There are special forms employed by certain entities; these consist of classes assigned to:

a) some series issued by the Interstate Commerce Commission

b) boards, commissions, and committees established by act of Congress or under authority of an act of Congress, not specifically designated in the executive branch nor as completely independent agencies

c) the several publications of the Congress and its committees

d) multilateral international organizations in which the United States participates

e) publications of the President and the Executive Office of the President including committees and commissions established by executive order and reporting directly to the President.

The classification and designation of the special forms will be taken up in succeeding chapters as the publications themselves are discussed. Although the SUDOCS class scheme, like other notation systems, presents an initial appearance of difficulty, it becomes easily comprehensible with frequent use. The librarian puzzling over a certain form has only to refer to the latest revised edition of *An Explanation of the Superintendent of Documents Classification System* (GP 3.2: C 56/8), a brochure prepared by specialists in the Public Documents Department Library.

Mailing Duties

A third major function of the Superintendent of Documents is the distribution service his Office performs for members of Congress and government agencies. SUDOCS maintains mailing lists, including the list for the *Congressional Record*, and performs mailing operations upon request of any government agency.

As an agency of the Congress, the GPO is ever reminded, through the power of appropriations, of its primary allegiance. Accordingly, although the Superintendent of Documents is responsible for what are referred to as "by law" mailings, which include agencies as well as the Congress, the latter gets first priority. For example, over 40,000 copies of the quotidian *Congressional Record* are printed; Senators and Representatives are authorized a number of extra copies and they may in turn designate constituents to receive these extra copies. The responsibility for maintaining the mailing lists is the Superintendent's. Publications to be distributed to federal agencies include the *Federal Register*, *Public Papers of the President*, *U.S. Government Manual*,[27] and the *Weekly Compilation of Presidential Documents*. All of the "by law" mailings that fall within the jurisdiction of the Office of the Superintendent are pursuant to the appropriate sections in Title 44 of the *United States Code*.

During fiscal year 1973 an effort was made to modernize mailing lists by conversion from the Elliott Stencil system to an automated system. Departmental mailing lists, as well as subscription files, were successfully converted by mid-1973; and all production for mailing is now provided from Videograph machine or the IBM 360 for 3x5" mailing labels.[28]

Distribution to Depository Libraries

For the more than 1,000 designated depository libraries, this function of the Office of the Superintendent is of paramount importance. In the following chapter the provisions under which the depository library program is administered will be discussed.

REFERENCES

1.   *100 GPO Years*, pp. 75-76.
2.   Kling, p. 112.

3.   *100 GPO Years*, p. 75.
4.   Kling, p. 112.
5.   *100 GPO Years*, p. 75.
6.   Kling, p. 131.
7.   *Library of Congress Information Bulletin* 31: 349 (August 4, 1972).
8.   By early 1974 less than ten percent of the collection had been unpacked and processed. A letter prepared by the Special Libraries Association and the Government Documents Round Table (GODORT) of the American Library Association was sent to the Archivist urging that additional staff be assigned to complete the project. See *Documents to the People* II: 12-13 (February 1974).
9.   *100 GPO Years*, p. 76.
10.   The major policy changes related to price increases as they affect sales procedures were outlined by the Superintendent in *Illinois Libraries* 56: 264 (April 1974).
11.   Kling, p. 114.
12.   By 1974 retail bookstores numbered 23, including six in the Washington, D.C., area, with several new locations projected for FY 1975.
13.   *Legislative Branch Appropriations for 1972* (House), pp. 323-24.
14.   Ibid., p. 323.
15.   Kling, p. 122.
16.   *Publishers' Weekly* (March 20, 1972), p. 42.
17.   *RQ* 10: 341 (Summer 1971).
18.   To expedite order processing and in general streamline the several operations of the Office of the Superintendent, the Public Documents Department was reorganized in 1974. The new organization chart was published in *Public Documents Highlights* (GP 3.27:3), April 1974, p. 3.
19.   *100 GPO Years*, p. 83.
20.   Kling, p. 129.
21.   The publications of the Congress are the primary exception to the alphabetical listing; these are subdivided both by form (serial set, laws, documents, reports) and by issuing entity (House and Senate committees).
22.   House and Senate public bills and resolutions (excluding amendments) were listed by number only in the MC from December 1947, until November 1965.
23.   These commercial aids will be discussed in more detail in Chapter 5.
24.   An account of criticism of the MC and GPO response is found in the May and September 1973 issues of *Documents to the People*. See also an excellent article "The *Monthly Catalog* and Bibliographic Control of United States Government Publications" by L. C. Schwarzkopf in the January/April 1974 combined special issue on federal documents in *Drexel Library Quarterly*.
25.   Remarks by W. H. Lewis, Superintendent of Documents, delivered at the annual conference of the Information Industry Association in Washington, D.C., March 19, 1974.
26.   The *Monthly Catalog* (GP 3.8; Item 557) is sold by SUDOCS. The *Selected List* (GP 3.17/4; Item 556) is available on deposit, as were *Price Lists* (GP 3.9; Item 554).

27.   Formerly titled *U.S. Government Organization Manual*. The 1973/1974 edition dropped the word *Organization*, according to the compilers, "to reflect a continuing attempt to direct the Manual to the general public rather than to the specialist in government."

28.   *Annual Report of the Public Printer, FY 1973*, p. 29.

3

DEPOSITORY LIBRARY SYSTEM

With the subsequent growth and shifting of population and the various changes in the boundaries of Congressional districts, many depository libraries are not now located so as to serve the districts for which they were originally designated. But other depository libraries cannot be selected under the present law for the new and large centers of population. . . . On the other hand, many districts apparently do not desire or cannot assume the burden of having a depository for government publications. . . . The . . . vacant designations cannot, however, be assigned to libraries in other districts. Consequently many important libraries are compelled to obtain government publications by haphazard importuning of Congressmen and the departments.

The selective privilege granted depository libraries a few years ago has also disclosed the fact that many of the present designations are either unwilling or lack the facilities to provide sufficient space for adequate deposits of government publications, thereby making their designation as depositories of little service to the public.

—Annual Report of the Public Printer, 1926

INTRODUCTION

Before designated depositories were established, and before the Printing Act of 1895 set up a systematic approach, special legislation was passed at various times, which provided for the printing of copies of the House and Senate *Journals*. These were printed in sufficient number to be distributed to the executives of the several states and to each of the state and territorial legislatures. Provision was also made at times to supply the acts, documents, and reports, as well as the *Journals*, to incorporated universities, colleges, and historical societies. We look upon the number of documents deposited in the early nineteenth century with bemusement. During the 13th Congress, 2d session, a resolution was adopted embodying earlier ad hoc legislation that directed "for every future Congress" a limit of two hundred in addition to the usual number, "and this, of course, was more than sufficient for the needs at that early day."[1] Joint resolutions of 1840 increased that number to three hundred. By contrast, during fiscal year 1973 the number of publications distributed to depository libraries was 12,490,228.

In the mid-nineteenth century, the Secretary of the Interior was charged with the distribution of publications to institutions, which now included public and school libraries, atheneums, literary and scientific societies, and boards of trade. During that time Congress and the departments had authority to continue their own distribution policies. These had become so indiscriminate that the first Superintendent of Documents asserted that publications were disbursed "with such liberal prodigality as to cheapen them in the estimation of the people at large." Unsolicited documents "were not only not appreciated but were regarded with contempt." Urging a more rational policy, he noted that "on the one hand, horse or cattle books were sent to districts in which automobiles and electric cars held sway and where cattle were represented only in butcher shops and dairies. On the other hand, rural districts were flooded with *Flags of Maritime Nations* . . . instead of books published specially for their use."[2]

Librarians unhappy with the unsolicited receipt of documents "of every nature" for their designated institutions had to wait until 1922 for relief from what the first Superintendent called "chronic document indigestion." The appropriation for that fiscal year provided that libraries could select those categories of publications most suitable for their clientele, and the selective deposit system was born.

The plan that had evolved with its several amendments by 1962 included 594 depository libraries, located in all of the states and most of the territories. The mechanics of distribution allowed "at least one mailing a day" to every depository. But changes in the demographic pattern, owing to redistricting and to economic shifts, created the need for new depositories in areas where no vacancies for an additional designation existed. Moreover, depository libraries could not dispose of documents no longer needed nor able to be housed properly, and some librarians complained that they lacked important "non-GPO" publications, which were excluded from depository distribution. On the other hand, they faulted the existing system for its inadequacies in supplying important GPO documents. In response to these and other complaints the GPO and the Superintendent applied their efforts to effect new legislation. The result, the Depository Library Act of 1962, represented the most significant major changes in depository legislation in over six decades.[3]

The 1962 legislation was long overdue; although the 1895 Act as amended had served libraries, its usefulness had been compromised by time and changing needs. The 1962 statute brought about some necessary changes but also left unresolved some crucial problems. When enacted it was greeted with guarded optimism by the library community generally. Now that it has (with minor amendments) been in operation for over a decade, critical appraisal can be more measured and objective. This is the law by which designated depositories are presently governed, and an understanding of its provisions is central to the professional task—even though one might wish the law were more responsive to the problems of documents librarianship.

THE ACT OF 1962

Approved August 9, 1962 (76 *Stat.* 352), the legislation amended various sections of Title 44. The act is currently the guide for librarians administering a depository collection.

Number of Congressional Designations

Congressional and senatorial designations were increased from one to not more than two, including the Resident Commissioner from Puerto Rico. Moreover, "the Commissioner of the District of Columbia may designate two depository libraries in the District of Columbia, the Governor of Guam and the Governor of American Samoa may each designate one depository library in Guam and American Samoa, respectively, and the Governor of the Virgin Islands may designate one depository library on the island of Saint Thomas and one on the island of Saint Croix."[4]

Classified List of Items

The Superintendent "shall currently issue a classified list of Government publications in suitable form, containing annotations of contents and listed by item identification numbers ... to facilitate the selection of only those publications which may be needed by designated depository libraries." Before the use of 3x5" Item cards (see Chapter 4), the classified list was issued in pamphlet form and carried descriptive annotations. Few Item cards carry annotations today.[5]

Special Designations

The Act permitted additional depository libraries within executive departments and independent agencies "to the extent that the number so designated does not exceed the number of major bureaus or divisions of the departments and independent agencies." The head of each executive department or independent agency must justify to the Superintendent his need for additional depository status. Moreover, these depositories may dispose of unwanted publications after first offering them to the Library of Congress and the Archivist of the United States.[6]

Size of Collection

The 1962 Act increased from 1,000 to 10,000 the number of non-government publications a library must have to minimally qualify as a depository.[7]

Postage

The Superintendent of Documents' appropriation now defrays the postage cost which, under previous legislation, the depository libraries had been required to assume. This had been a sore point with librarians.[8]

Regional Depositories

The perennial complaint of squeezed space reflected unhappiness under the laws in effect prior to 1962. The Office of the Superintendent had provided minuscule relief in permitting the disposal of "so-called ephemeral material . . . without the need for other specific authorization." Furthermore, permission had been granted depositories "to substitute commercially-produced microfacsimile reproductions for depository copies, where the library maintained suitable reading equipment, provided the material was adequately indexed for reference use."[9] But the problem of keeping the vast majority of documents throughout all eternity remained until the establishment, in 1962, of the regional depository concept.

The new law formalized a pilot program in effect in Wisconsin and New York State, a voluntary regional depository arrangement "which made it possible for other depositories in the areas involved to be more liberal in disposing of some parts of their depository collections." So successful were these experimental ventures that the regional concept was made part of the 1962 legislation.

Non-GPO Publications

Of potential import was a provision in the 1962 Act which read: "Government publications, except those determined by their issuing components to be required for official use only or for strictly administrative or operational purposes which have no public interest or educational value and publications classified for reasons of national security, shall be made available to depository libraries through the facilities of the Superintendent of Documents for public information. Each component of the Government shall furnish the Superintendent of Documents a list of such publications it issued during the previous month, that were obtained from sources other than the Government Printing Office."[10]

Of these several changes, the most significant were the increase in congressional designations, the regional depository concept, and the provision to include non-GPO documents in depository shipments. The increase in representative and senatorial designation has resulted in a dramatic growth in the number of depository libraries. For fiscal year 1973 the designation had reached 1,121.[11] Testimony of officials before congressional committees leaves the impression that GPO finds adequate the monies allocated to service depositories. Space, however, remains the most crucial problem: spokesmen for the Public Printer have insisted that room to store and work with depository publications has barely increased since the 1962 legislation.[12]

THE ROLE OF REGIONAL DEPOSITORIES

The designation, functions and administrative duties of regional depository libraries are set forth in 44 *U.S.C.* 1912:

> Not more than two depository libraries in each State and the Commonwealth of Puerto Rico may be designated as regional depositories, and shall receive from the Superintendent of Documents copies of all new and revised Government publications authorized for distribution to depository libraries. Designation of regional depository libraries may be made by a Senator or the Resident Commissioner from Puerto Rico within the areas served by them, after approval by the head of the library authority of the State or the Commonwealth of Puerto Rico, as the case may be, who shall first ascertain from the head of the library to be so designated that the library will, in addition to fulfilling the requirements for depository libraries, retain at least one copy of all Government publications either in printed or microfacsimile form (except those authorized to be discarded by the Superintendent of Documents); and within the region served will provide interlibrary loan, reference service, and assistance for depository libraries in the disposal of unwanted Government publications. The agreement to function as a regional depository library shall be transmitted to the Superintendent of Documents by the Senator or the Resident Commissioner from Puerto Rico when the designation is made.

> The libraries designated as regional depositories may permit depository libraries, within the areas served by them, to dispose of Government publications which they have retained for five years after first offering them to other depository libraries within their area.

The Superintendent publishes a brochure of instructions designed to provide guidance for all depository libraries. Duties as set forth in the Act are expatiated upon in this pamphlet. For regionals, the functions outlined in the following paragraphs are significant.

Discard Policy

If, after retention for at least five years, a selective depository wants to discard publications received on deposit, the regional library should ask the depository to prepare a list of the publications, showing the Item number, series title, and approximate extent of the holdings to be disposed of. Copies of these lists should be forwarded to the Superintendent. Disposition is to be made as follows: "Publications should be first offered to other depository libraries in the State or States, then to some other library or educational institution in the vicinity or area which would be able to make them available to the public and to which requests might be referred. Failing to find such a recipient after reasonable effort, they may be disposed of in any appropriate manner. However, if such disposition should take the form of sale, either as secondhand books or waste paper, the proceeds with a letter of explanation should be sent to the Superintendent of Documents since all depository publications remain the property of the United States Government."

Moreover, "the Regional Library can refuse to grant permission for disposal of any publication that it feels should be kept for a longer period of time by one of its depositories." While this is a dubious interpretation of the law, its putative intent is to give the regionals authority to insure that discard decisions are made in a responsible manner by selective depositories. The instructions enjoin regionals to "prepare guidelines and issue any special instructions which they deem necessary for the efficient operation of depositories within their jurisdiction and which will enable the library to better serve the needs of the community where it is situated."[13]

Interlibrary Loan and Reference Service

The Superintendent's instructions do not expand or clarify this provision of the 1962 Act. In Senate hearings on the Act it was argued that interlibrary loan might occasion a decrease in the number of Items selected by the participating libraries. Proponents of the clause, however, argued the opposite: ILL would stimulate increase in selection of a larger and wider variety of Items. The former argument was based on the fear that selective depositories would unduly rely upon the regional for materials they themselves ought to select. The latter argument stated that the disposal provisions would have a liberating effect upon the selective libraries and would allay the obsession with space.

There is a larger problem, however. Should the regionals provide interlibrary loan only to the other *depository* libraries within their region or to all libraries within the geographical jurisdiction? Neither the law nor the Superintendent's instructions provide guidance on this issue.

Reference service is somewhat more difficult to define than interlibrary loan. The absence of specificity in the instructions suggests that the regionals are to decide what is appropriate. From regional to local depository, "reference service" is often synonymous with interlibrary loan. Personal, one-to-one service is defined and carried out variously according to user need and personnel considerations.

Other Kinds of Assistance

Neither the law nor the instructions deny to the regional initiatives that a dedicated librarian with regional responsibility might conceive. Regional depositories can, and do, make periodic visits to selective depositories, assist on Item selection, organize and conduct workshops, seminars and conferences, compile regional union lists, and issue newsletters and announcements.

Federal Libraries

As noted, 44 *U.S.C.* 1907 designates as depositories the libraries of the executive departments, independent agencies, and service academies. Most federal libraries are located in the District of Columbia; a few are in other states. Disposal policy for these entities are by law a function of the Library of Congress and the Archivist. What of interlibrary loan and reference service? The instructions are not specific on this, nor do they suggest other kinds of assistance from the regionals.

Oddly, not all of the states have regional depositories. A decade after enactment of the 1962 legislation, only 41 regional depositories existed in but 35 states. Moreover, seven states have two regionals, but there is no necessary correlation with population. The three states with the greatest number of selective depositories—California, New York, and Ohio—have one regional, whereas Arizona and New Mexico have two regionals. Some states, such as Colorado and Maine, serve contiguous and nearby states that do not have regionals.

To become a regional a library must already be a designated depository. States without regionals cannot participate in the crucial discard policy, nor can they receive interlibrary loan or reference services. Reluctance to assume regional responsibility may be based upon lack of resources, the burden of keeping publications permanently, or general apathy. Many librarians think that the logical choice for a regional depository is the state library. But only 15 state libraries have become regionals. As one regional librarian noted, "A regional library should be a research library with significant collections in many subjects, including federal documents." How the library's documents collection is organized, to what extent it is capable of providing services, its accessibility to a community, and its peripheral extensions—all these are factors that would influence choice of a regional. The majority of regionals are academic libraries, but this does not suggest that the pattern has been the result of logic; adventitious circumstances have often played a part in the formation of regional depository library services.[14]

RESPONSIBILITIES OF SELECTIVE DEPOSITORIES

The word "selective" refers to *all* designated depository libraries that are not regionals, yet a selective depository may, if it so chooses, subscribe to every Item the Superintendent offers for deposit. The term "partial depository" is also used to describe a library having selective status, and the two terms may be considered synonymous in this context.

Designation

Official depository status may be conferred 1) by the U.S. Representative of the congressional district or his predecessor; 2) by one of the U.S. Senators of a state, or his predecessor; 3) by virtue of the fact that the library is a state library or a land-grant college library; or 4) by a special act of Congress.

Selection

Partial depositories are admonished to select only those Items, or categories, of documents best suited to their clients' needs. It is advised that Items be selected cautiously "so that there will be no waste of Government funds and so that you can give proper custody to those you do select and make them readily available to your patrons."[15]

Care and Treatment

Government publications should be managed in much the same way as privately published materials. The Superintendent recommends that documents circulate, that periodicals not be segregated merely because they are government publications, and that government pamphlets be kept in vertical files if that is the library's policy for similar commercial materials. It is the Superintendent's desire that unbound documents be included in the regular binding policy of the library. Lost or worn documents "should be subject to the same replacement policy as the library maintains for non-Government materials."[16] To implement these egalitarian notions about documents that are to be retained at least five years and are the property of the federal government poses difficulties for the conscientious librarian.

Periodic Reports

Pursuant to 44 *U.S.C.* 1909 "the designated depository libraries shall report to the Superintendent of Documents at least every two years concerning their condition." This is accomplished by the use of a questionnaire to depository institutions. Its purpose is to determine whether libraries are providing proper custody of documents received and whether the publications are being used to best advantage. Other questions elicit information helpful to the Superintendent in refining and improving his administration of the depository program. Newly designated depositories are also asked to complete the biennial questionnaire, even though they must submit to the Superintendent a six-month "Check of Condition" report (Public Documents Department, Investigative Series No. 4) designed specifically for newly designated institutions. In the biennial report space is set aside for comments by documents librarians.

The law further requires the Superintendent to make firsthand investigation of depository libraries "for which need is indicated." During 1972, one hundred depository libraries were inspected personally by representatives of the GPO; some of these libraries were notified of a coming visit, others were not. The Superintendent thus relied upon the remaining one thousand libraries themselves to judge the effectiveness of their program.

Termination of Status

Any depository library has the right to relinquish its depository privilege. Conversely, the Superintendent may terminate depository status if the library fails to meet the standards required by law. Upon termination by request or for cause, the library must secure instructions from the regional concerning disposition of the documents on hand. However, "if the library wishes to keep permanently certain publications which were received under the depository program, it may do so. A list of these holdings should be submitted to the Regional Depository and/or the Superintendent of Documents if the library is not served by a designated Regional, with an accompanying statement to this effect."[17]

Classification

Use of the SUDOCS class scheme is not mandatory for depository libraries. The Superintendent adds that "any library should carefully weigh [the SUDOCS scheme] against other classification schemes before adopting it." Generally, smaller depository libraries will integrate government publications into the general collection and, of course, use the classification system of the larger unit. Large depository collections tend to segregate their documents and employ the Superintendent's scheme. There are all kinds of exceptions to this pattern. Some periodicals, significant monographs, and important reference tools are categories that will be integrated into all general collections. The librarians must simply use common sense and good judgment in their decisions. Because extra copies of many publications can be obtained for sale from SUDOCS or the issuing agency, and from one's Representative, many combinations of separation and integration may be employed.

Substitution of Microform

Permission is granted to all designated depositories to substitute micro-copies for any holdings of federal documents, so long as they are properly indexed, easily located, and readily accessible to patrons. Of course, proper reading equipment must be available for whichever type of microform is substituted for the hard copy. Libraries substituting microcopies must send a list of the materials involved to the Public Documents Department Library and must also notify the regional. Part II of the 1973 biennial report was designed to determine how much interest documents librarians showed in the distribution of publications in microform by the Superintendent.[18]

Discard Policy

In addition to the disposal of publications by partial depositories after five years, *all* depository libraries may dispose of certain kinds of material on a continuing schedule. The instructions mention "some of the types of material which may be disposed of":

1. Daily *Congressional Record*, after bound volumes are received.
2. Slip laws, after bound *Statutes* are received.
3. House and Senate bills and resolutions, one year after the adjournment of the Congress.
4. Any materials which are cumulated in later issues, such as *Supplements* to the *United States Code*, *Digest of Public General Bills*, etc.
5. Any publication upon receipt of a revised edition.
6. Supplanted loose-leaf pages when new inserts arrive.
7. Separates, upon receipt of final bound volumes.
8. House and Senate *reports* and *documents*, upon receipt of the bound volumes of the serial set.
9. Compilations of laws and regulations issued by various agencies, upon receipt of new editions.
10. Lists and indexes of publications of various agencies, upon receipt of *complete* new editions. Small spot lists, such as announcements, may be discarded at the end of six months or when they have lost their timeliness.
11. Annual or biennial publications of a statistical nature which merely revise figures or information and bring them up-to-date, upon receipt of a new issue. This permission does not apply to annual reports of departments or agencies.
12. Material which has an expiring-effect date, such as Civil Service examination announcements. Only the latest issues need be kept.
13. Any publication superseded by another which is stated to contain similar information.
14. *Calendars of the House of Representatives*, upon receipt of a new issue. However, the Monday issue contains an index while the other daily issues do not. The final issue of each session of Congress should be kept. All issues of the Senate *Calendar of Business* must be retained, since this publication is not cumulative.[19]

It is important to note that libraries do *not* have to discard these kinds of materials. It is frustrating to the researcher not to have bills and resolutions for earlier Congresses, in order to be able to reconstruct the process and language of failed legislation. It is annoying not to have earlier editions of important publications, whose several revisions reflect cultural, economic, or political changes in our society. The knowledgeable documents librarian will exercise intellectual caution before discarding materials, especially those which cannot easily or inexpensively be recaptured in microform.[20]

NON-GPO PUBLICATIONS

The so-called non-GPO documents consist of those printed or processed materials emanating from executive and independent establishments in Washington and field offices and produced by the agencies' own printing or mimeographing equipment or under contract. The law requires that every issuing unit of government furnish the Superintendent a copy of these publications, so long as they are not confidential in nature or administrative in character. Unless the Public Documents Department Library receives a copy, the document cannot be indexed for citation in the *Monthly Catalog*. Indeed, it is estimated that non-GPO documents constitute from 55 to 90 percent of the total number of federal publications. Some documents of government agencies are controlled through the indexes that cover technical report literature: *Scientific and Technical Aerospace Reports*, *Government Reports Index*, and ERIC's *Resources in Education*. But the citations reported in the technical literature abstracting and indexing services include information from all sources. Those reports generated by a recognizable unit of the federal government are entered, if received, in the *Monthly Catalog*. Consequently, there is duplication of indexing.

The Library of Congress since 1967 has been sending to the Superintendent copies of the non-GPO imprints it receives. Most of these have been selected for entry in the *Monthly Catalog*. Moreover, the Library has published editions of *Non-GPO Imprints Received in the Library of Congress in [year]: A Selective Checklist*. These *Non-GPO Imprints* checklists contain entries for publications not listed in the *Monthly Catalog* or in the other technical indexing and abstracting services mentioned above. Compiled in LC's Exchange and Gift Division, the brochures are sent to all depository libraries and are otherwise available for sale from the Library's Card Division. Their utility is minimal, since they include such a relatively small percentage of the total non-GPO and non-depository production.

When this provision of the 1962 legislation was being considered, Carper W. Buckley, then Superintendent of Documents, waxed pessimistic over the ability of his office and the participating agencies to implement the program in a satisfactory manner. Buckley envisioned vast production and budgetary problems; his fears were not unfounded. A paltry sum of $57,000 was allowed by the Appropriations committee to begin the non-GPO program on a trial basis with two participating units, the Bureau of the Census and the Department of the Interior. The operation was not begun until January 1965, when distribution of the first Census Bureau publications produced outside the GPO was made. By

May 1, 1966, "more than 650,000 copies of Census Bureau publications had been distributed to the depositories."[21] Fiscal 1972 and 1973 estimates placed at about 150,000 the number of non-GPO documents sent annually to depository libraries.

Producing the extra Census data for libraries initially taxed the in-house capabilities of that bureau. Interior also found it difficult to distribute its Bureau of Mines Circulars and Reports of Investigations. Such situations resulted in an ironical solution. Under the 1962 Act the non-GPO publications sent to the Superintendent were to be funded by the participating agency. The Commerce Department found it necessary to send some of its preliminary Census reports to GPO to be printed "to relieve the pressure on its own printing facilities." Interior's field printing plant in Pittsburgh decided to issue a weekly bulletin incorporating certain series, "to be printed at GPO." The provisions of the law appeared to "force more departmental printing into GPO," which incidentally, would then be funded by GPO rather than by the participating units. Thus we watched the ludicrous situation of "non-GPO" documents being printed at the GPO, the *reductio ad absurdum* of the intent of the Act.[22]

After a decade, the Deputy Superintendent of Documents could report to a congressional committee, with regard to non-GPO documents, that "we are currently working with the Library of Congress, Environmental Protection Agency, Board of Governors of the Federal Reserve System, and the Department of Agriculture. We have brought in the Bureau of the Census, Department of the Interior, Department of Labor, and the Department of State. Hopefully, as we can get the cooperation of the other agencies, we will be able to bring more and more of these publications into the program."[23]

Cooperation is likely to be grudging at best so long as there remain critical problems of funding and printing facilities. Buckley has noted, however, that there may be a partial solution to the problem:

> The future distribution of Non-GPO publications to depository libraries may be affected significantly by the establishment throughout the United States of Regional Printing Procurement Offices of the Government Printing Office. It has been my understanding that the printing produced through these regional offices is that which would have been produced in earlier years in Government departmental and field printing plants. If so, such printing will become GPO printing and its distribution to the depositories will be governed by the same procedures followed in the distribution of publications produced in the main GPO plant in Washington.[24]

Examples of some non-GPO categories now being distributed to subscribing depository libraries are shown in Table 1 (page 41).

Table 1

CATEGORIES OF NON-GPO SERIES
AVAILABLE ON DEPOSIT

Issuing Agency	Category	Item Number
Census	Census of Mineral Industries, Preliminary Reports	158
	Construction Industries: Advance Industry Reports	133-D-1
	Current Industrial Reports	142-A
	Small Area Data Notes	148-C
Interior	Fishery Products Reports	611-E
	International Petroleum Annual	642-A
	Mineral Trade Notes	638-B
Labor	Background Facts on Women Workers in the U.S.	783-C-1
	Employment Service Statistics	754
	Family and Property Law	781-A
	Occupational Safety Aids	765-G

NON-DEPOSITORY PUBLICATIONS

To understand the depository system, one must be aware of what it excludes. Many publications are printed by the facilities of the GPO or through GPO contract but are not offered as depository items. These may properly be called "non-depository publications" to distinguish them from "non-GPO publications." Except for the trickle of non-GPO publications that make their way into depository libraries under a prescribed Item, these two categories have in common their lack of availability to libraries under the depository program.

Every publication listed in the *Monthly Catalog* which is not indicated by the "dot" or "bullet" symbol (●) must be procured by other than depository means. 44 *U.S.C.* 1902 states that all government publications shall be made available to depository libraries "except those determined by their issuing components to be required for official use only or for strictly administrative or operational purposes which have no public interest or educational value and publications classified for reasons of national security." One is aware of the tortured arguments over the withholding of information for reasons of national security. But what Solomons in their "issuing components" can judge with foreknowledge the kinds of documents lacking in "public interest or educational value"? This is the crucial problem; it has created a system that unnecessarily complicates acquisition and bibliographic control. Moreover, it often abets a contravention of the spirit of the Printing Act of 1895 and the Depository Library Act of 1962.[25]

Consequently, even regional depository librarians cannot rely upon the depository apparatus for building a collection that will be wholly responsive to the needs of the libraries' heterogeneous clientele. Commercial firms and government units outside of GPO's jurisdiction have moved into this twilight zone in an attempt to service the needs of libraries. Although a number of non-depository publications can be obtained free from the issuing agency or from one's elected Representative, many documents are elusive and their acquisition is time-consuming. Some of the more widely used sources for securing non-depository publications are listed below.

National Technical Information Service

The publications sold by the National Technical Information Service (NTIS) will be discussed in more detail in Chapter 8. Formerly known as the Clearinghouse for Federal Scientific and Technical Information, the publications sold by NTIS are indicated in the *Monthly Catalog* by an "at" sign (@). A few technical reports so indicated are nevertheless sold by the Superintendent. In a given series, one report may be a depository item and the others may not. *Scientific and Technical Aerospace Reports*, a semi-annual indexing service prepared by NASA, lists ten times the number of NASA publications found in the MC, but this journal is itself a depository item sold by SUDOCS. There is a Kafkaesque unreality about this sales, indexing, and distribution pattern.[26] Of greater consequence, however, is the present ominous trend in which more and more titles that were formerly available to libraries on deposit are now handled by commercial firms. Like the exorbitant price increases, this pattern reflects a form of indirect censorship.

The Documents Expediting Project

Familiarly known as "DocEx," the project is an acquisition service for publications not offered by the Superintendent on deposit. DocEx does not distribute what NTIS sells, while NTIS does not sell what the Expediter distributes. If an issuing agency offers a publication for sale, DocEx does not include it in its acquisition policy.

Although the project was begun in 1949, the Library of Congress did not assume total responsibility for the operation until 1968. Presently DocEx is managed in the Federal Documents Section of LC's Exchange and Gift Division. Subscribers to DocEx are eligible to participate in four principal services: current materials; special requests; agency mailing lists; and special offers.

Current materials include the elusive Committee Prints of Congress and various agency publications such as the materials issued by the Tennessee Valley Authority, the Bonneville Power Administration and the Air Force Academy. Special requests may include sales items now out-of-print at GPO and from the agencies if they fall into categories regularly handled by the project. Subscribers' names can be placed on agency mailing lists for specific serial publications and committee calendars. DocEx also makes special offers of older congressional publications from time to time; lists of these are compiled, sent to member libraries, and distributed on a first-come-first-served basis.

Of the participating libraries, most are depositories and the vast majority are academic libraries. Membership is on an annual basis, and fees range from $175 to $525 on a sliding scale based on the quantity of distributed materials.[27] To facilitate listing of congressional Committee Prints in the *Monthly Catalog*, DocEx sends the prints it has secured from the several committees to the Public Documents Department Library. These are sent in separate shipments on a priority basis for permanent retention and indexing. Librarians can secure prints by writing the committees when the prints are abstracted in *CIS/Index* or cited in the *Monthly Catalog*. But to the extent that DocEx gathers elusive materials for libraries otherwise too burdened or too geographically isolated to collect these publications, it performs a useful service.

Readex Microprint

Of the several commercial sources that make documents available in microform, Readex Microprint Corporation serves libraries' needs perhaps most systematically. Launched in 1950, the Readex Microprint publishing program provides complete depository publications from 1953 and non-depository publications from 1956 as listed in the *Monthly Catalog*.

The project is a cooperative venture. All documents, including those secured by DocEx, are assembled in the Office of the Superintendent in the order in which they appear in the MC. The materials are forwarded to the Photoduplication Service of the Library of Congress, which films them at Readex's expense. Thus the materials are arranged by the entry number of the *Monthly Catalog*, which serves as the index to the microprint collection.

Microprint is received by libraries in plastic boxes the shape and size of a royal octavo volume (6½ x 10") with the contents labelled. Because they are shelved in the same manner as books, no expensive or specially designed equipment is needed for storage; the environmental conditions suitable for books meet the requirements for Microprint. A Readex Universal Micro-Viewer must be purchased to magnify the images. To obtain hard copy from Microprint, a Dennison-Readex Unitform Enlarger-Printer produces enlarged electrostatic copies from the microform. Fortunately, the Micro-Viewer also functions for microfiche, microcards, aperture cards, and other unitized forms, both opaque and transparent.

The cost of subscribing to a year's supply of depository and non-depository publications on Microprint runs over $6,000, not counting the cost of the viewer. Readex offers a number of separate units at varying prices: the publications of individual agencies, the *Federal Register*, the Serial Set, and so forth.

Other Categories

Certain important publications, notably maps, are almost exclusively sold or issued by the several agencies responsible for their production, and they are generally not available on deposit.[28] Occasionally a document is sent to depositories and then withdrawn. A 1965 Army manual on booby traps was recalled in 1970. In 1973 a manual with detailed information on how U.S. Customs Bureau officers search for drugs and other contraband items was retrieved from depository libraries by Customs agents. The agents were dispatched to pick up the books directly from the subscribing institutions. Presumably these dangerous tomes are still on Readex Microprint, and can be converted to hard copy at less than five cents a page.

PROBLEMS AND PROSPECTS

An ad hoc committee on the depository library system was created by the ALA Council at its January 1973, Midwinter Meeting. After a year's intensive study, the committee prepared a report calling for significant changes in the Depository Act of 1962. The report was accepted by the Council on January 25, 1974. Because of its far-reaching implication, further study was indicated. The report is herewith reproduced in its entirety:

The ALA Ad Hoc Committee on the Depository Library System recommends that:

1. To insure optimal access of federal information to all citizens, the present depository library system should be strengthened and expanded into a comprehensive network of local and regional depositories, with a national federal depository library at the head of the system.

2. The National Depository Library collection should consist of all publications produced at the expense of the federal government, regardless of format, method of reproduction or source, including security classified documents which will be held from public release until declassified. This collection should be maintained as a permanent archive for reference and

photocopy services for depository libraries and for the general public.

3. The National Depository Library should provide the depository library network, libraries in general, and the public with complete bibliographic control of all publications produced at government expense. This bibliographic data should be made available for inclusion in any other regional or national library network.

4. A permanent Council on Depository Libraries should be established to consult with the National Depository Library on all aspects of the depository library system. The Council should include document librarians, federal printing officials, and representatives of library associations and of the federal library community.

5. The National Depository Library, in conjunction with the Council on Depository Libraries, should be authorized to designate additional depositories based on each library's demonstrated need and ability to meet the national depository standards. Before a library can achieve depository status in this manner, it must obtain the approval of the regional depository library, the appropriate state library agency, and the Council on Depository Libraries. Present provisions for designating depository status will not be affected.

6. National standards of performance which all depository libraries must meet to obtain or continue depository status should be established by the Council on Depository Libraries and administered by the National Depository Library.

7. Regional depositories should continue to be charged with a) receiving and retaining at least one copy of all federal government publications made available to depositories, and b) providing local depository libraries with interlibrary loan service, reference service, and assistance in the disposal of unwanted documents. In addition, the regional depository libraries should assume the responsibility for conducting periodic inspection of depository libraries in their areas to insure compliance with national standards.

    Regional depository libraries should also provide advisory services and training programs to local depository libraries requesting them.

    In order to carry out these responsibilities the regional depositories should be provided with federal funds, on a formula basis, which should include such factors as number of libraries in the region, type of libraries in the region, distance involved, and actual dollars expended in performing legal responsibilities.

8.   Depository libraries should be offered, at no cost to them, the following:

a) All publications produced at the expense of the federal government regardless of format, method of reproduction, or source. Exceptions should include: 1) security classified documents (available when declassified) and 2) publications produced for obvious internal office use. An option should be given to depository libraries to receive documents in paper or microform; some publications may be provided in both forms.

b) Reference tools, including adequate indexes designed to be used with federal documents. This should include quasi-official and commercial publications essential to the operation of a depository library. The selection of the tools should be made by the depositories from a list compiled by the National Depository Library in conjunction with the Council on Depository Libraries.

c) Equipment needed to insure easy and efficient access to publications in microform.

9.   Funds should be provided to the National Depository Library to purchase for the depository libraries the items mentioned in the immediately preceding section. Adequate guidelines should be established by the National Depository Library in conjunction with the Council to govern the provision of these items to depository libraries.[29]

The above recommendations, though they may pose political and bureaucratic problems difficult if not impossible to overcome, provide the library community with an outline for protracted discourse on a subject central to documents librarianship. There is a consensus that the current patchwork policies can only continue to vitiate that section of the law which states that "depository libraries shall make Government publications available for the free use of the general public."[30] Unless major conceptual changes are wrought by GPO—changes that identify as paramount the right of access to information generated by government—libraries will always have less than satisfactory depository arrangements.

REFERENCES

1.   U.S. Congress. Joint Committee on Printing, *Government Depository Libraries*, Committee Print, 93d Cong., 2d Sess., rev. April 1974 (Washington: Govt. Print. Off., 1974), p. 4.

2.   *100 GPO Years*, pp. 79, 90.

3.   Carper W. Buckley, "Implementation of the Federal Depository Library Act of 1962," *Library Trends* 15: 27-28 (July 1966).

4.   44 *U.S.C.* 1905.

5. 44 *U.S.C.* 1904. The policy of the Public Documents Department Library is to annotate Item cards only when the Item category is not self-explanatory.

6. 44 *U.S.C.* 1907. Curiously, the Library of Congress is not part of the designated depository system, but acquisition of U.S. documents both for use within the Library and for purposes of international exchange is accomplished pursuant to 44 *U.S.C.* 1718, 1719.

7. 44 *U.S.C.* 1909.

8. Buckley, p. 29.

9. Ibid., p. 28.

10. 44 *U.S.C.* 1902.

11. Public Law 92-368 provided for the designation of the highest appellate court in each state as a depository library. Bills have been introduced that would increase the number of congressional designations from two to three, and that would provide for the designation of accredited law school libraries as depositories.

12. *Special Libraries* 64: 211 (April 1973).

13. U.S. Superintendent of Documents, *Instructions to Depository Libraries* (rev. April 1973; Washington: Govt. Print. Off., 1973), pp. 3-4.

14. For an excellent study of these problems, see LeRoy C. Schwarzkopf's *Regional Libraries and the Depository Library Act of 1962* (June 1972, ED 066 177) and his summary remarks in *Documents to the People* 1: 17-19 (September 1973).

15. *Instructions to Depository Libraries*, p. 1.

16. Ibid., pp. 1-2.

17. Ibid., pp. 5-6.

18. It was reported in *Public Documents Highlights* 3: 2 (April 1974) that favorable response by librarians and approval by the Joint Committee on Printing would result in microfiche distribution of depository documents, as desired, "by early 1975."

19. *Instructions to Depository Libraries*, pp. 14-16.

20. The Advisory Council to the Public Printer on Depository Libraries criticized these revised *Instructions* and requested that they be rewritten. By mid-1974 the Superintendent was acting upon the Council's recommendations.

21. Buckley, p. 33.

22. Ibid., p. 34.

23. *Legislative Branch Appropriations for Fiscal Year 1972* (Senate), p. 327. The Department of State, however, advised that all of its publications in the specified categories at that time were in fact being produced by the GPO.

24. Comment (p. 5) on the author's article "The Government Printing Office and Non-GPO Publications," *Government Publications Review* 1: 1-5 (Fall 1973).

25. Of little value is the explanation given in *Public Documents Highlights* 3: 4 (April 1974): "When a publication is sent to the GPO, a work jacket (or envelope) containing the specifications, number of copies to be printed, and delivery instructions, is prepared. At this time, if the publication is of educational value, and not of an administrative or confidential nature, enough depository copies are ordered printed for Libraries which are on the list to receive that particular Item. This is a standard procedure."

26.   A typical example of this inconsistency can be discerned in the sales and distribution pattern of NASA's SP-Series. In the February 1973 issue of the *Monthly Catalog*, one notes that a conference on manual control held at the University of Southern California is a depository Item (830-I), while in the same SP-Series a colloquium on the physics of space environment held at the University of Alabama is available only through NTIS.

27.   Alma Mather, "The Documents Expediting Project," *Illinois Libraries* 53: 390-93 (June 1971).

28.   However, a library may obtain Geological Survey map depository status by written request to the U.S.G.S. Publications Division, 12201 Sunrise Valley Drive, Reston, Virginia 22092.

29.   *Library of Congress Information Bulletin* 33: A39-40 (February 8, 1974); *Documents to the People* II:10,13 (February 1974). The ad, hoc committee comprised representatives from the ALA Council, ACRL Law and Political Science Section, Interdivisional Committee on Public Documents of GODORT, and the Legislation Committee, and recommended that its life be continued in order to develop further the implementation of these proposals. At the ALA conference in New York in July 1974, the language of the report was refined somewhat. The Legislation Committee added a separate recommendation advising that the plenary body develop data that would substantiate the need for change, and also that the body provide a cost estimate for implementation.

30.   44 *U.S.C.* 1911.

4

ADMINISTERING DOCUMENTS COLLECTIONS

However wide the coverage and various the form, United States government publications have in common the fact that they are issued by some agency of the federal government for some purpose connected with the public interest. The occasional controversies as to whether issuance of one or another specific publication is in the public interest are not significant against the background of the vast resources of the publications of the government. Over the lengthening years of the nation's history they have come to be an invaluable heritage, worthy of the best efforts of their custodians to organize and make available their wealth of information. In considering the proper organization and administration of these diverse publications in a library, the community of their origin and purpose is an important factor.

—Ellen Jackson, *A Manual for the Administration of the Federal Documents Collection in Libraries* (Chicago: American Library Association, 1955)

INTRODUCTION

This introduction to the mechanics of administering collections of federal publications will first consider the procedures involved in managing selective depository libraries and will then proceed to methods of building a public documents collection without benefit of depository status.[1] Keep in mind that this discrete division is somewhat oversimplified, since many techniques used to acquire and control documents not sent on deposit are used by depository as well as non-depository institutions. Moreover, we will be discussing the machinery of handling publications received in hard copy rather than the storage and retrieval of documents in microform.

Until 1942 the numbers that corresponded to groups or categories of publications available to depository libraries were carried on the "Depository Invoice" sent to participating institutions. In September 1942 the Invoice was discontinued and the November 1942 issue of the *Monthly Catalog* began indicating by a solid circle (sometimes called a "black dot" or "bullet") those documents available to depositories; an "Item number" was also given.

Let us look at a typical entry in the *Monthly Catalog*:[2]

17483 United States Government organization manual, 1972/73.
       Revised July 1, 1972 [1972.]   viii+710p.
       (Published by Office of Federal Register,
       National Archives and Records Service.)
       [Includes Constitution of United States
       with amendments. Revised annually.]
       * Paper, $3.00.   ● Item 577
              GS 4.109:972

The asterisk and price indicate that the publication is for sale to individuals and institutions by the Superintendent of Documents; the black dot means that the *Manual* will be deposited with those libraries that already subscribe to Item 577. In Chapter 3 we noted that since 1922 libraries have been given the choice of selecting or rejecting categories of publications based upon user needs. The "Item" is the apparatus by which the Superintendent controls and distributes publications to designated depositories. As is so common in the area of government documents, the concept of an "Item" is not as crystal clear as librarians would wish. But it is the foundation unit of depository selection and control, and as such is the appropriate locus of inquiry into depository management.

DEPOSITORY LIBRARY PROCEDURES

Items

Items may be considered generic categories, but they do not reflect the number or ratio of publications to Items. The Item (577) that stands for the *U.S. Government [Organization] Manual* accounts for that publication alone. That is, libraries that have chosen to receive Item 577 will get the annual edition of the *Manual* and nothing else in that category. On the other hand, a subscription to Item 770 will insure deposit of twelve issues of the *Monthly Labor Review* magazine during the year, while Item 557 covers the dozen issues of the *Monthly Catalog*.

Other Items reflect types of publications with an indeterminate number of copies. Item 323 covers Army Regulations, and an institution may receive over one thousand different regulations during the course of a year. Item 1006, public bills and resolutions of the Congress, will result in shipments of over 20,000 individual pieces during a Congress. Items that cover areas such as the Treaty Series or Supreme Court Decisions will also vary in number depending upon the degree of activity of those agencies.

More annoying than the categories involving series of a necessarily unspecified number of publications are the many documents issued under the rubric "General Publications." As noted in Chapter 2, these are unnumbered and of a miscellaneous nature, and they are assigned the digit "2" in the SUDOCS classification scheme. Since the category is designed as a catch-all, its very nature precludes advance knowledge of the content of the monographs that will be issued under the Item. Of this potpourri, librarians have complained that "a depository must keep a lot of unimportant pamphlet material in order to be sure it obtains the more substantial publications in each Item category. Such Items are time consuming to weed, take up much shelf space, and would not have to be distributed on deposit in the first place if the Items were broken down more minutely."[3] *The National Atlas of the United States of America*, this nation's first official atlas, was offered as a general publication of the U.S. Geological Survey. Accordingly, libraries that did not subscribe to Item 621 had to pay $100 for this important work.

Item Cards

The Superintendent's vehicle for making Items available to depository libraries consists of a deck of 3 x 5" cards, with one card for each series or category of publications available for selection by depositories. Each card gives the Item number, issuing agency, series title, SUDOCS class number, information on the series when necessary, and space for the library's assigned depository number.

Two sets of cards, arranged numerically by Item number sequence, are furnished to depository libraries at the time of their designation. One set is retained by the library, the other is used to make selections. Items desired by the library are decided upon, and one of the two cards is sent back to the Public Documents Department Library properly identified with the library's depository number. Newly designated depository libraries should make their selection of Items within thirty days from the time the deck is received.

The assigned Item number remains the controlling designation for that category regardless of a change of title or reorganization of the issuing agency. The Item concept, however, is not static. Periodically the Superintendent will notify depositories of new series available for selection. Notification is usually made on a special survey that is distributed approximately once a month with the shipping list. Two 3 x 5" cards are then sent to libraries for each new Item listed, along with a sample copy of the publication whenever possible. The depository library returns one card if the publication is desired; a time limit is specified on the survey.[4]

Libraries will always possess a complete duplicate set of Item cards, for amendments to selection can be made at any time.[5] Publications cannot be furnished retroactively, but selections may also be discontinued by written request, citing the Item number and series title of the Item to be dropped, along with the library's assigned depository number. Items that become inactive or are discontinued as a result of reorganization are announced by a card that serves to replace the superseded Item (Figure 5).

Figure 5

ITEM CARDS

```
Item No. 231-J

  INTERNATIONAL COMMERCE BUREAU, Commerce Dept.

International Marketing Information Service    C 42.31/2:
  Country Market Survey

Series will contain 11 country surveys. These publications will
evaluate the opportunities and pitfalls of doing business in each
country and region. Each survey will contain a complete and authori-
tative analysis on the industrial base, banking, finance structure,
natural resources development, import/export patterns, distribution,
facilities and trade practices.
                                      Depository Library No. _____
```

```
  Item 582-J

    HOUSING AND URBAN DEVELOPMENT DEPARTMENT

  HUD Clearinghouse Service HCS - (Series)    HH 1.35:




            Depository Library No. _____
```

Figure 5 (Cont'd)

Item No. 209

INACTIVE OR DISCONTINUED ITEM

DO NOT SELECT

A list arranged alphabetically by the Superintendent of Documents classification scheme, entitled *List of Classes of United States Government Publications Available for Selection by Depository Libraries*, is revised approximately once a year and furnished to depository institutions. This *List of Classes* updates the Item cards and should be consulted when making new selections to determine whether the series is still active (Figure 6, page 54).[6]

Shipping Lists

The Daily Depository Shipping List is perhaps the single most important internal working document for the administration of depository collections. Begun August 1, 1951, the lists include *all* depository publications distributed each day except the *Federal Register*, the daily *Congressional Record*, the House and Senate *Calendars*, the *Weekly Compilation of Presidential Documents*, the *Daily Statement of the Treasury* and the daily *News Digest* of the Securities and Exchange Commission; these publications, all depository Items, are mailed automatically by another section of the Office of the Superintendent.

The Shipping List serves as an invoice for the day's shipment. Upon receipt of a package, the indicated Item numbers should be checked against the library's selections (that is, the active Item card file) to determine whether any Items have been omitted from the shipment. The list provides such basic information as the Item number, title of the publication and sales price if applicable, and classification number (Figure 7, page 55).[7]

Figure 6

LIST OF CLASSES OF UNITED STATES GOVERNMENT
PUBLICATIONS AVAILABLE FOR SELECTION
BY DEPOSITORY LIBRARIES

EP 2.13:	Project Register, Distribution by River Basin of Projects Approved under Sec. 8 of Federal Water Pollution Control Act (Public Law 660, 84th Cong.) as amended 607-E
EP 2.14:	Cost of Clean Water [annual report to Congress] 473-A-2
EP 2.15:	Northwest Shellfish Sanitation Research Planning Conference, Proceedings 473-A-5
EP 2.17:	Inventory Municipal Waste Facilities, Co-operative State Reports 473-A-1
EP 2.19:	Estuarine Pollution Study Series 607-C-2
EP 2.20:	Sewage Facilities Construction (annual) 498-A
EP 2.21:	Digest of State Program Plans (fiscal year) 473-A-6
EP 2.24:	Fish Kills Caused by Pollution (annual) 496-C
EP 2.25:	Pesticide Study Series 498-A-1
EP 2.26:	Technical Studies Report, TS (series) 473-A-8

Solid Waste Management Office

EP 3.5:	Laws 487-A-5
EP 3.9:	Bibliographies and Lists of Publications 487-A-3
EP 3.10:	State Solid Waste Planning Grants, Agencies, and Progress Report of Activities 487-A-4

Air Programs Office

EP 4.2:	General Publications 483-E-1
EP 4.8:	Handbooks, Manuals, Guides 483-E-2
EP 4.9:	Air Programs Office Publication, AP-(series) 483-E
EP 4.9/2:	Air Programs Office Publication, APTD-(series) 483-E
EP 4.10:	Air Pollution Report, Federal Facilities 483-E
EP 4.11:	Air Pollution Abstracts 483-E-3
EP 4.12:	Addresses 483-E-4
EP 4.13:	Air Pollution Training Courses 483-E-6

Pesticides Office

EP 5.2:	General Publications 473-B-1
EP 5.8:	Handbooks, Manuals, Guides 473-B-2
EP 5.9:	Health Aspects of Pesticides Abstract Bulletin 475-M
EP 5.11/	EPA Compendium of Registered Pesticides, Volumes 1 to 5 473-B-3

Radiation Office

EP 6.2:	General Publications 431-I-18
EP 6.9:	Radiological Health Data and Reports (monthly) 498-B
EP 6.10:	RO/EERL [Eastern Environmental Radiation Laboratory] (series) 498-B-3

EP 6.10/2:	ORP/SID [Surveillance and Inspection Division] (series) 483-M
EP 6.10/3:	ORP/CSD [Criteria and Standards Division] (series) 431-I-13
EP 6.10/4:	EPA/ORP (series) 431-I-21

Technology Transfer

EP 7.2:	General Publications 473-C-1
EP 7.8:	Handbooks, Manuals, Guides 473-C-3
EP 7.9:	Technology Transfer, the Bridge Between Research & Use [Newsletter] 473-C-2
EP 7.10:	EPA Technology Transfer Seminar Publications 473-C-1

FINE ARTS COMMISSION

FA 1.	Reports and Publications 432

FARM CREDIT ADMINISTRATION

FCA 1.1:	Annual Report 430-J-1
FCA 1.2:	General Publications 430-J-2
FCA 1.3:	Bulletins 430-J-3
FCA 1.4:	Circulars (numbered) 430-J-4
FCA 1.4/2:	——(letter-numbers) 430-J-4
FCA 1.22:	Production Credit Associations, Summary of Operations 430-J-5

FEDERAL HOME LOAN BANK BOARD

FHL 1.1:	Annual Report 595
FHL 1.2:	General Publications 596
FHL 1.6:	Regulations, Rules, & Instructions 597
FHL 1.6/2:	Handbooks, Manuals, Guides 597
FHL 1.27:	Journal of Federal Home Loan Bank Board (monthly) 597-A

FEDERAL MEDIATION AND CONCILIATION SERVICE

FM 1.1:	Annual Report 433
FM 1.2:	General Publications 434

FEDERAL MARITIME COMMISSION

FMC 1.1:	Annual Report 233
FMC 1.2:	General Publications 432-L-1
FMC 1.6:	Regulations, Rules, and Instructions 237
FMC 1.10:	Reports (decisions) 233-A
FMC 1.11:	Approved Conference, Rate & Interconference Agreements of Steamship Lines in Foreign Commerce of United States 432-L

FEDERAL POWER COMMISSION

FP 1.1:	Annual Report 435
FP 1.2:	General Publications 436
FP 1.5:	Laws 437
FP 1.6:	Rules of Practice & Procedure 439
FP 1.7:	Regulations, Rules, & Instructions 439
FP 1.7/2:	Uniform Systems of Accounts Prescribed for Natural Gas Companies 439
FP 1.10:	FPC R [Rate] (series) 438-A
FP 1.12:	FPC P [Power] (series) 435-D

Figure 7

DAILY DEPOSITORY SHIPPING LIST

LIBRARY,
PUBLIC DOCUMENTS DEPARTMENT,
U.S. GOVERNMENT PRINTING OFFICE,
WASHINGTON, D.C. 20402

**DAILY DEPOSITORY
SHIPPING LIST**

Claims for nonreceipt of publications on this list under item numbers previously selected by a library must be postmarked within ten days of the date of receiving it. (Instructions to Depository Libraries, Revised September 1967, page 9.)	Shipping List _____ 7314 _____ Shipment of May 15, 1974

Item No.		Class
4	AIB No. 363, Science for Living, Jan.1974 *$1.45 S/N 0100-03177	A 1.75:363
40-A-1	Agricultural Science Review Vol.11, No.2, 2nd Quarter 1973 *75c	A 94.11:11/2
231-B	Overseas Business Reports Nos. 73-61 *30c; 73-62 *30c	C 57.11:
270	Government Reports Index Vol.74, No.4, Feb.22,1974	C 51.9:74/4
294	Federal Personnel Manual Bulletin 296-17, supp. 296-31, May 9,1974 *on sub	CS 1.41/4:296-31/btn. 296-17
431-I-1	National-Wide Roster of Professional Minority Consulting Firms, Feb.1974	EP 1.2:M 66/2
572	CFR Title 47, Telecommunication, pts.20-69, rev. 10/1/73 *$4.05	GS 4.108:47/pt.20-69/ 973
616-A	Wildlife Review No.150, Sept.1973	I 49.17:150
622	New Publications of the Geological Survey List 788, Mar.1974	I 19.14/4:788
1017	Hearing: Overseas Private Investment Corporation	Y 4.F 76/1:Ov 2/5
1025-A	Hearings: 1975 NASA Authorization, Pt.2, Serial No.25	Y 4.Sci 2:93-2/25/pt.
1039	Hearing: ACDA Authorization	Y 4.F76/2:Ar 5/15 C3
1040	Hearings: Energy Information Act, Pt.3 - Appendix, Serial No. 93-34	Y 4.In 8/13:93-34/pt. C3
1051-A	Nuclear Science Abstracts Vol.29, No.4, Feb.28,1974 *$3.25	Y 3.At 7:16/29-4

* For Sale by the Superintendent of Documents

SEE SEPARATE SHEET FOR SURVEY 74-4, MAY 1974

Claims

On Figure 7, note the boxed statement that appears to the left of the Shipping List number and date. Special claim forms are provided, but the Superintendent does not guarantee that claims will be honored, even if the ten-day deadline for claiming non-receipt is met; sometimes the supply of the publication has been exhausted. Moreover, claims cannot be honored in the case of publications for which Item cards were received by the Superintendent after the specific publication within that category has gone to press.

It is not unusual for the Superintendent to send out a second shipment of depository Items on the same day. When this occurs, the Shipping List so indicates and is assigned the next consecutive number. Often the package in which the invoice arrives does not include all of the publications shipped. Military regulations, public laws, and House and Senate public bills and resolutions, for example, are frequently packaged separately, but the initial Shipping List for that day will note that this separate packaging will arrive in the second shipment.

Corrections

The Shipping List also serves as a notice of mistakes made on previous lists; errors are inevitable but are well within the parameters of an operation this large. Usually corrections are minor, involving errors made in class number, prices, and similar bibliographic data. More annoying are mistakes involving publications that were distributed under the wrong Item number. Here is an example from a 1967 Shipping List:

SPECIAL NOTICE CONCERNING JAG LAW REVIEW, distributed November 28, 1967, 1st Shipment, S.L. 4551.

This publication was listed on the shipping list under the correct item number but was inadvertently distributed under Item No. 327-B. Libraries selecting Item No. 327-B but not Item No. 427-B who received copies of this publication in their shipment are requested to return their copy to the Library, P.O. Box 1533, Washington, D.C. 20013, so that we may complete distribution to those libraries selecting Item 427-B but not 327-B. Libraries selecting both item numbers may disregard this notice since they have received a copy and are not involved.

Non-GPO Publications

Under the provisions of the 1962 Act, non-GPO publications are identified as such; they are often enclosed in a separate package if they comprise a lengthy series (Figure 8, page 57).

Classification Changes

The Shipping List provides the librarian with the earliest notification of a change in SUDOCS class number due to merger or reorganization. New classification numbers, including discontinued series, are published in the *Monthly Catalog* and are eventually incorporated into the next edition of the *List of Classes*, but the Shipping List provides librarians with the information on the most current basis.

Figure 8

NON-GPO ITEM ON SHIPPING LIST

Shipping List 5416   PAGE -2-   First Shipment of January 15, 1970

Item No.   Class

```
1008-A     91/1:Senate Reports: 628
1008-B     91/1:House Reports 620
1037       Hearings: Planning - Programming - Budgeting, Pt.5     Y 4.G74/6:P69/4/pt.5
```

BEING MAILED IN ONE SEPARATE PACKAGE BUT AS PART OF THIS SHIPMENT

```
135        1967 Census of Manufactures, NON-GPO                  C 3.24/8:
           MC 67(P)-19A-2, Ammunition, Except for Small Arms, n.e.c.
           MC 67(P)-20H-4, Animal and Marine fats and oils
           MC 67(P)-39C-4, Carbon paper and inked ribbons
           MC 67(P)-34C-3, Fabricated platework (boiler shops)
           MC 67(P)-30A-4, Fabricated rubber products, n.e.c.
           MC 67(P)-23E-8, Fabricated textile products, n.e.c.
           MC 67(P)-22C-1, Finishing plants, cotton
           MC 67(P)-20I-4, Food preparations, n.e.c.
           MC 67(P)-20C-6, Fresh or frozen packaged fish
           MC 67(P)-22B-5, Knit Fabric mills
           MC 67(P)-34A-1, Metal cans
           MC 67(P)-28D-2, Polishes and sanitation goods
           MC 67(P)-29F-1, Raw Cane Sugar
           MC 67(P)-24A-4, Special product sawmills, n.e.c.
           MC 67(P)-24C-5, Wood preserving
```

*For sale by the Superintendent of Documents

The "Monthly Survey"

The Superintendent's *Instructions* outlines the procedure for subscribing to new series. New Item cards, described above, are accompanied by a survey list and samples if available. Item number, title of publication, and class number are given. It happens now and then that a serial publication will be offered in mid-year—for example, Volume 13, Number 6. Since there is no retroactive distribution of documents for deposit, the library that desires the periodical, newsletter, or abstracting service must purchase it (if that is possible) or scrounge back issues to obtain a full run. Moreover, the meager information describing the new Item offered, especially in the case of the "General Publications," forces depositories to accept many new categories on faith. On the other hand, if a library decides that the content of the publications it is receiving under the new Item is not germane to its clientele, the Item may be discontinued.

Insufficient Copies

Occasionally the Superintendent will notify libraries that a particular publication to which they have duly subscribed has been printed in an insufficient amount; not all depositories designated to receive that document will actually receive it. When this happens, the Public Documents Department tries to fill the shortage from sales stock if the publication is for sale. If it is not, an attempt is made to secure it from the issuing agency. The GPO does *not* go back to press to make up the deficiency.

These are the salient features of the Shipping List. Neither the law nor the Superintendent's *Instructions* mentions a required retention period for the lists, but many libraries keep their copies for two years before discarding. It must be reiterated that every depository library receives a copy of each Daily Depository Shipping List, even though it is possible that a given list would contain no Items selected by a particular institution. For regional depository libraries, the Shipping List is a complete survey of Items received on deposit.

Bibliographic Control

Cataloging

Large depository libraries have abandoned attempts to catalog fully each document acquired. The great volume of publications, their diversity of subject and form, and the high cost of cataloging have made total cataloging prohibitive. The Superintendent's class number is now supplied by the Library of Congress on their catalog cards. Cataloging-in-Publication (CIP), which provides for the printing of cataloging information in each individual document as published, was reluctantly made a part of the Library's cataloging procedures. But one cannot rely upon the Library of Congress to catalog anywhere near the total number of documents that appear in the *Monthly Catalog* and the other lists and indexes that provide the bibliographic apparatus for federal publishing.[8]

Classification

In Chapter 2 we mentioned briefly the options of controlling documents either in a segregated collection or incorporated into the larger library holdings. Central to any decision of the use of the SUDOCS class scheme in a separate collection is the role of the *Monthly Catalog*. As a *book catalog*, MC reduces reliance on outside cataloging and classification schemes that may not be wholly adequate. Modified cataloging is viable; active reference service to clients is stimulated. Like materials do become separated when class numbers are left alone in a segregated collection, but the principle of provenance does not lend itself to "browsing" in any event. All classification options are characterized by various drawbacks as well as advantages, and librarians must choose the system most appropriate to their needs.[9]

Record Keeping

Many are the varieties of records maintained by librarians involved in the technical services aspect of government documents. Because an estimated 80 percent of government publications are serial in nature, depository libraries use "form" cards for these kinds of publications and another card (often a Library of Congress catalog card) for non-serial publications with a Cutter number.

Among the types of form catalog cards would be a card numbered from 0 to 99 in 10 columns, used for checking in and recording holdings of numbered publications in series that use a simple consecutive numbering system. This form, as Figures 9 through 13 show, can be used for ordinary numbered publications (which themselves may be separate monographs) in a series, for series like Army Regulations, for serial numbering systems with a numbered prefix, such as the Department of Commerce's Overseas Business Reports, for daily serials with an issue number, like the *Federal Register*, or for series with subdivisions that are numbered, such as Bulletin 1725, Area Wage Surveys for metropolitan areas.

Figures 14 and 15 are examples of typical form variations for daily serials that do not have a volume or issue number (*Daily Statement of the Treasury*) and recurring serials that are issued periodically on a weekly to semi-annual schedule (*Commerce Today*). Still another form card is maintained for annual reports and serials issued on a fiscal-year schedule (Figures 16 and 17).

A plain catalog card, either homemade or supplied by the Library of Congress, is usually used for monographs. Examples of kinds of separates for which plain cards may suffice are shown in Figures 18, 19, and 20. On the monograph cards, depository libraries can provide as much information as they think necessary. Library of Congress printed cards are often used for congressional hearings and committee prints and for any monographs that are integrated in the main library collection.

A number of depository libraries maintain only one set of records, with few if any added entries for titles or subjects. Records are arranged either in shelflist order or alphabetically by government author. If shelflist order is used, librarians must prepare a new card whenever there is a change in SUDOCS class number. If government author arrangement is followed, librarians must prepare a new card when a change in class number also results in a change in author or title of a series. In both situations the librarian must enter cross references for both the old and the new record cards.[10]

In view of the controversy surrounding the organization of the documents collection in relation to the library's overall holdings, it must be stated again that such factors as the mission of the institution, its space, personnel, and clientele are crucial. The ultimate criterion is a pragmatic one: that organization is best which provides adequate internal control and effective reader services.

Figure 9

RECORD CARD: NUMBERED PUBLICATIONS

U.S. Bureau of Labor Statistics

L 2.3

Bulletin

15 0	15 10	15 20	15 30	15 40	15 50	15 60	15 70	15 80	15 90
1	11	21	31	41	51	61	71	81	91
2	12	22	32	42	52	62	72	82	92
3	13	23	33	43	53	63	73	83	93
4	14	24	34	44	54	64	74	84	94
5	15	25	35	45	55	65	75	85	95
6	16	26	36	46	56	66	76	86	96
7	17	27	37	47	57	67	77	87	97
8	18	28	38	48	58	68	78	88	98
9	19	29	39	49	59	69	79	89	99

Cataloged   **Bound**

Analyzed

Figure 10

RECORD CARD: NUMBERED PUBLICATIONS

U.S. Dept. of the Army

D 101.9
680

Regulations. AR 680-

0	10	20	30	40	50	60	70	80	90
1	11	21	31	41	51	61	71	81	91
2	12	22	32	42	52	62	72	82	92
3	13	23	33	43	53	63	73	83	93
4	14	24	34	44	54	64	74	84	94
5	15	25	35	45	55	65	75	85	95
6	16	26	36	46	56	66	76	86	96
7	17	27	37	47	57	67	77	87	97
8	18	28	38	48	58	68	78	88	98
9	19	29	39	49	59	69	79	89	99

Cataloged   Bound

Analyzed

Figure 11

RECORD CARD: NUMBERED PUBLICATIONS

U.S. Dept. of Commerce

C1.50
72

Overseas Business Reports. OBR 72-

0	10	20	30	40	50	60	70	80	90
1	11	21	31	41	51	61	71	81	91
2	12	22	32	42	52	62	72	82	92
3	13	23	33	43	53	63	73	83	93
4	14	24	34	44	54	64	74	84	94
5	15	25	35	45	55	65	75	85	95
6	16	26	36	46	56	66	76	86	96
7	17	27	37	47	57	67	77	87	97
8	18	28	38	48	58	68	78	88	98
9	19	29	39	49	59	69	79	89	99

Cataloged   Bound

Analyzed

Figure 12

RECORD CARD: NUMBERED PUBLICATIONS

U.S. Office of the Federal Register

GS4.107
36

Federal Register, vol. 36, no.-

0	10	20	30	40	50	60	70	80	90
1	11	21	31	41	51	61	71	81	91
2	12	22	32	42	52	62	72	82	92
3	13	23	33	43	53	63	73	83	93
4	14	24	34	44	54	64	74	84	94
5	15	25	35	45	55	65	75	85	95
6	16	26	36	46	56	66	76	86	96
7	17	27	37	47	57	67	77	87	97
8	18	28	38	48	58	68	78	88	98
9	19	29	39	49	59	69	79	89	99

Cataloged   Bound

Analyzed

Figure 13

RECORD CARD: NUMBERED PUBLICATIONS

L2.3
1725

U.S. Bureau of Labor Statistics

Bulletin no. 1725-(nos.)

0	10	20	30	40	50	60	70	80	90
1	11	21	31	41	51	61	71	81	91
2	12	22	32	42	52	62	72	82	92
3	13	23	33	43	53	63	73	83	93
4	14	24	34	44	54	64	74	84	94
5	15	25	35	45	55	65	75	85	95
6	16	26	36	46	56	66	76	86	96
7	17	27	37	47	57	67	77	87	97
8	18	28	38	48	58	68	78	88	98
9	19	29	39	49	59	69	79	89	99

Cataloged   Bound

Analyzed

Figure 14

RECORD CARD: DAILY SERIAL

Daily   T1.5   U.S. Treasury Dept.
             974   Daily Statement of Treasury

	1	2	3	4	5	6	7	8	9	10	11	12	13	14	15	16	17	18	19	20	21	22	23	24	25	26	27	28	29	30	31
January																															
February																															
March																															
April																															
May																															
June																															
July																															
August																															
September																															
October																															
November																															
December																															

DEMCO NO. 28-145

Figure 15

RECORD CARD: WEEKLY–SEMI-ANNUAL SERIAL

YEAR	Vol.	Jan.	Feb.	Mar.	Apr.	May	June	July	Aug.	Sept.	Oct.	Nov.	Dec.	T-p. & Ind.
19 70														
19 71														
19 72														
19 73														
19 74														

C1.58

U.S. Dept. of Commerce

Commerce Today

Cataloged

Bound   Lib. 8-1,100 Aug., 1960

Figure 16

RECORD CARD: CALENDAR YEAR SCHEDULE

FT 1.1

U.S. Federal Trade Commission

Annual Report

1970	1980	1990	2000	2010	2020
1971	1981	1991	2001	2011	2021
1972	1982	1992	2002	2012	2022
1973	1983	1993	2003	2013	2023
1974	1984	1994	2004	2014	2024
1975	1985	1995	2005	2015	2025
1976	1986	1996	2006	2016	2026
1977	1987	1997	2007	2017	2027
1978	1988	1998	2008	2018	2028
1979	1989	1999	2009	2019	2029

CATALOGED

ANALYZED

Figure 17

RECORD CARD: FISCAL YEAR SCHEDULE

HE 5.25

U.S. Office of Education
Education Directory, Part 3.
Higher Education.

1940-41	1950-51	1960-61	1970-71	1980-81
1941-42	1951-52	1961-62	1971-72	1981-82
1942-43	1952-53	1962-63	1972-73	1982-83
1943-44	1953-54	1963-64	1973-74	1983-84
1944-45	1954-55	1964-65	1974-75	1984-85
1945-46	1955-56	1965-66	1975-76	1985-86
1946-47	1956-57	1966-67	1976-77	1986-87
1947-48	1957-58	1967-68	1977-78	1987-78
1948-49	1958-59	1968-69	1978-79	1988-89
1949-50	1959-60	1969-70	1979-80	1989-90

Cataloged   Bound

Analyzed   Lib. 41-2M Mar. 1945

Figure 18

RECORD CARD: SEPARATES

D7.6/6   U.S. Dept. of Defense. Defense Supply
            Agency.

            DSA regulation.   DSAR...

4140.35   4140.46
4100.2   4140.43
4145.3
5805.3
4140.27
3200.1
4115.3
4140.37

Figure 19

RECORD CARD: SEPARATES

D7.6/4	U.S. Dept. of Defense. Defense Supply Agency.
	Federal item identification guide.
W36/2	Miscellaneous waxes, oils, & fats. 1971.
M41/5	Material handling equipment ...1971.
G51	Gloves, mittens, and sleeves. 1971.

Figure 20

RECORD CARD: SEPARATES

Y4.Ar5/2	U.S. Congress. House. Committee on Armed Services.
	United States-Vietnam relations, 1945-1967: study prepared by the Dept. of Defense. 1971. 12 books. (Committee print 92d Cong. 1st sess.)
	"The Pentagon Papers"

NON-DEPOSITORY LIBRARY PROCEDURES

Acquisition

The smaller library can build a suitable collection of United States public documents without the problems that characterize the selective depository. All of the following procedures can be and are used by depository libraries if integration or subject departmentalization demands the acquisition of extra copies of publications. But an aggressive policy of securing government publications will yield good results for the non-depository library with a relatively small purchasing budget, despite higher GPO prices.

Coupons

Coupons in the denomination of five cents may be purchased from the Superintendent and used in lieu of a money order or check. Because so many of the vertical-file kinds of publications (*Growing Raspberries*, ten cents) are cheap as well as useful, coupons provide an easy mode of purchase. The Superintendent sets no limit to the amount in coupons that libraries or individuals may purchase from his office, but since prices of documents are subject to change without notice, problems in remittance may arise from time to time.

Deposit Account

The problem of incorrect remittance is avoided by libraries that open an account with the Superintendent. Over 60,000 individuals and institutions have a deposit account with SUDOCS: it is the most suitable and convenient way to purchase publications for both depository and non-depository libraries alike. An account may be opened for a minimum of $25. A deposit account number is assigned and the library is sent a supply of Deposit Order Blanks (Figure 21). Depositors fill out the appropriate information (the stock number may be substituted for the catalog number), send one copy of the form to SUDOCS, and include periodical orders on a form *separate from other publications*. Usually the top half of the form is returned to the library, along with a transaction slip, after the library has received the publications. The returned form serves as an invoice and the transaction slip acts as a bank statement showing previous and closing balance. Since the Superintendent does not maintain a file of depositors' orders, only one invoice is returned. When the transaction form shows a dwindling balance, the library simply sends a check or money order as one would replenish a personal bank account.

The method is simplicity itself. Price increases, or any information that might have been erroneously indicated on the deposit order blank, can be corrected at the Office of the Superintendent. A checklist on the reverse of the order blank provides information on exhausted stock and other variations on the theme of unavailability. When, for example, the Superintendent underestimates

Figure 21

DEPOSIT ORDER BLANK

DEPOSIT ORDER BLANK

To: Superintendent of Documents,
Government Printing Office,
Washington, D.C.   20402

BEFORE USING THIS ORDER FORM, read the important information on the reverse side.

Deposit Account No. ....

Date ....

Order No. ....

	FOR OFFICE USE ONLY	
	Number of Books	Sales
Mailed............		
To Be Mailed Later............		
Sub..............		
Refund...........		
Coupons.......		
Postage...........		

PLEASE PRINT OR TYPE DEPOSITOR'S NAME, STREET ADDRESS, CITY, STATE, AND ZIP CODE IN THE UNSHADED AREA ABOVE.

CATALOG No.	QUANTITY DESIRED	TITLE OF PUBLICATION	PRICE PER COPY	TOTAL
				$............

FOR ADDITIONAL SPACE ATTACH ANOTHER SHEET.   TOTAL AMOUNT OF ORDER........ $............

IS YOUR BALANCE SUFFICIENT TO COVER FUTURE ORDERS? PLEASE CHECK YOUR LATEST TRANSACTION SLIP.

FOR PROMPT, ACCURATE SHIPMENT please fill in the following mailing label—Please PRINT or typewrite

SD-172-70

U.S. GOVERNMENT PRINTING OFFICE
DIVISION OF PUBLIC DOCUMENTS
WASHINGTON, D.C.   20402

OFFICIAL BUSINESS

RETURN AFTER FIVE DAYS

POSTAGE AND FEES PAID
U.S. GOVERNMENT PRINTING OFFICE

RDER No. ....

Name ....

Street Address ....

City, State, and ZIP Code ....

OUR ACCT. No. ....

the popularity of a publication, it may be sold out even if the librarian places an order for it promptly. In this case a Delayed Shipment Notice (Figure 22) is returned with the invoice, and the Superintendent's mimeographed apologies. In the case of periodicals, an Expiration Notice is sent reminding one to renew, and this renewal, of course, can be charged to one's deposit account.

Figure 22

DELAYED SHIPMENT NOTICE

UNITED STATES GOVERNMENT PRINTING OFFICE
DIVISION OF PUBLIC DOCUMENTS
WASHINGTON, D.C. 20402

DELAYED SHIPMENT NOTICE

We are indeed sorry that, due to the unprecedented demand for the publications listed in our recent announcement, we are temporarily sold out of a number of these items. These items are indicated on your order by a green check mark.

We have placed rush reprint orders for additional copies, and your request has been scheduled to receive immediate attention as soon as the first copies come off the press.

Your original letter or order is returned, and we shall appreciate your keeping it as a receipt until you receive all of the publications you have ordered.

We sincerely regret the inconvenience this delay may cause you.

SUPERINTENDENT OF DOCUMENTS

Discounts

As noted in Chapter 2, institutions that purchase 100 or more copies of a single publication going to one address are eligible for a 25 percent discount, on condition that they "adhere to the public sales price set by the Superintendent of Documents and that publications shall not be overprinted with any advertising matter." Publications purchased in bulk, however, can be sold for *less* than the indicated sales price as a service or promotional device. The library has the right to return materials that have not proved popular, while it can earn up to 25 percent profit on the sale of the documents.

Other Order Forms

White order blanks, samples of which are found in the *Monthly Catalog* and occasionally in other government publications, are similar in format to the blue Deposit Order Blank and are to be used by libraries that do not have a deposit account. In addition, the *Selected U.S. Government Publications* has a special order form for publications listed in each issue. SUDOCS requests that these special forms be mailed separately, one list to an envelope; the forms are color coded and so organized as to facilitate distribution from the warehouse.

Issuing Agencies

Non-depository libraries with specialized mission, such as scientific information centers, will rely upon indexing and abstracting services other than the *Monthly Catalog*. But it is unlikely that small libraries serving a general clientele will find need for NTIS publications. School libraries, however, will find useful some agency periodicals in the field of education and, of course, the ERIC materials that are available on microfiche or in hard copy from the microfiche. The numerous publications listed in the *Monthly Catalog* that are available from the issuing agency are indicated by a plus sign (+). They cannot be ignored in the non-depository library's acquisitions policy, regardless of the size of the library or the type of clientele. Some agencies maintain library mailing lists, but there is no uniform policy.

Congress

Your elected Representative is an inestimably valuable source for securing government documents. Provided the Congressperson or Senator has a capable and cooperative staff, this source should be used for publications that cannot be obtained expeditiously (or at all) through other channels. A call placed to a Representative's secretary will often cause the needed document to materialize more swiftly than any other procedure. Although PL 93-191 has placed some restrictions on members' franking privileges, by law they are permitted free distribution of many kinds of publications. Service to libraries on an ad hoc basis is not only legitimate but effective. Although it is not politic to bombard one's Representative or Senator with requests for documents, a judicious understanding with a member will contribute significantly to collection building.

Selection

Liberated from the tyranny of the Item, the non-depository library's selection of U.S. public documents becomes an autonomous pleasure. In addition, participation in the selection of individual publications engenders familiarity, which in turn broadens one's reference capabilities.

The primary tools for the small library are the triad of guides issued by the Public Documents Department, the *Monthly Catalog, Selected U.S. Government Publications*, and *Price Lists*.[11] The catalogs of the several departments and agencies round out the basic government tools at one's disposal. A host of secondary sources—non-government publications—serves the librarian in the selection process. Some of the prominent, useful commercial guides are indicated below to exemplify the scope of services available for an eclectic, collection-building endeavor.

Body

Alexander C. Body's *Annotated Bibliography of Bibliographies on Selected Government Publications and Supplementary Guides to the Superintendent of Documents Classification System* (the author: 925 Westfall, Kalamazoo, Michigan) has been appearing since 1967. Well-balanced and thorough, the basic volume and periodically issued *Supplements* cover a variety of bibliographies published by federal agencies, with extensive annotations. These guides are good starting points for collection needs.

Leidy

W. Philip Leidy's *A Popular Guide to Government Publications* (New York: Columbia University Press) has appeared in several editions and cites over 2,000 publications, excluding works with detailed statistics or documents of a technical nature. Sales publications and free agency materials are included, and topics from Aging to Carpentry to Wildlife are represented.

Pohle

Linda C. Pohle's *A Guide to Popular Government Publications for Libraries & Home Reference* (Littleton, Colorado: Libraries Unlimited, 1972) may be used to supplement Leidy's editions. Arrangement is alphabetical by broad subject, with a subject index that also includes some titles.

Wynkoop

Sally Wynkoop is an indefatigable compiler of useful government sources. Her *Government Reference Books* appears biennially (Libraries Unlimited, 1970, 1972, 1974) and has covered the periods 1968/69, 1970/71, and 1972/73. The more than 1,000 entries, briefly annotated, are arranged under broad areas (social sciences, science and technology, humanities, general reference, and periodicals), with further subdivisions by specific subjects. The index is a personal author/title/subject approach. Wynkoop has also issued a *Subject Guide to Government Reference Books* (Libraries Unlimited, 1972) which includes not only current reference sources but earlier publications of reference value.

Two guides that purport to serve the non-depository library as well as the larger depository collection are Ellen Jackson's *Subject Guide to Major United States Government Publications* (Chicago: American Library Association, 1968) and Sylvia Mechanic's *Annotated List of Selected Government Publications Available to Depository Libraries* (New York: Wilson, 1971). The former lists titles "which appear to be of permanent importance from the earliest period to the present" and "is intended for reference librarians, for library school students learning the nature and extent of the resources of government publications, and for librarians who, under the new provision for regional depository libraries, will be able to borrow from a regional depository." Mechanic's compilation is arranged by Items, with a series/title index, and includes some 500 Items basic for depository selection. But the author "has kept in mind not only the needs of depository libraries but also those of small and medium-sized public and college libraries and public library branches ... as a selection guide and as a tool for both direct reference and interlibrary loan."

Indexes

Certain indexes such as PAIS (*Public Affairs Information Service. Bulletin*) are well known for their coverage of government materials. But such standard, popular indexes as *Readers' Guide* are skimpy in coverage because they index so few government magazines.[1][2] A sampling of reviewing activity through *Book Review Index* shows that government publications are covered in a variety of sources, which may roughly be divided into the categories of general magazines and library-oriented periodicals. Because the small, non-depository library is apt to be on the lookout for the exoteric rather than the arcane publication, the librarian is advised to have some acquaintance with the general as well as the specific reviewing sources.

General Magazines

The disappearance of the "general" magazine leads to terminological problems, but popular government publications that are useful in a non-depository collection are noted in the pages of *Changing Times: The Kiplinger*

Magazine, U.S. News & World Report, and *Good Housekeeping,* as well as in the more specialized issues of *The Living Wilderness, Negro History Bulletin,* and *American City Magazine.* Indeed, the ubiquity of government involvement in all aspects of national and personal affairs suggests that at some time or other documents will be listed—in passing or in depth—in a majority of periodicals. Of course, when a government report or monograph attains some controversy or notoriety, it will be reviewed in the newspapers, on radio and television, and in almost all journals of opinion.

Library-Oriented Periodicals

News of government publications, ranging from brief notes to annotations to longer expositions, is found either on a regular or a recurring basis in several periodicals devoted to librarianship. Among these magazines are *Publishers' Weekly, Choice, Library Journal, Booklist, RQ, LRTS, Special Libraries* and *Reference Services Review.* Of special note are *Documents to the People,* a newsletter, and *Government Publications Review,* a quarterly. The former, available to individual members of the American Library Association and institutional members who belong to the Government Documents Round Table, is issued four times a year and is a treasure trove of significant activities in the world of government documents, including not only federal publications, but those of states, municipalities, the United Nations and its agencies, and foreign governments. Summaries of Task Force groups in each of these areas are given, as is the latest information on documents librarians' continual struggle to be heard in the decision-making processes of the GPO, the Superintendent of Documents, and the Library of Congress.

Government Publications Review (New York: Pergamon, 1973 to date) is the first magazine to be devoted entirely to the publishing activity of governments. Articles cover the availability and use of government documents at all levels: federal, state, province, municipal, United Nations, and other countries. The magazine includes reviews of current government publications and commercial publications in aid of primary materials.

Increased interest in government publications has spawned a growing body of literature that offers comment on the documents themselves. Recency becomes a problem here. As good as the book-length guides are, they inevitably suffer the obvious handicap of obsolescence. Biennial updating of these guides seems at least the minimal effort needed to compensate for the ineluctable ravages of title, edition, and price changes of government documents.

Government Periodicals

A category that is often overlooked in selection is that of the government periodical itself. A number of government magazines geared to a popular audience contain annotations or reviews of other government publications. *American Education,* for example, contains a section called "Recent Publications," in which documents available from the Office of Education or from the

Superintendent are briefly annotated. *Children Today* has a section titled "In the Journals," which summarizes articles in various government publications relevant to the editorial interests of the magazine. The *Department of State Bulletin* has a "Publications" feature that provides annotations of State Department materials available from SUDOCS or from the agency.[13]

If it is true that the elusive document precisely needed for information or knowledge is often found through a procedure more serendipitous than systematic, it is also true that there is no shortage of selection tools for a small, non-depository library. But reliance upon secondary sources, however useful, should not be considered a substitute for the librarian's own initiative in seeking out primary information.[14]

Storage, Retrieval, Use

As noted, the small library generally distributes its documents collection throughout the holdings, which means that government publications are classified and cataloged in the same manner as the general collection. Materials of a so-called "ephemeral" nature are often stashed away in vertical files.

In the large depository library, retrieval and reference service demands a librarian who is specially trained in documents. In the non-depository library, however, documents work is simply another function of general reference, so all the librarians must know enough about government publications to provide assistance. At the same time, the technical processes in an integrated collection are subsumed in the general method used for all the publications that the library acquires and houses.

The non-depository library enjoys an independence not permitted the depository institution, and this freedom can be harnessed in the service of creative librarianship. Those provisions of the law regarding retention and disposal, for example, do not obtain in the non-depository situation. The range of professional activities—acquisitions, selection, cataloging and classification—may be carried out without the constraints of depository regulations. Regardless, therefore, of the size of the library or its lack of depository status, the skill needed to manage a non-depository documents collection is not qualitatively different from the technique used in the research library. Indeed, it may be a more demanding task to administer in exemplary fashion a collection based upon purchase rather than upon deposit.

REFERENCES

1.   A newly published book devoted entirely to this aspect of government documents is *Administration of Government Documents Collections*, by Rebekah M. Harleston and Carla J. Stoffle (Littleton, Colo.: Libraries Unlimited, 1974).

2.   Issue of February, 1973, p. 57. As noted in Chapter 2, the 1973/74 edition of the *Manual* foolishly dropped the word *Organization*.

3.   Alphonse F. Trezza, "The Documents Workshop: A Review and a Look Ahead," *Illinois Libraries* 53: 428 (June 1971).

4.   *Instructions to Depository Libraries*, pp. 7-9. It has been estimated that the Superintendent provides sample copies for only 50 percent of the new Items offered in the Monthly Survey.

5.   Ibid., p. 9. Exceptions include certain cases where material has been printed in earlier years and held for later binding, such as decisions of courts and some of the agencies. The Serial Set, which is bound from slip reports and documents issued earlier, is available to depository libraries that selected the bound volumes prior to the beginning of the session of Congress covered.

6.   As Figure 6 shows, the *List of Classes* leaves no room to add the many new Items introduced between revisions. In 1973 an estimated 3,000 or more Items were available, but the Superintendent is often careless about notification of discontinued or dormant Items.

7.   In 1974 the Superintendent discontinued making the Shipping Lists available to non-depository libraries, which had found them valuable for acquisitions, prompt classification, cataloging information, and general awareness. However, librarians' complaints forced SUDOCS to reinstate subscription to the Lists.

8.   Current developments in CIP are excellently covered in the April 1974 issue of *Illinois Libraries*, pp. 313-18.

9.   For a spirited discussion of the pros and cons of using the SUDOCS class scheme when reorganization forces a classification change, see Robert M. Simmons, "Handling Changes in Superintendent of Documents Classification," *Library Resources & Technical Services* (LRTS) 15: 241-44 (Spring 1971); reaction to this article in a letter from L. C. Schwarzkopf, LRTS 16: 95-97 (Winter 1972); Simmons' response, LRTS 17: 354-56 (Summer 1973); and a final rebuttal by Schwarzkopf, LRTS 17: 356-58 (Summer 1973).

10.   Jack W. Lyle, "Utilizing the Superintendent of Documents System Without Reclassification," LRTS 16: 497-99 (Fall 1972) and response, letter from L. C. Schwarzkopf, LRTS 17: 359-60 (Summer 1973). Figures 9-20 are examples of cards used in administering the documents collection at the University of Maryland's McKeldin Library.

11.   Obviously, if the *Price Lists* are not resurrected from their moribund status, they will become valueless in selection.

12.   This shortcoming appears to be rectified by the *Index to U.S. Government Periodicals* (Chicago: Infordata International Incorporated). Arranged by author and subject, the quarterly issues index over 100 federal government periodicals, many of which are not indexed anywhere. The first issue covered the period January-March 1974, and there will be an annual cumulation.

13.   See the author's contribution to government periodical annotations in Bill Katz's, *Magazines for Libraries* (2d ed.; New York: Bowker, 1972), pp. 378-98, et passim.

14.   Commercial services like C. W. Associates of Washington, D.C., are eager to relieve librarians of their professional responsibilities in selection by offering standing order packages for numerous GPO and NTIS series.

5

GENERAL GUIDES TO FEDERAL PUBLICATIONS

When the members of the Joint Committee on Printing of the 47th Congress commenced the direction of the work thus entrusted to them, they were in the position of Christopher Columbus when he steered westward on his voyage of discovery, confident that a new world existed, but having no knowledge of its distance or the direction in which it lay. . . . On the first of March, 1883, the work was placed under the superintendence of the subscriber, with directions to follow the plan approved by the committee, and to employ fourteen gentlemen, who were designated. . . . Unfortunately, not one of the clerks employed possessed any experience in the performance of such work, and some proved to be so entirely incompetent that no use could be made of what they did; but by the patient and diligent application of the others, 63,063 books, pamphlets, and documents were found and catalogued.

—Preface to Ben Perley Poore's *Descriptive Catalog of the Government Publications of the United States, September 5, 1774–March 4, 1881* (48th Cong., S. misc. doc. 67)

INTRODUCTION

The bibliographic apparatus of United States public documents, that often unwieldy aggregate of instruments and materials designed to control the large and various publications of government, exhibits a complex and irregular pattern. Indexes, lists, guides, and bibliographies—even those purporting to be comprehensive—fall short of the bibliographic ideal. Indeed, as one learns more of the problems associated with the control of publications, the inadequacies in the apparatus seem to increase. One is reminded of Tennyson's Ulysses who, in the poem of the same name, viewed experience's vistas with some despair; mastering the apparatus of documents is like gazing upon

an arch wherethro'
Gleams that untravell'd world whose margin fades
For ever and for ever when I move.

This chapter will introduce the reader to some of the more important retrospective and current guides intended to organize the several kinds of publications. By way of introduction, the student is advised to consult one or more of the fundamental background works, which have been prepared with care by authorities in this field. The short discussion of background works is followed by an enumeration of the significant signposts toward that elusive bibliographical ideal.

Background Sources

Even a list of guides to the guides cannot claim to be complete. Allowing, however, for the date of publication, there are resources that have attempted to bring order out of the apparent chaos. Two texts stand out in this endeavor. Boyd and Rips[1] is a standard, basic introduction to federal publications. A wealth of detail on the departmental and agency publications, in addition to good coverage of the Congress, courts, and executive office, gives this seminal but outdated work its value. Schmeckebier and Eastin[2] contains an abundance of historical information, with excellent sections on congressional publications and federal laws. An inadequate index limits the effectiveness of this otherwise detailed and meticulous text. A comprehensive, annotated guide compiled by John Brown Mason[3] provides a useful bibliographic checklist, a departure point for further inquiry. James Bennett Childs has an excellent summary of United States government publications in his survey of the bibliographic structure of worldwide government publishing.[4] Price and Bitner is the outstanding text on the documents and citations of statutory and administrative law.[5]

The literature of librarianship contains many articles about government publications. Important collected works include the July 1966 issue of *Library Trends*; the June 1971 issue of *Illinois Libraries*; the January-April 1974 issue of *Drexel Library Quarterly*; and the April 1974 issue of *Illinois Libraries*. The latter periodical is quite likely the magazine *par excellence* in this profession for its preëminent attention to the publications of government.

Monographs of a scholarly nature, in addition to the works cited above, include a recent study sponsored by the U.S. Office of Education, which proposed a research design for analyzing and examining the use, bibliographic control, and distribution of federal, state and local documents.[6] The report contained a lengthy bibliography, which was reprinted in the June 1971 *Illinois Libraries*.

These accounts of the documents process complement the works noted in the preceding chapter, which attempt to afford control over the content of federal publications. Some of the general references that follow will be invoked again in later chapters as their significance impels more detailed analysis. Important instruments of control not included in this section will be given appropriate coverage in the chapters that ensue, for the bibliographic mosaic must be assembled piece by piece.

CATALOGS, INDEXES AND CHECKLISTS

Government Documents

Poore

Pursuant to a law enacted in 1882, which authorized the preparation of a "Descriptive Catalogue of all publications made by the authority of the government of the United States and the preceding government of the Colonies, and all departments, bureaus and offices thereof, from July 4, 1776 to March 4, 1881,"[7] Ben Perley Poore and a ragtag group of helpers assembled "the first and only attempt to make a complete list of all government publications—executive, legislative, and judicial";[8] the result was *A Descriptive Catalogue of the Government Publications of the United States, September 5, 1774–March 4, 1881.* The volume was 1,392 pages, consisting of 1,241 pages of catalog and 151 pages of index. The index was euphemistically deemed "far from complete or satisfactory. It is sufficient to condemn it to state that there are no cross references."[9] Moreover, Poore's *Catalogue* omitted many departmental publications.

Poore's is arranged according to the publication's date of issue. Each entry is annotated, but the chronological format mandates a superior index. Because of the lack of differentiation and specificity in the index, the *Catalogue* is time-consuming drudgery to use. First issued as Senate Miscellaneous Document 67, 48th Congress, 2d session, Poore's *Catalogue* has since been reissued in a 1962 Johnson reprint.

Greely

Adolphus Washington Greely was a soldier, scientist, and arctic explorer who published works on meteorological, electrical, and geographical subjects, and who found time to supervise a compilation of congressional publications for the early Congresses. Entitled *Public Documents of the First Fourteen Congresses, 1789-1817—Papers Relating to Early Congressional Documents*, it was issued in one volume as Senate Document 428, 56th Congress, 1st session. A supplement was published in Volume 1 of the *Annual Report* of the American Historical Association for 1903; the two studies were reprinted in one volume by Johnson in 1963.

Although there is some overlapping with Poore, Greely's list pertains to publications of Congress and not necessarily to those ordered compiled or printed by Congress. Arrangement is chronological by Congress, followed by a 45-page index of names (but not subjects). The compiler endeavored to give a complete listing for the period 1789-1817, but there are many omissions; no attempt was made to include departmental publications as such.

Checklist

After Ames (see below) had directed and supervised the publication of two earlier editions of a checklist for both departmental and congressional publications, the Superintendent of Documents in 1911 issued the *Checklist of United States Public Documents, 1789-1909* (Kraus reprint, 1962). The *Checklist* reproduced the shelflist in the Public Document Department Library. It is arranged in three sections: congressional edition by serial number; departmental edition by SUDOCS class number; and miscellaneous publications of Congress. Planned in two volumes, the index volume was never issued. Librarians and those conversant with government structure are best equipped to handle this source. The failure of earlier compilers to include departmental documents is significantly remedied by the *Checklist*.

Tables and Index

Picking up where Greely stopped, the *Tables of and Annotated Index to the Congressional Series of United States Public Documents* was published in 1902 (Mark Press reprint, 1963) and lists publications of the 15th to the 52d Congresses, 1817-1893. The first section of the book, the "Tables," gives series information, with notes on contents and on omission or duplication in the Serial Set. The second section, the "Index," is a useful reference by subject and name, with the accompanying serial number of the bound congressional set.[10]

The index is deliberately selective, covering little more than 50 percent of the numbered *documents* and *reports* issued from 1817 to 1893. The compilers expressed their disdain for many congressional materials. In the preface it is noted that an effort was made "to extricate the more important documents from the scattered mass of worthless matter which composes nearly one half the congressional set."[11] Like Greely's compilation, the *Tables and Index* includes only congressional publications. However, because many executive publications were issued in their "Congressional edition," the guide has limited usefulness in this area. The peculiarities of issuing publications in more than one edition will be discussed in the next chapter.

Ames

Poore's comprehensive general catalog included publications up to 1881, and John Griffith Ames carried the listing from that year to 1893, the first edition covering the years 1889-1893. Ames, who was the Superintendent of Documents in the Interior Department, called his second edition *Comprehensive*

Index to the Publications of the United States Government. It was brought out in 1905 in two volumes (issued as House Document 754, 58th Congress, 2d session; Edwards reprint, 1953, 2 volumes in 1). But, like Poore, Ames omitted a number of departmental publications. Arrangement is alphabetical by subject with a personal name index at the end of volume 2. The usefulness of the index, as opposed to Poore's, is manifest: subordinate sections of a book are indexed separately, and serial numbers are given in tables under the subject "Congressional Documents" in volume 1.

Document Catalog

Covering the years 1893-1940, this biennial work, whose title was *Catalogue of the Public Documents of the . . . Congress and of All Departments of the Government of the United States for the Period from March 4, 1893 to December 31, 1940,* is an analytic dictionary catalog. It represents the first truly systematic effort to record public documents issued by the federal establishment.

The *Document Catalog* is a joy to use. Entries are under both personal and governmental authors, subject, and frequently title. It includes a complete list of executive orders issued during the period covered. Proclamations are listed, as are periodicals that were issued regularly. Processed as well as printed documents made available to the Superintendent are included, but no claim to completeness is made for the processed materials. A list of government offices appears at the end of each catalog to serve as a guide to government organization. Beginning with the 56th Congress, the serial number was included in brackets to permit easy access to the bound volumes of the Serial Set.

For all its accuracy, however, the *Document Catalog* was doomed by a fatal dose of overenthusiasm in the 1895 legislation, which mandated the publishing of the *Monthly Catalog* during the very years when the *Document Catalog* was being compiled. From the beginning it was three years late in appearing; World War I retarded publication of its biennial editions to the extent that they appeared nine years after the close of the Congress covered. It was finally discontinued with Volume 25, issued in 1947 but covering the 76th Congress (1939-40).

Document Index

An alphabetical subject (or inverted title) listing for the congressional documents and reports only, the full title was *Index to the Reports and Documents of the . . . Congress, with Numerical Lists and Schedule of Volumes, 1897-1933.* Libraries that have the *Document Catalog* rarely need to use this sessional tool, unless the client has only the number of the document or report. This publication was superseded by the *Numerical Lists and Schedule of Volumes.*

Numerical Lists

The *Numerical Lists and Schedule of Volumes* is simply that section of the *Document Index* consisting of the reports and documents in numbered sequence (the "Lists"), and a grouping of numbered reports and documents by volumes (the "Schedule") of the congressional set. Since 1933 the *Numerical Lists* has been the only *sessional* key to the bound volumes known as the Serial Set. Lists and schedules for an entire Congress were included in the biennial *Document Catalog*, but owing to its increasingly tardy appearance, libraries that subscribed to the Serial Set needed a more prompt key. With the discontinuance of the *Document Catalog*, the *Numerical Lists* and the *Monthly Catalog* now furnish the information necessary to pursue the congressional *reports* and *documents*. Because of its essential value in this respect, the *Numerical Lists* will be considered in more detail in the next chapter.

Monthly Catalog

Current use of this basic source was discussed in Chapter 2. Historically, the *Monthly Catalog* was created by the Printing Act of 1895, wherein the Superintendent of Documents was directed "to prepare and publish a Monthly Catalog of Government publications, which shall show the publications printed during a month, where obtainable, and the price thereof." However, the same Act instructed the Superintendent "to prepare and print at the close of each Congress a Comprehensive Index [*Document Catalog*] of public documents [and] to prepare and print at the close of each regular session of Congress a Consolidated Index [*Document Index*] of congressional documents."[12] Thus the *Monthly Catalog* was not intended to compete with the *Document Catalog* or *Document Index*. The *Monthly Catalog* was to remedy the haphazard system of distribution and sales and provide "a reasonably early notice of all works printed by the government and how they could be obtained."[13] The *Document Catalog*, a "retrospective" tool virtually from its inception, was to be the exemplary bibliographic achievement. But as the cost of compiling and printing the biennial work grew ever more burdensome, and as the *Monthly Catalog* improved its coverage,[14] however slowly, the Superintendent was compelled to reexamine both programs. Upon his recommendation to the Joint Committee on Printing, the latter index became the single official source of publications as mandated by Section 62 of the 1895 Printing Act.

A privately published work in ten volumes known as *Hickcox's Monthly Catalogue* was the precursor of the monthly publication.[15] Between 1941 and 1947 three supplements to the *Monthly Catalog* were issued "to cover publications which had been omitted from the *Monthly Catalog* and which would have appeared in the biennial *Document Catalog*."[16] The internal improvements beginning with the issue of September 1947, the reemergence of personal authors in 1963, the decennial indexes—all have been measures designed to make the *Monthly Catalog* a tool fully justifying the discontinuance of the *Document Catalog*. But those who mourn the demise of the magnificent *Document Catalog* are not wholly irrational in their grief.

The foregoing attempts to place the general catalogs, indexes and checklists in chronological sequence by period covered, an arrangement that is graphically presented in Table 2 (see page 82); the works are referred to by popular (short) title. Another perspective on the sequence is shown below.[17]

Executive *and* Congressional Publications	Congressional Publications Only
Poore Ames Checklist Document Catalog Monthly Catalog	Greely Tables and Index Document Index Numerical Lists

Because of the limitations inherent in each of these resources, the librarian will often have to direct the client to more than one source, especially if the client is seeking citations prior to 1893. Moreover, the only way to become familiar with the construction of the early indexes and lists is through much practice in the working situation.

Commercial Publications

The bibliographic apparatus produced by the government has always fallen short of the inclusive ideal; if our Tennysonian metaphor is true, it is likely always to remain so. Commercial ventures have attempted to bridge the gap, but with varying degrees of success. Some prominent examples follow.

Andriot

John Andriot has been the greatest single *individual* resource outside of the government for control of federal documents. A one-man "cottage industry" (Andriot calls his operation "Documents Index"; the address is simply P.O. Box 195, McLean, Virginia), his guides for documents librarians have appeared for well over a decade and have provided invaluable assistance to technical and readers' services.

It is difficult to say which of Andriot's sources is most renowned. His annual *Guide to U.S. Government Publications*, a multi-volume work, gives basic information for the more than 2,000 agencies of government that issue series, including periodicals. Arrangement is by SUDOCS class number with government author and title indexes. Entries are annotated; additional information includes brief agency histories. Andriot issues this *Guide* in looseleaf form so that changes in organization may be reflected without awaiting the expense of a complete, new edition.

Table 2

CHRONOLOGY OF GENERAL CATALOGS, INDEXES
AND CHECKLISTS

	1775	1880	1880	1890	1900	1930	1940	Present
Poore	(1776)	(1881)						
Greely	(1789)	(1817)						
Checklist	(1789)			(1909)				
Tables and Index	(1817)		(1893)					
Ames	(1881)		(1893)					
Document Catalog			(1893)			(1940)		
Document Index			(1895)		(1933)			
Monthly Catalog			(1895)					
Numerical Lists					(1933)			

Andriot's *Guide to U.S. Government Statistics* has appeared less regularly than the serials volumes. In 1973 the fourth edition of *Statistics* appeared after a dozen years.[18] *Statistics* is an annotated guide to over 1,700 recurring U.S. government publications "from 1-page releases to huge compilations of historical data." Over 3,000 titles in major statistical numbered series are listed. For each agency Andriot provides basic statistical serials in SUDOCS class order with information as to the kinds of statistical data given. There is a subject index, but it is not a detailed, analytical one.

Andriot's most recent venture is entitled *Checklist of Major U.S. Government Series*, a projected 20- to 30-volume set of checklists covering the major series, both numbered and unnumbered, published by departments and independent agencies. Volume I, *Department of Agriculture*, was issued in 1973 and covered 23 prominent numerical series currently being issued by the department and its subordinate agencies. Priority in this series will be given to those agencies that do not publish cumulative lists of their series on a periodic basis. *Checklist* has a title index, and Andriot plans to add subject indexes to subsequent editions.

Carrollton Press

Briefly noted in Chapter 2 was Carrollton Press's *Cumulative Subject Index to the Monthly Catalog of U.S. Government Publications, 1900-1971*, a single-alphabet index to more than one million publications listed in the *Monthly Catalog* for those years. In 15 hard-copy volumes, the *Cumulative Subject Index* eliminates the necessity of piecemeal searching for citations that formerly required using the 21 biennial *Document Catalogs* and the decennial and annual indexes to the *Monthly Catalog*. Moreover, the headings and forms of entry, which differ between the *Document Catalog* and the *Monthly Catalog*, have been made uniform. Cumulating annual supplements will be published until such time as a large cumulation can be integrated into the main index.

Checklist '70 (published by Carrollton under the imprint of U.S. Historical Documents Institute) completes the task begun by the *Checklist of United States Public Documents, 1789-1909* which, as we noted, served to remedy the failure of Poore's *Catalog* and Ames' *Index* in coverage of agency documents. According to Boyd and Rips, a fourth edition of the 1909 *Checklist* had long been "the aid to government publications most needed by librarians," and this large bibliographic lacuna was finally filled with the publication of *Checklist of United States Public Documents, 1789-1970*, popularly known as *Checklist '70*.

Remember that for the 1909 *Checklist*, the index volume was never issued. *Checklist '70* has five index volumes in hard copy to accompany 118 microfilm reels on which are contained approximately 1,200,000 shelflist cards arranged in SUDOCS classification order. This, of course, is the shelflist of the Public Documents Department Library. The 1909 *Checklist* was organized in this fashion, but, until *Checklist '70*, the updating had to be partially accomplished by homemade indexing or by using the heroic listings of Mary Elizabeth Poole.[19] The five index volumes provide access to the microfilm as follows: Volume I, *Superintendent of Documents Classification Number Index*, accumulates the names of over 8,000 current and non-current government authors in SUDOCS class order; Volume II, *U.S. Government Author-Organization Index, 1789-1970*, is arranged alphabetically by the official names of the active and inactive government authors; Volume III, *Departmental Keyword Indexes to U.S. Government Author-Organizations*, is organized by departments and subdivided by agencies; Volume IV, *U.S. Government Serial Titles, 1789-1970*, is an annotated alphabetical listing of some 18,000 current and discontinued titles in the Serials Card File of the Public Documents Department Library;[20] and Volume V, *Master Keyword Index to the Publication-Issuing Offices of the U.S. Government, 1789-1970*, consists of title and KWIC/titles to the *Checklist*. *Checklist '70* issues semi-annual cumulative updating index volumes. Its advent fulfills the promise of the third edition after six decades of bibliographic silence.

A recent Carrollton Press guide is entitled *The National Union Catalog of U.S. Government Publications Received by Depository Libraries* (NUC/GP), the first edition having appeared in 1974 in four volumes. Holdings of most government documents are not included in the standard union lists such as the *National Union Catalog, Union List of Serials*, or *New Serial Titles*. NUC/GP lists for each Item the individual depository libraries that are receiving the publications in that Item category as of November 1973. The real value of NUC/GP will not be felt until it becomes a "retrospective" tool, when its value for interlibrary loan will be manifest.

Pierian Press

Noted also in Chapter 2 were the decennial and quinquennial personal author indexes to the *Monthly Catalog* in four volumes covering the years 1941-1970. Edited by Edward Przebienda and published by Pierian Press (Ann Arbor, Michigan), the *Cumulative Personal Author Indexes* consist of alphabetical lists of all personal names that have appeared in the entries of the *Monthly Catalog* for those years. Authors in these lists include virtually every relationship—editor, compiler, translator, researcher, joint author, lecturer—of personal authorship to publication cited, including a systematic author approach to Joint Publications Research Service translations.

The *Cumulative Personal Author Indexes* are significant because from September 1947 to December 1962 personal authors were omitted from the *Monthly Catalog* index, including the two decennial cumulative indexes (1941-50 and 1951-60). Prior to September 1947, personal authors were included in a limited fashion. The *Document Catalog* (1893-1940) included personal authors. With the publication of Carrollton Press's subject index and Pierian Press's personal author indexes, access to the *Monthly Catalog* is immeasurably improved.

Congressional Information Service

Like Carrollton and Pierian, the Congressional Information Service (CIS), a Washington, D.C., based commercial firm, is a relative newcomer to the bibliographic scene. Two significant tools have been created by CIS; one is concerned with control of congressional publications and the other with providing access to the ubiquitous statistical publications of the United States government.

CIS/Index collects all the publications of Congress and provides abstracts for them on a monthly basis. If *Checklist '70* now fills the gap in citing departmental publications since the 1909 *Checklist, CIS/Index* surpasses other congressional guides in its abstracting capabilities, although it is not a retrospective tool.[21]

Begun in 1970, *CIS/Index* consists of two parts: a Summary Section and an Index Section. The Summary Section publishes an abstract of the several types of congressional materials—hearings, prints, documents, reports, and executive documents and reports—excluding reports and hearings on private bills, publications primarily "ceremonial" in nature, internal housekeeping matters of the Congress, and the like. Note the basic bibliographic information provided and the brief description of the document's contents (Figure 23). A simple accession number system identifies the publication in both the Summary Section and the Index Section. In our example, S242-5 is CIS's own internal alphameric notation indicating that the publication is a committee print of the Senate Committee on Banking, Housing and Urban Affairs.

The Index Section offers access by subjects, names of witnesses, names of organizations represented by witnesses, names of individual and corporate authors, names of subcommittees, and popular names of bills, laws, and reports. Additional indexes offer cross-references by bill numbers, report numbers, document numbers, and names of committee and subcommittee chairmen. In our example, the committee print cited was found in the Index Section under both subject and primary government agency (Figures 24, 25).

Quarterly cumulative indexes include the documents covered during the previous three months. The *CIS/Annual* is more than a cumulation of a year's *CIS/Index* coverage; it contains a guide to multi-volume hearings issued by Congress during the year, plus added bibliographic data for the entries—Library of Congress card number and *Monthly Catalog* entry number—which were not available in the monthly issues. Using the annual, one can trace the development of a Public Law through previous Congresses back to 1970, since the annual provides specific references to all congressional documents in which the legislation or the need for it is discussed in any detail. *CIS/Highlights*, a brochure sent to subscribers in advance of the monthly index, contains announcements of documents of more than routine interest, annotated and arranged by broad subject headings.[22]

American Statistics Index was first published as an annual in 1973; subsequent editions have been announced and indexed in monthly supplements and cumulative indexes throughout the year until the next annual; in this pattern ASI is roughly comparable to *CIS/Index*.

Figure 23

CIS/INDEX: SUMMARY SECTION

S242   Prints
BANKING, HOUSING AND
URBAN AFFAIRS
Committee, Senate

**S242-5   THE CENTRAL CITY
              PROBLEM AND URBAN
              RENEWAL POLICY.**
Feb. 16, 1973.   93-1.
$2.00; $2.35 ppd.   ●Item 1035.
viii+370 p.   Y4.B22/3:C49/4.

CRS study, prepared for the *Subcom on Housing
and Urban Affairs*, analyzing the problems of the
central city. Focuses on history, operations, and
policies of the urban renewal program and the
related model cities program administered by
HUD. Includes analyses of economic and social
characteristics of central city populations, cities'
fiscal problems, property and business invest-
ments, housing abandonment, manpower training programs, and LEAA in central cities.

   Report is in two main parts: first part (p. 19-
134) summarizes and analyzes the data provided
in greater detail in the second part (p. 135-431).
Includes tables throughout.

   Appendices (p. 342-370) include:

a. "The Inner City Environment" chapter 6
   from Council on Environmental Quality 2d
   annual rpt, Aug. 1971 (p. 344-362).

b. "A Health Profile of the Urban Poor" excerpt
   from Our Urban Environment and Our Most
   Endangered People, by EPA (p. 363-370).

Figure 24

CIS/INDEX: INDEX SECTION (SUBJECT)

Housing
   Central cities problems, S242-5
   Elderly housing programs and needs,
      S142-2
   see also Construction industry
   see also Federal aid to housing
   see also Low income housing
   see also Mortgages

Figure 25

CIS/INDEX: INDEX SECTION (GOVERNMENT AGENCY)

Department of Housing and Urban Development
Central cities problems, S242-5
Exec Reorganization Plan No 1, 1973,
  H401-11.4
Fed housing policies review, J841-9

The comprehensive scope of ASI dwarfs the efforts even of the admirable Andriot. The annual is in two parts. Part 1, the Index Section, provides references to subjects, individual and corporate authors, publications, specific articles, and tables. A "category index" permits searching by census divisions and Standard Metropolitan Statistical Areas (SMSA's), by commodities and income, and by age, race, sex, educational attainment, etc. The Index Section also offers access to publications and individual articles when only the title or report number is known. From the index the user is referred by accession number to the Abstract Section, where detailed information about the content of the publication is given (Figure 26, page 88).

ASI claims to cover the full statistical output of the federal government, just as *CIS/Index* purports to include all congressional materials save minor publications. The only exclusion in ASI involves publications "which are considered to be of extremely limited interest." The significant sources of statistics include the major statistical agencies; analytic, research, and regulatory agencies that produce studies based on the data collected by the major agencies; and judicial and legislative sources, including many standing, select, and special committees of Congress.[23] Publications screened include periodicals, annuals and biennials; surveys and reports; articles of a statistical nature appearing in selected journals; series; regional and field office publications of agencies; and even publications of non-statistical agencies that report relevant data. *ASI Annual* also contains a "Guide to Selected Standard Classifications" which includes census regions, Consumer Price Index cities, etc. And, like *CIS/Index*, ASI makes available the publications that it indexes on microfiche; subscribers may purchase the entire collection or select groupings, including a retrospective service of special and irregular statistical publications going back, where appropriate, ten years or more.

Computerized text processing permits both *CIS/Index* and ASI a recency not found in many resource tools of comparable scope. Indeed, these indexes are exemplars of what the twin technologies of electronic data processing and microreproduction can accomplish when harnessed in the service of information needs. ASI's thesaurus was built on the base of the one developed for *CIS/Index*; the descriptors are maintained, too, by computer-assisted methods.[24]

Other

Omnibus guides to reference sources inevitably list many government publications and works about documents. Standard classics like Winchell's *Guide*

Figure 26

AMERICAN STATISTICS INDEX: ABSTRACT SECTION

6742
BUREAU OF LABOR STATISTICS: MANPOWER AND EMPLOYMENT
Current Periodicals

6742-5   EMPLOYMENT SITUATION
Monthly.   Approx. 20 p. †
ASI/MF   L2.53/2:(date).
1907(74).

Monthly press release providing current statistics on U.S. labor force size and characteristics. Data include total employed and unemployed, Vietnam War veteran employment status, and breakdowns by industry for employment, hours, and earnings.

Release is usually issued in first week of the month and covers data for the previous month, with comparisons to the same month of the previous year. An annual review is issued in Dec. Releases in Mar., June, Sept., and Dec., provide quarterly averages. Beginning Mar. 1974 issue, quarterly issues also include 1 text table on employment status of Spanish heritage persons and comparisons with white and black workers.

Contents:

a. Summary analysis with 1 table highlighting the employment situation.

b. 12 tables, listed below, followed by approximately 20 charts which supplement tabular data.

Data on the labor force, total employment, and unemployment are derived from the Census Bureau sample survey of households. Payroll, employment, hours, and earnings data are collected by State agencies from payroll records of employers. Both surveys are described in the technical notes of the BLS monthly publication *Employment and Earnings* (see 6742-2).

This abstract updates previous abstracts for this publication.

TABLES:

[Tables are for past month and same month of previous year. Seasonally adjusted data are also included for the past 2 months and for selected months of the previous year.]

ESTABLISHMENT DATA

A-1. Employment status of the noninstitutional population by sex and age, by race, quarterly.

A-2. Major unemployment indicators, seasonally adjusted [includes sex, race, occupation, and major industry group].

A-3. Selected employment indicators [includes sex, occupation, major industry, and class of worker].

A-4. Duration of unemployment of unemployed persons.

A-5. Reasons for unemployment.

A-6. Unemployment by sex and age.

A-7. Employment status of the civilian noninstitutional population, seasonally adjusted quarterly averages [by sex, age, and race].

A-8. Persons not in labor force, by whether they want jobs, current activity, and reasons for not seeking work, seasonally adjusted quarterly averages [by sex and race].

to *Reference Books* (8th ed.; Chicago: American Library Association, 1967) and its supplements (1968–), and Wynar's *American Reference Books Annual* (Littleton, Colorado: Libraries Unlimited, 1970–) should not be overlooked. Over the years a number of catalogs, indexes, and guides (some of which are not treated here) have been issued; these are noted in several sources, among them Ellen Jackson's *Subject Guide to Major United States Government Publications* (1968), pp. 159-75; Sylvia Mechanic's *Annotated List of Selected United States Government Publications Available to Depository Libraries* (1971), pp. 392-95; and J. B. Mason's *Research Resources, Volume 2* (1971), pp. 11-16.

* * *

The commercial sources of bibliographic control are as expensive as they are useful, a strong argument for federal subsidy to libraries to defray cost of purchase. Thanks in no small measure to technology, bibliographic control has come a long way since the Heraclean but inadequate efforts of individuals like Poore and Ames. Yet expanding the scope and quality of control and retrieval of government information seems only to reveal the need for more and better systems. Indeed, the sheer amount of information has grown more rapidly than the apparatus that seeks to render it manageable. The task often resembles the one designed to punish Sisyphus.

REFERENCES

1. Anne M. Boyd, *United States Government Publications* (3d ed. rev. by Rae E. Rips; New York: Wilson, 1949).
2. Laurence F. Schmeckebier and Roy B. Eastin, *Government Publications and Their Use* (2d rev. ed.; Washington: Brookings, 1969).
3. John Brown Mason, *Research Resources: Annotated Guide to the Social Sciences, Volume 2* (Santa Barbara, California: ABC-Clio, 1971).
4. J. B. Childs, "Government Publications (Documents)," in Allen Kent, et al. (eds.) *Encyclopedia of Library and Information Science, Vol. 10* (New York: Marcel Dekker, 1973), pp. 38-53.
5. Miles O. Price and Harry Bitner, *Effective Legal Research* (3d ed.; Boston: Little, Brown, 1969).
6. Bernard M. Fry, et al., *A Research Design for a Comprehensive Study of the Use, Bibliographic Control, and Distribution of Government Publications* (Bloomington, Indiana: Graduate Library School, Indiana University, 1970; OEC-0-70-2746-506).
7. W. F. Willoughby, "Government Publications," *Yale Review* (August 1896), p. 159.
8. Schmeckebier, p. 6.
9. Willoughby, p. 160.
10. The Serial Set will be analyzed in Chapter 6.
11. Schmeckebier, p. 33.
12. *100 GPO Years*, p. 76.
13. Willoughby, pp. 163-64.
14. For instance, after 1936 there was a pronounced increase in the number of "processed" publications cited in the *Monthly Catalog*.
15. John H. Hickcox, *United States Government Publications: A Monthly Catalogue* (Washington: W. H. Lowdermilk, 1885-1894). Irregularly issued over this period, it contains many entries not listed elsewhere.
16. Schmeckebier, p. 26.
17. Bearing in mind the omission of many departmental publications and the overlapping periods covered.
18. In the foreword to his 3d edition (1961) Andriot declared his hope to issue the guide biennially, a wish that went palpably unrealized.
19. From 1895 to 1924 the *Monthly Catalog* did not include class numbers. Poole has added these missing SUDOCS numbers to a "classes-added" reprint

edition of the *Monthly Catalog of U.S. Government Publications, 1895-1924*, published by Carrollton Press in 30 clothbound volumes. Furthermore, the U.S. Historical Documents Institute has issued Ms. Poole's famous *Documents Office Classification* in three clothbound volumes. This "definitive" fourth edition of her *oeuvre* had been published previously by University Microfilms (Ann Arbor, Michigan) in what amounted to Xeroxed copies of her notebooks.

20.   Also published as *Bibliography of U.S. Government Serial Publications, 1789-1970* by compilers Daniel and Marilyn Lester.

21.   Those bibliographic tools designed primarily for tracing legislation through Congress will be analyzed in Chapter 6.

22.   CIS offers all the indexed materials on microfiche, including a complete collection of public and private bills and resolutions.

23.   Andriot's statistical *Guide* (4th ed.), for example, is skimpy in coverage of congressional statistical publications.

24.   James B. Adler, editor and publisher of *CIS/Index* and ASI, has written of the genesis and development of the tools in the *Journal of Micrographics* 4: 239-45 (May 1971) and *Review of Public Data Use* 1: 38-43 (April 1973).

6

LEGISLATIVE BRANCH MATERIALS

What is the spirit that has in general characterized the proceedings of Congress? A perusal of their journals, as well as the candid acknowledgments of such as have had a seat in that assembly, will inform us, that the members have but too frequently displayed the character, rather of partisans of their respective States, than of impartial guardians of a common interest. . . .

—The Federalist, XLVI (Madison)

The necessity of a Senate is not less indicated by the propensity of all single and numerous assemblies to yield to the impulse of sudden and violent passions, and to be seduced by factious leaders into intemperate and pernicious resolutions.

—The Federalist, LXII (Madison)

INTRODUCTION

The framers of the Constitution had no major doubts about Congress as *primus inter pares*. In historical fact Congress antedates both the presidency and the judicial branch. The first federal Congress made the arrangements for counting the ballots of the first electoral college and for inaugurating George Washington and John Adams as the first executive officers. The office of Attorney General and the Departments of War, State, and Treasury were established by acts of the first Congress. Congressional legislation was needed to erect the system of federal courts and to establish the Supreme Court. It is no accident of organization or style that the framers began the noble document with that unequivocal statement, "All legislative powers herein granted shall be vested in a Congress of the United States which shall consist of a Senate and House of Representatives."

Congress, in addition to its committees, carries in its marsupial pouch six agencies whose officers are charged with specific duties and functions under its direction. We have discussed the duties of the Government Printing Office and its ward, the Public Documents Department, in Chapters 1 and 2. The other units are the Architect of the Capitol, Botanic Garden, Cost Accounting Standards Board, General Accounting Office, and Library of Congress.[1] Brief descriptions of the activities of these units are found in the *United States Government Manual*, and detailed accountability is set forth in the annual *Legislative Branch Appropriations* hearings. This chapter will consider first the administrative units under the Congress that publish materials of more than routine interest and importance, and then discuss the several documents that issue from the House and Senate. Finally, the legislative process will be assayed, with reference to the indexes and guides published by both government and private companies in aid of tracing legislation.

GENERAL ACCOUNTING OFFICE

Established in 1921, this arm of Congress was created to oversee the expenditures of the executive branch; its audit authority extends to all departments and agencies of the federal government. The GAO has been called the watchdog of Congress, and its investigative audits are often newsworthy, although they range from multi-million dollar cost overruns for weapons systems to relatively minor peccadilloes of venal or naive public servants. Although some of its investigative activities turn up embarrassing or scandalous matters, the GAO operates to effect greater economy and efficiency in government. When Congress labors on the annual appropriations bills, GAO staffers act as consultants; if an area of government activity is of particular interest to a congressional committee or member, the GAO may be asked to make a special investigation.

A handful of items are available from GAO on deposit. Among them are the *Annual Report of the Comptroller General* (GA 1.1; Item 543), which includes highlights of fiscal year activities and statistical appendixes; a General Publications Series (GA 1.2; Item 545); and Handbooks, Manuals and Guides (GA 1.14; Item 545-A).

Decisions of the Comptroller General of the United States (GA 1.5/a) is a monthly that is sold by SUDOCS. The March, September, and December issues include index digests, and the June issue contains cumulative tables. Annual bound volumes covering the fiscal year are on deposit (GA 1.5; Item 544). The *Index-Digest of the Published Decisions* (GA 1.5/3; Item 546) is published quinquenially and includes tables to the laws, court opinions, and other references cited in the Comptroller General's decisions.

The *Joint Financial Management Improvement Program* (GA 1.12; Item 546-A) is an annual report detailing the Comptroller General's activities in prescribing principles and standards for accounting to be followed by executive branch departments and agencies. GAO's *Policy and Procedures Manual for Guidance of Federal Agencies* (GA 1.6/10) is the official medium through which the Comptroller General promulgates uniform procedures to be followed by the federal agencies. It is issued in looseleaf form in Titles 1-8, and subscription through SUDOCS includes the basic manual and supplements. *GAO Review* (GA 1.15; Item 544-A), a quarterly, contains articles on accounting in general and specifically on accounting and auditing activities of the Office and its employees. Regulations codified under GAO are found in Title 4, Chapters I and II of the *Code of Federal Regulations*.

LIBRARY OF CONGRESS

In 1800 Congress passed a law appropriating $5,000 "for the purchase of such books as may be necessary for the use of Congress" and the Library of Congress was born. In an act of 1802, a librarian was authorized to take charge of the library, "to be appointed by the President of the United States solely." From these modest beginnings, the Library of Congress (LC) today is a huge operation with six major departments, numerous divisions within each department, and seven offices that report directly to the Librarian of Congress. The library's extensive collections now total over 64 million pieces, and its several issuing units produce a variety of publications, over forty of which are made available on deposit.

Office of the Librarian

The *Annual Report of the Librarian of Congress* (LC 1.1; Item 785) for the fiscal year includes reports of the activities of the departments. It is supplemented by the *Quarterly Journal of the Library of Congress* (LC 1.17; Item 788), a handsomely designed and illustrated journal covering the various activities of LC. *Library of Congress Publications in Print* (LC 1.12/2; Item 785-A) is not annotated but is a complete listing of in-print documents; a detailed index affords access to the alphabetical-by-title arrangement.[2]

The *Library of Congress Information Bulletin* (LC 1.18) is issued by LC's Card Division and is free to educational or publicly supported libraries and research institutions. Although the weekly is intramural in much of its content, it has a great deal of information useful to librarians. Regular features include announcements of significant acquisitions, forthcoming events to be held at LC, and news from the GPO and Superintendent of Documents. *New Serial Titles* (LC 1.23/3) continues the *Union List of Serials* after December 31, 1949, and is available on subscription from LC's Card Division. Various *Accessions List* (LC 1.30/) compilations provide a continuing record of the publications acquired by LC's American Libraries Book Procurement Centers, which are located in individual countries. They are available to libraries in varying periodicities, and are largely Public Law 480 projects in countries such as India, Ceylon, Israel, United Arab Republic, Nepal, and Pakistan.

General Reference and Bibliography Division

The General Publications Series (LC 2.2; Item 806-C) contains a number of useful monographs, while the Handbooks, Manuals, and Guides Series (LC 2.8; Item 806-B) features guides to published official records of various countries.[3] *Children's Books* (LC 2.11; Item 806-I) is an annual list of books published during the year in the United States for children from preschool through junior high school. A brief synopsis of the books is given in addition to the standard bibliographic data. Of outstanding reference value is the *Guide to the Study of the United States of America* (LC 2.2; Un 3/4; Item 806-C), a comprehensive listing of bibliographical studies on the United States. In it are described approximately 10,000 books reflecting the development of life and thought in this country.

Copyright Office

Bulletins Series (LC 3.3; Item 790) and Information Circulars Series (LC 3.4; Item 802-A) are worthwhile items to receive because they include pamphlets concerning general instructions on copyright procedures and copyright law. But the most important series for depository institutions is the *Catalog of Copyright Entries* (LC 3.6/5), a massive record of books and other copyrighted material deposited in LC.

Now in its third series, the *Catalog* is divided into several parts. Part 1, Books and Pamphlets (Item 791), lists copyrighted domestic and foreign books, pamphlets, serials, and periodical articles—including cartoons and columns published in magazines and newspapers. Part 2, Periodicals (Item 793), lists both domestic and foreign magazines. Parts 3 and 4 (Item 794) list lectures or similar productions prepared for oral delivery, including certain forms of television and radio scripts. Part 5 (Item 795) lists musical compositions. Part 6, Maps and Atlases (Item 797), lists domestic and foreign cartographic works. Parts 7-11A (Item 798) consist of works of art, prints, pictorial illustrations, and drawings or sculptural works of a scientific or technical character. Part 11B (Item 799) lists commercial prints and labels, and Parts 12-13 (Item 800) cover domestic and foreign motion pictures and filmstrips. The copyright law (Title 17, *United States Code*) divides these categories into thirteen broad classes (A-M) that do not exactly parallel the *Catalog*'s issuing segments. *Cumulative Series* (LC 3.8; Item 803-A) cover entries over a period of time, and are often available for sale by SUDOCS.[4] The basic bibliographic information in the *Catalog of Copyright Entries* is somewhat different from that given in the *National Union Catalog*, and Part 1 of the *Catalog* duplicates information in NUC; but the *Catalog* is a splendid retrospective tool.

Manuscript Division

The Presidents' Papers Index Series (LC 4.7; Item 811-B) is an ambitious project authorized by Congress in 1957. It charges the Librarian of Congress with arranging, indexing, and microfilming all of the papers of United States Presidents in LC's collections. The indexes are essentially of names of correspondents with descriptive information about each document and a key to where on the microfilm it is reproduced. As of 1973, the Index Series had made available to scholars the indexed papers of 16 Presidents from Washington to Coolidge.

Congressional Research Service

The Library of Congress, as its name suggests, serves on a priority basis the members of Congress. The Congressional Research Service (CRS), formerly known as the Legislative Reference Service, functions exclusively for the legislative branch. As a result, most of the research done by this unit eventually appears in the several kinds of publications in the congressional series, including committee prints.[5]

One important tool for tracing legislation is prepared by the Bill Digest Unit, American Law Division, Congressional Research Service. Titled *Digest of Public General Bills and Resolutions* (LC 14.6; Item 807), its purpose is to summarize briefly the essential features of public bills and resolutions with their changes during the legislative process. Published during each session of a Congress, the *Digest* cumulates in five or more issues, with bi-weekly supplements as needed and a final edition at the conclusion of each session. The *Digest* is for sale by the Superintendent.

The cover page of each issue includes the numbers of all measures introduced on and prior to dates indicated after each category of congressional measures. Each cumulative issue is divided into seven parts:

"Part I: Status of Measures Receiving Action." Each measure which has become law is listed numerically by Public Law number. Other measures that have received action are then listed by bill or resolution number. For the measures a digest is given as well as a brief legislative history indicating, if applicable, 1) date reported and report number; 2) dates considered; 3) dates passed; 4) conference action; and 5) approval date or veto. Because bills and resolutions carry throughout an entire Congress, Part I, in the cumulative issues for the second session, also reflects action in the first session.

"Part II: Public Law Listing." This section contains a numerical listing of all enactments through the then current Congress indicating both bill and Public Law number.

"Part III: Digests of Public General Bills and Resolutions." House and Senate measures are separately categorized as to bills, joint resolutions, concurrent resolutions, and (simple) resolutions. Measures are listed by category in numerical order as introduced. If a measure is identical to one introduced in the same session and previously summarized, reference is made to the prior digest. For measures having multiple sponsors, only the member whose name appears first on the bill is indicated (see Part IV). Because of the present limitation on the number of co-sponsors (25) permitted in the House, there may be reference to several identical measures having the name of the same original sponsor (Figure 27).

Figure 27

DIGEST OF PUBLIC GENERAL BILLS AND RESOLUTIONS, 93D CONG., 1ST SESS., SUPPLEMENT NO. 2 TO FIRST ISSUE

SENATE BILLS   S. 604

S. 580. Mr. Percy, et al.; 1/26/73. Judiciary.

A bill to amend title 18 of the United States Code by adding a new chapter 404 to establish an Institute for Continuing Studies of Juvenile Justice. (BILL TITLE ONLY; DIGESTED IN SUBSEQUENT ISSUE)

S. 581. Private.

S. 582. Mr. Scott (Pa.), et al.; 1/29/73. Finance

A bill providing social services for the aged. (BILL TITLE ONLY; DIGESTED IN SUBSEQUENT ISSUE)

S. 583. Mr. Ervin; 1/29/73. Judiciary.

A bill to promote the separation of constitutional powers by securing to the Congress additional time in which to consider the rules of evidence for U.S. courts and magistrates, the amendments to the Federal Rules of Civil Procedure, and the amendments to the Federal Rules of Criminal Procedure which the Supreme Court on November 20, 1972, ordered the Chief Justice to transmit to the Congress. (BILL TITLE ONLY; DIGESTED IN SUBSEQUENT ISSUE)

S. 584. Mr. Bayh; 1/29/73.
Interior and Insular Affairs.

A bill to amend the act entitled "An Act to provide for the establishment of the Indiana Dunes National Lakeshore. (BILL TITLE ONLY; DIGESTED IN SUBSEQUENT ISSUE)

S. 585. Mr. Moss; 1/29/73. Commerce.

A bill to amend section 303 of the Communications Act of 1934 to require that radios be capable of receiving both AM and FM broadcasts. (BILL TITLE ONLY; DIGESTED IN SUBSEQUENT ISSUE)

S. 586. Mr. Dominick, et al.; 1/29/73.
Labor and Public Welfare.

A bill to amend the Occupational Safety and Health Act of 1970. (BILL TITLE ONLY; DIGESTED IN SUBSEQUENT ISSUE)

certain officers in the Executive Office of the President be subject to confirmation by the Senate. (BILL TITLE ONLY; DIGESTED IN SUBSEQUENT ISSUE)

S. 591-593. Private.

S. 594. Mr. Hruska; 1/29/73. Judiciary.

A bill to amend the Immigration and Nationality Act to provide for waiver of excludability for certain aliens. (BILL TITLE ONLY; DIGESTED IN SUBSEQUENT ISSUE)

S. 595. Private.

S. 596. Mr. Burdick; 1/29/73. Judiciary.

A bill to improve judicial machinery by revising the certiorari jurisdiction of the Supreme Court. (BILL TITLE ONLY; DIGESTED IN SUBSEQUENT ISSUE)

S. 597. Mr. Burdick (by req.); 1/29/73. Judiciary

A bill to provide for the appointment of additional district judges. (BILL TITLE ONLY; DIGESTED IN SUBSEQUENT ISSUE)

S. 598. Mr. Burdick, et al.; 1/29/73.
Interior and Insular Affairs.

A bill to donate to the Devils Lake Sioux Tribe, Fort Totten Reservation, some submarginal lands of the United States, and to make such lands part of the reservation involved. (BILL TITLE ONLY; DIGESTED IN SUBSEQUENT ISSUE)

S. 599. Mr. Burdick, et al.; 1/29/73.
Interior and Insular Affairs.

A bill to provide that certain lands shall be held in trust for the Standing Rock Sioux Tribe in North Dakota and South Dakota. (BILL TITLE ONLY; DIGESTED IN SUBSEQUENT ISSUE)

S. 600. Mr. Jackson, et al.; 1/29/73.
Interior and Insular Affairs.

"Part IV: Sponsor Index." A reference by subject is provided to all public and private bills and resolutions sponsored by each member of Congress. A one-word or brief phrase description of the subject-matter of public measures is followed by the bill number or numbers pertaining to that subject entry.

"Part V: Subject-Matter Index." A reference is provided to all public bills and resolutions in a given subject area. Preceding the subject index is a list of the principal subject headings used. Although the subject listing is not all-inclusive, it provides access to most areas.

"Part VI: Specific-Title Index." Arranged alphabetically according to the first substantive word of the title.

"Part VII: Identical Bill Index." All measures that are identical in both language and content are included here. They appear under the number of the first such bill in the current session with cross referencing made for succeeding bills.

The manifold uses of the *Digest* make it one of the more widely used guides to the legislative process. Moreover, it is the only tool that actually offers summaries, or digests, of the text of the legislation. In the summary section of this chapter, we will discuss the role of the *Digest*, with other guides, in tracing legislation.

Processing Department

Subject Headings Used in the Dictionary Catalogs of the Library of Congress (LC 26.7; Item 823) and *Library of Congress Classification Schedules* (LC 26.9; Item 819) had in the past been completely handled by the Subject Cataloging Division. The responsibility for the sale and distribution of these cataloging aids has now been transferred to the Card Division.

The cumulative author list of the *National Union Catalog* (LC 30.8) and the *Library of Congress Catalog: Books, Subjects* (LC 30.8/3) are subscription items from the Card Division, as is the well-known *Monthly Checklist of State Publications* (LC 30.9; Item 816). The latter, LC's oldest serial publication, presents a record of state documents issued during the previous five years that have been received by the Library. An index to the monthly issues appears only annually; periodicals issued by state agencies are listed in the June and December issues. As an ordering tool, the *Checklist* is of limited value, since LC receives from the states only a fraction of the total publications produced at that governmental level.[6]

GENERAL PUBLICATIONS OF THE CONGRESS

Generally, materials initiated by or required by the Congress fall into two categories: 1) publications of the Congress as a whole, and 2) publications of the committees or subcommittees of Congress.[7] Moreover, the Superintendent's notation scheme for publications of the Congress employs a *classified* and a *designated* symbol system, or a combination of both.

The Congressional Record

The *Congressional Record* (X/a; Item 994) is issued daily when Congress is in session, and includes a fortnightly index. A bi-weekly edition is compiled for members of Congress only. A permanent, bound edition (X; Item 993) is issued in many volumes, but due to revision and rearrangement, its pagination, which is continuous throughout the session, differs from that of the daily edition.

The members' privilege of revising remarks or expunging material from the *Record* extends not only to the bound edition but to the daily issues. Moreover, members may be granted "leave to print" material so long as it is relevant to the legislation under debate. Unfortunately, the Public Printer does not identify in the *Record* remarks that were revised or not actually delivered on the floor.

The *Record* consists of four sections: the proceedings of the House and of the Senate; the Extensions of Remarks; and the Daily Digest. Each section is paged continuously and separately during each session, and each page in each section is preceded by a letter prefix as follows: "S" for Senate, "H" for House, "E" for Extensions of Remarks, and "D" for Daily Digest.

It costs over $200 to print each page of the daily *Record*. In 1972 the Joint Committee on Printing had to remind members not to include extraneous matter in the proceedings section. Exceptions included "(a) excerpts from letters, telegrams, or articles presented in connection with a speech delivered in the course of debate; (b) communications from State Legislatures; and (c) addresses or articles by the President and the members of his cabinet, the Vice President, or a Member of Congress."[8]

The Extensions of Remarks section contains traditionally extraneous matter, although "germane" material does appear in this section if printing requirements obtain. All the news that fits may show up in the Extensions of Remarks: newspaper articles; poetry of dubious esthetic quality; tributes to Abraham Lincoln, Vince Lombardi, or a local constituent; reprints from books and magazines—a potpourri of trivia mixed with some important documentation.

Until the 90th Congress, 2d session, this section was called the Appendix. Separately paged, it formed a part of both the daily and the permanent editions from the 75th Congress, 1st session, through the 83d Congress, 2d session. Beginning with the 77th Congress, 1st session, each page number was preceded by the designation "A." With the 84th Congress, 1st session, the Appendix pages were *omitted* from the permanent edition. Thus from 1955 to 1968 material in the Appendix could be consulted only in the daily edition. The *index* to the permanent edition, however, cited references to Appendix material appearing in the daily edition. Libraries were forced to retain the Appendix pages from the daily edition and shelve them in proper sequence with the permanent edition. After the Appendix was omitted from the permanent edition, materials considered germane to legislation were inserted in that edition at the point when the legislation was under discussion. With the 90th Congress, 2d session, the "Appendix," now the Extensions of Remarks, was restored to the permanent edition of the *Record*. Moreover, beginning with that Congress and session, the last page of each daily edition has carried an alphabetical listing of members whose extended remarks appear in that issue, with page numbers.

The Daily Digest section includes "Highlights" of the legislative day, chamber action which summarizes bills introduced and reported, resolutions agreed to, quorum calls, bills signed by the President, committee meetings, and a schedule of House and Senate meetings for the following day.

The bi-weekly Index and the master index for the bound edition of the *Record* are composed of two parts: an index to the proceedings, including material in the Extensions of Remarks; and a History of Bills and Resolutions. The index has a subject and name approach. The History is arranged by bill number. Bill number references are cumulative, however, so that with the latest index one can trace the history of a bill in page references to its introduction, committee report, debate, amendment(s), and enactment or defeat of the measure.[9]

Amendments proposed in the House are noted in the Proceedings section. Although most of the work on bills is done in committee, only a summary of committee activity appears in the Daily Digest. The Digest, however, does include names of witnesses testifying before committee.

The *Record* contains recurring features of some reference value, such as a list of members with state and party affiliation; standing committees with names of members; U.S. judicial circuits with justices assigned and their territories; the various appellate courts and judges; names and home addresses of official reporters; Supreme Court justices and their home addresses; and the several laws and rules in effect for publication of the *Record*.

When Congress is in session, the visitor in the gallery of either chamber of the Congress sees the proceedings and debates being taken down by official reporters. By law the *Record* is supposed to be substantially a verbatim report of proceedings. But the privileges of "leave to print," revision (including the expunging of material), and alteration of members' remarks serve to define and qualify the word "substantially."

Congressional debates reported in earlier sets of the presently titled *Congressional Record* began with the *Annals of Congress* (1789-1824), followed by the *Register of Debates* (1824-37) and the *Congressional Globe* (1833-73), the first five volumes of which overlap the *Register*. The current cost per page includes the expense of all versions of the *Record*—daily, cost of indexing, bi-weekly index, bound copy indexing, and the total production cost of the bound volumes. Title 44 of the *United States Code* allows each Senator 100 copies of the daily *Record* and each Representative 68 copies. These extra copies are furnished on request; they are not sent to a member unless he or she designates a constituent that the *Record* be mailed to. Some members send their extra copies to libraries and educators as well as to government agencies. Moreover, Title 44 authorizes the distribution of 3,451 sets of the bound volumes of the *Record*, including 505 sets for the Vice President (who is nominally President of the Senate) and Senators, and 1,311 for House members.

Journals of the House and Senate

Like the *Congressional Record*, the House *Journal* (XJH; Item 1030) and Senate *Journal* (XJS; Item 1047) are assigned a classed notation but also have a series designation.[10] The journals of Congress are the only publications required by the Constitution. Article I, Section 5 states: "Each House shall keep a Journal of its Proceedings, and from time to time publish the same...." Consequently, the *Journals*, not the *Record*, are the official documents for the proceedings of Congress.

Both journals are published at the end of a session. The House *Journal* has appendixes that include proceedings subsequent to *sine die* adjournment, Rules of the House, questions of order decided in the House for that session, and a History of Bills and Resolutions. The Senate *Journal* has a History of Bills and Resolutions, arranged similarly to the House *Journal*: bills, joint resolutions, concurrent resolutions, and resolutions are organized by number, title, and action. The *Journals* have a name/subject/title index.

The House *Manual*, which contains the annotated rules of the House of Representatives, notes that members may decide what proceedings will be included in the *Journal*, "even to the extent of omitting things actually done or recording things not done." Nevertheless, the rules suggest that the *Journal* "ought to be a correct transcript of the proceedings of the House."[11] Rule IV of the Senate simply states that "the proceedings of the Senate shall be briefly and accurately stated in the *Journal*. Messages of the President in full; titles of bills and joint resolutions, and such parts as shall be affected by proposed amendments; every vote, and a brief statement of the contents of each petition, memorial, or paper presented to the Senate, shall be entered."[12] Because the *Journals* are putatively a faithful record of activities, excluding debates, they provide easier access to retrospective procedural information than does the *Congressional Record*.

House General Publications

This category is classified but not designated. The notation Y 1.2 is followed by a Cutter number; Item 998 covers documents issued in this series. Many of the publications carried in this category are available for sale through the Superintendent, and most of the individual issues are compilations of laws grouped in related subjects: agriculture, bankruptcy, interstate commerce, social security, veterans, etc. A prominent exception is the quadrennial *Platforms of the Democratic Party and the Republican Party* (Y 1.2:P 69/year), prepared by the Clerk of the House of Representatives. It contains the text of the platforms adopted by the two parties at their respective national conventions held to nominate the presidential candidates.

The several compilations of laws cumulate and are updated irregularly. A typical example of a publication under this Item is *Laws Relating to Securities Commission Exchanges and Holding Companies* (Y 1.2:Se 2/973), which contains the texts and extracts of Public Laws from 1933 to 1970 that relate to the Securities and Exchange Commission, securities, stock exchanges, and holding companies. This publication, like the others in this series, is compiled under the supervision of the Superintendent of the House Document Room.

A series of publications covering House members has been recently made available to depository libraries. Titled *Annual Reports of Political Committees Supporting Candidates for House of Representatives* (Y 1.2/4; Item 998-C), it is compiled under the direction of the Clerk of the House and issued pursuant to the provisions of the 1971 Federal Election Campaign Act (PL 92-225, February 7, 1972). The Superintendent of Documents has been offering these reports for sale as separates.

House Calendars

Rule XIII of the House *Manual* delineates the handling of business reported from committees. The official document conveying this aspect of the legislative process is the *Calendars of the United States House of Representatives and History of Legislation* (Y 1.2/2; Item 998-A), which is published daily when the House is in session. Each issue is cumulative, and in every Monday issue there is a subject index of all legislation, both House and Senate, which has been reported by the committees and acted upon by either or both of the chambers, with the exception of Senate resolutions not of interest to the House and special House reports. Because of its ease of use and its cumulative features, many documents librarians find the *Calendars* to be the single most useful tool for the tracing of a bill's history.

Sections include "Bills in Conference" and "Bills Through Conference," both arranged by *date*, with bill number, title of bill, House and Senate conferees, conference report number, and action taken. For "Bills Through Conference" additional information includes public or private law number and date of approval. Following those tables, the various calendars are represented. The documents librarian will find the *Union Calendar* and *House Calendar* to be of the greatest value for the legislative matters.[13] They are arranged by date with bill or report number, member and committee, title, and calendar number. Tables are also provided for the *Private Calendar*, *Consent Calendar*, and *Calendar of Motions to Discharge Committees*.

Tables on public and private laws are included, arranged by Congress and law number, referencing the bill number. Of perhaps most significance is a section entitled "Numerical Order of Bills and Resolutions Which Have Passed Either or Both Houses, and Bills Now Pending on the Calendars." Arranged numerically (and easily accessible through the subject index) by House bills, joint resolutions, concurrent resolutions, and resolutions, followed by similar tables for the Senate, it gives each bill's history to date. Similar or identical bills, and bills having reference to each other, are indicated by numbers in parentheses. Reference features include Special Legislative Days and Status of Major Bills, a table giving the legislative history of the bill, divided into Legislative Bills and Appropriation Bills.

The final edition of the *House Calendar* includes a list of bills that failed to become law as well as a summary of actions on all House and Senate bills and resolutions for the complete Congress. Issued biennially, it provides a Status of Major Bills table for each session of the Congress and notes vetoes as well. For bills that become law, the final edition of the *House Calendar* has a numerical listing of Public Law numbers, referencing bill numbers.

Senate General Publications

Classified in Y 1.3, publications in this series are new or recurring monographs compiled in the Senate Library under the direction of the Secretary of the Senate. Of reference value are the following documents in this category (Item 998):

Presidential Vetoes (Y 1.3:V 64). Subtitled a *List of Bills Vetoed and Action Taken Thereon by the Senate and House of Representatives, First Congress through the Ninetieth Congress, 1789-1968*, this publication is the only source of vetoes in one location.

Nomination and Election of the President and Vice-President of the United States (Y 1.3:P 92). This publication, issued quadrennially with supplements between presidential elections as needed, includes an analysis of election laws prepared by staffers of the Congressional Research Service.

Factual Campaign Information (Y 1.3:C 15). Every two years one-third of the Senate faces re-election; this publication is revised biennially or as needed to serve Senators in their campaigns.

Cumulative Index of Congressional Committee Hearings (Y 1.3:H 35/2/yr./supp. no.). Although the *Monthly Catalog* and *CIS/Index* list hearings, this publication lists hearings (not confidential in character) and most committee prints in a series of volumes providing retrospective bibliographic control. The basic volume, *Index of Congressional Committee Hearings Prior to January 3, 1935, in the United States Senate Library*, has been out of print for many years but is available as a 1969 Kraus Reprint. The *Cumulative Index of Congressional Committee Hearings* for the 74th through the 85th Congresses was issued in 1959, followed by the *Quadrennial Supplement* for the 86th and 87th Congresses in 1963, and the *Second Quadrennial Supplement* for the 88th and 89th Congresses. The *Third Quadrennial Supplement* covered the 90th and 91st Congresses and was composed for the first time on the GPO's Linotron 1010 phototypesetting machine. Moreover, the index arranged by committees was generated automatically by a computer program that sorted the subject data by Senate, House, joint, select, and special committees and rearranged the subject matter alphabetically within the committee.

The current index follows basically the format used in earlier volumes, with the addition of some earlier hearings that have been identified. Hearings are indexed by subject; Senate committees; House committees; joint, select, and special committees; and bill numbers. The Appendix indexes committee prints by subject; title; Senate committees; House committees; and joint, select, and special committees. Corrections to earlier volumes are listed. Volume numbers are those assigned by the Senate Library for reference to its own collections, but depository libraries find the *Cumulative Indexes* useful as a checklist and a reference tool.

In many instances the titles assigned to hearings by corresponding committees of the House and Senate lack uniformity, even though the subject matter under consideration is identical. Moreover, the title does not always describe adequately the contents of a hearing. This supplement has attempted and largely succeeded in overcoming these deficiencies by uniform subject headings and adequate cross-references.[14]

Like its House counterpart, the Senate has a series, for each member, of *Annual Reports of Political Committees Supporting Candidates for [the] Senate* (Y 1.3/5; Item 998-C).

Senate Calendar of Business

Less important than the House *Calendars* in tracing legislation, the *Senate Calendar of Business* (Y 1.3/3; Item 998-B) should be a selection of large depository libraries. Designated by Congress and Calendar Number following the

Y 1.3/3 classification, the *Calendar of Business* is not cumulative and does not have an index; it is issued daily when the Senate is in session.

Pursuant to Rule VIII in the Senate *Manual*, there is a section in the Senate *Calendar* called "General Orders," which organizes legislation by order number, bill number and sponsor, title, and report number. "Bills in Conference" is a section arranged by date sent to conference, with bill number, brief title, Senate and House conferees, Senate report number, and current status. A separate table gives "Status of Appropriation Bills" and is arranged by bill number with brief title and legislative history to date. Ready reference information in the *Calendar of Business* includes the members and office locations of the Senate standing, special, and select committees.

Public Bills and Resolutions

The classification Y 2 was originally assigned for congressional bills and resolutions, followed by the Congress, session, and bill or resolution number. Libraries that use this classified and designated combination would have, for example, an alphameric notation of Y 2. 90/1:H.R. 8629 assigned to a typical bill introduced in the House (Figure 28). The category of public bills and resolutions is made available to depository libraries under Item 1006.

Defining accurately the borderline differences between *public* and *private* bills has been a vexing problem for lawmakers and scholars. The principal criterion of division seems to be legislative intent with an effort toward historical consistency and precedent. A bill that becomes law does not carry an indication of whether it is public or private, yet the Office of the Federal Register, in issuing the *Statutes at Large*, makes precisely that distinction. Save for the scholar-specialist's needs, libraries have little call for private bills or laws, although peculiarly House and Senate *reports* on private bills are available on deposit in unbound form (Item 1008-B) and in the bound volumes of the Serial Set (Item 1007-B).[15]

Bills (H.R.; S.)

The term *bill* is used in enacting new legislation or in amending previous legislation, and appears in the form shown in Figure 28. It is by far the most common form of legislation. Bills may originate in either the House or the Senate, except revenue raising bills which, according to the Constitution, must originate in the House. It is also customary, but not necessary, that general appropriation bills originate in the House.

The various stages of a bill in the legislative process are officially described in the House *Manual*, Section 983, and will be discussed later in this chapter.[16] Bills and amendments, either in summary form or the text itself, may be printed in the *Congressional Record*. Roll-call votes are recorded in the *Congressional Record* where a roll call is required, tallied swiftly in the House by its electronic voting system. The Legislative Reorganization Act of 1970 (PL 91-510, October 26, 1970) requires that a breakdown of *teller votes* be recorded upon

Figure 28
BILL: INTRODUCED PRINT

90TH CONGRESS
1ST SESSION

H. R. 8629

IN THE HOUSE OF REPRESENTATIVES

APRIL 17, 1967

Mr. CELLER introduced the following bill; which was referred to the Committee on the Judiciary

A BILL

To amend the Act of July 4, 1966 (Public Law 89–491).

1   *Be it enacted by the Senate and House of Representa-*

2 *tives of the United States of America in Congress assembled,*

3 That the Act of July 4, 1966 (80 Stat. 259), is hereby

4 amended as follows:

5   1. By adding in section 2 (b) (3) the words "the

6 Secretary of Commerce," after the words, "the Secretary

7 of Defense,".

8   2. By deleting in section 3 (d) the words "two years

9 after the date of the enactment of this Act," and inserting

10 in lieu thereof "July 4, 1969.".

I

request of one-fifth of a House quorum; when this occurs, the results are also published in the *Record*.

Joint Resolutions (H.J. Res.; S.J. Res.)

At one time the joint resolution was used for purposes of general legislation; but the two houses finally concluded that a bill was the proper instrumentality for this purpose. However, the legal effect of joint resolutions is the same as that of bills. They may be used for "incidental or inferior" legislation, such as establishing the date for the convening of Congress, or "unusual" legislation, such as the Tonkin Gulf Resolution (H.J. Res. 1145, adopted August 7, 1964). The prescribed form of joint resolutions uses the word "resolved" rather than the phrase "be it enacted."

Amendments to the Constitution are proposed in the form of joint resolutions (Figure 29). Their passage through the legislative process is similar to that of ordinary joint resolutions, except for the two-thirds vote of both houses required by Article V of the Constitution. While all other joint resolutions, like bills, must be signed by the President to become law, constitutional amendments do not require his signature. After ratification by the legislatures of three-fourths of the states, the amendment is filed with the Administrator of General Services, who is responsible for its certification and publication.

Concurrent Resolutions (H. Con. Res.; S. Con. Res.)

This form does not have the force of law. Concurrent resolutions are used for matters in which the two chambers have a mutual interest. They are used to express an opinion, a "sense of" the House and Senate. They are identified and/or published in the *Congressional Record*, and later appear in the journals of the two chambers. Although they do not require the signature of the President, they are published in the *Statutes at Large* (Figure 30, page 107).

Resolutions (H. Res.; S. Res.)

Known as "simple" resolutions, they govern the action of only one house and are used for the concern only of the chamber passing them. They affect procedural matters of the body to which they relate, need no presidential signature, and may be found in the *Congressional Record*, and later appear in the House and Senate *Journals* (Figure 31, page 108).

The majority of bills are printed only once. About 12 percent are reprinted at various steps in the legislative process. The first printing is known as the "introduced print," but when reported from committee there is a "reported print" with calendar number and House or Senate report number indicated. When passed by one body and sent to the other house, the bill is called "an act" and is known as a "referred (act) print." When reported from committee in that body there can be another printing. There are other variations and some

Figure 29

HOUSE JOINT RESOLUTION

92D CONGRESS
1ST SESSION

H. J. RES. 620

IN THE HOUSE OF REPRESENTATIVES

MAY 6, 1971

Mr. LENT introduced the following joint resolution; which was referred to the
Committee on the Judiciary

JOINT RESOLUTION

Proposing an amendment to the Constitution of the United States
relative to neighborhood schools.

1   *Resolved by the Senate and House of Representatives of*

2   *the United States of America in Congress assembled (two-*

3   *thirds of each House concurring therein)*, That the following

4   article is proposed as an amendment to the Constitution of the

5   United States to be valid only if ratified by the legislatures of

6   three-fourths of the several States within seven years after

7   the date of final passage of this joint resolution:

8   "ARTICLE —

9   "SECTION 1. No public school student shall, because of

10   his race, creed, or color, be assigned to or required to attend

11   a particular school.

VI—O

Figure 30

HOUSE CONCURRENT RESOLUTION

93D CONGRESS
1ST SESSION

H. CON. RES. 1

IN THE HOUSE OF REPRESENTATIVES

JANUARY 3, 1973

Mr. O'NEILL submitted the following resolution; which was considered and agreed to

---

CONCURRENT RESOLUTION

1   *Resolved by the House of Representatives (the Senate*

2   *concurring),* That effective from January 3, 1973, the joint

3   committee created by Senate Concurrent Resolution 63, of

4   the Ninety-second Congress, to make the necessary arrange-

5   ments for the inauguration of the President-elect and Vice

6   President-elect of the United States on the 20th day of

7   January 1973, is hereby continued and for such purpose

8   shall have the same power and authority as that conferred

9   by such Senate Concurrent Resolution 63, of the Ninety-

10   second Congress.

      V

Figure 31

HOUSE RESOLUTION

House Calendar No. 253

93D CONGRESS
2D SESSION

H. RES. 803

[Report No. 93–774]

IN THE HOUSE OF REPRESENTATIVES

FEBRUARY 1, 1974

Mr. RODINO, from the Committee on the Judiciary, reported the following resolution; which was referred to the House Calendar and ordered to be printed

---

RESOLUTION

1   *Resolved*, That the Committee on the Judiciary, acting

2   as a whole or by any subcommittee thereof appointed by the

3   chairman for the purposes hereof and in accordance with the

4   rules of the committee, is authorized and directed to investi-

5   gate fully and completely whether sufficient grounds exist for

6   the House of Representatives to exercise its constitutional

7   power to impeach Richard M. Nixon, President of the United

8   States of America. The committee shall report to the House

9   of Representatives such resolutions, articles of impeachment,

10   or other recommendations as it deems proper.

problems associated with the printing of bills, but librarians generally should have no trouble organizing the bills for public use.[17]

Of the some 25,000 bills and resolutions introduced during a Congress, over three-quarters originate in the House of Representatives. Libraries that subscribe to Item 1006 are required by the Superintendent to retain House and Senate bills and resolutions for one year after the close of the Congress. Institutions that find it burdensome to retain bills from earlier Congresses for research purposes may avail themselves of Readex Microprint (1956-1965) or Congressional Information Service's microfiche collection. It is important to remember that the life of a bill expires with the conclusion of a Congress. If it fails of passage and is reintroduced in a new Congress, it will be assigned a new number.

CONGRESSIONAL COMMITTEE PUBLICATIONS

The several standing, joint, and select or special committees of the House and Senate issue a large body of materials. They are both classed and designated. Numbered series are easily controlled. Other categories are somewhat elusive. The lack of uniformity in printing and distribution of publications of Congress causes problems in access and bibliographic control. Although virtually every congressional committee has been assigned an Item number for deposit, not all publications issued by committees are available on deposit.

Legislative Calendars

Individual committees issue calendars on an irregular schedule. Often overlooked in reference work because, unlike the House *Calendars* and the Senate *Calendar of Business*, they are not depository items, the committee calendars represent yet another index to legislation. Since they cumulate, the final issue covers an entire Congress. They are classed in Y 4. followed by a Cutter symbol for the specific committee, thus Y 4.Ed 8/1 (House Education and Labor Committee) or Y 4.J 89/2 (Senate Judiciary Committee), the alphameric notation that signifies congressional committee publications in general. Following the Cutter symbol, the calendars are designated by Congress and calendar numbers. A list of committees issuing calendars is found in the Appendix to the February issue of the *Monthly Catalog* under the heading "Legislative Calendars, United States Congress."

A typical legislative calendar includes presidential messages referred to committee; status of bills referred to committee on which action has been taken; miscellaneous publications by the committee; nominations before the committee and committee action; hearings held, arranged by bill number; House and Senate bills and resolutions referred to committee, arranged by date; and separate author and subject indexes.

Codes

According to Rule XI of the House (House *Manual*, Section 707), the House Judiciary Committee has the responsibility for "revision and codification of the Statutes of the United States." Divided into Title, Part, Chapter, and Section, the *United States Code* is the editorial reorganization of the "public, general and permanent laws of the United States in force." Just as administrative law in the *Federal Register* becomes codified in the *Code of Federal Regulations*, so the statutory law as evidenced in the *Statutes at Large* becomes codified in the *United States Code*.

Because the *United States Code* is issued by the House Judiciary Committee, it bears that committee's notation (Y 4.J 89/1) followed by the Cutter Un 3/3/ and designated by year and volume number. New editions of the *Code* have appeared about every six years since the first edition in 1926, and cumulative supplements are issued after a session of Congress. There is a popular name index to acts as well as a voluminous subject index, and tables of statutes included or repealed affords invaluable parallel reference aids.[18] Individual volumes are sold by the Superintendent, and for depository libraries the *Code* is available under Item 991. The House Judiciary Committee also issues the *District of Columbia Code* and *Supplements* (Y 4.J 89/1:D 63/24; Item 990), owing to the peculiar powers of Congress to legislate for the nation's capital.

Official Congressional Directory

The Joint Committee on Printing annually issues this important reference tool (Y 4.P 93/1:1; Item 992); like other seminal documents published by the federal government, its contents vary from time to time. General information found in the *Directory* includes biographical data of the "Who's Who" variety for members; standing, joint, select, and special committees with assignments of members;[19] foreign representatives and consular offices in the United States; chief officers of departments and independent agencies; Supreme Court and appellate courts membership; and members of the media entitled to cover the Congress. Maps of congressional districts by states and an individual name index round out the *Directory*. The publication is available for sale through the Superintendent.

Hearings

Whether hearings are investigatory or pursuant to legislation, they are made available to depository libraries (unless they are classified or otherwise limited in distribution). The Legislative Reorganization Act of 1970 mandated that committees holding hearings give at least one week's public notice of the date, place, and subject matter. Notice is published in the *Congressional Record*, in some journals, and in the Washington, D.C., newspapers. Witnesses are required to file with the committee clerk a written statement of proposed testimony at least one day prior to appearance. Open hearings permit broadcast by radio or television, "subject to committee rules." Since 1970, there has been no dramatic increase in the number of open hearings conducted by Congress.

Hearings do not constitute a real series, although some committees have serialized their publications for their own convenience. Some hearings are designated alphabetically, some numerically. Some series run through a session, some through a Congress. Hearings are classed in Y 4 and are often issued in "Parts" when multi-volumed.[20] The *Monthly Catalog* indexes hearings by title, committee, and subject. *CIS/Index*, the best tool for reference in this area, indexes hearings by subject, witnesses and their affiliations, committees and subcommittees, and bill and report numbers. For research prior to the advent of *CIS/Index* in 1970, the *Monthly Catalog* and the *Cumulative Index of Congressional Committee Hearings* (with its supplements) may be used. The only publication that gives an abstract of testimony with reference to page numbers is *CIS/Index*. Since individual volumes of hearings are indexed badly, this feature of *CIS/Index* cannot be praised highly enough.

Committee Prints

If hearings have no consistent serialization, committee prints are even more elusive. Many committee prints are issued without series designation or numbering. Some are offered to depository libraries, others are not. Some are placed on sale by the Superintendent, others may be requested from the committee, secured through one's Congressman, or ordered by subscription through the Documents Expediting Project. Readex Microprint, of course, picks up committee prints that have been indexed, by title, committee, and subject, in the *Monthly Catalog*. Like hearings, committee prints are most easily researched through *CIS/Index* by committee or subcommittee, subject, and often key names of individuals cited in the print. Again the abstracting feature of *CIS/Index* demonstrates its superiority as a reference tool for committee prints as well as hearings.

Committee prints are the background information for congressional committees. As such they are printed in limited quantity. Sometimes a committee print will, in its revised form, be reissued as a *document* or *report* and get into the numbered Serial Set. Since so many committee prints contain information of value to the public, their capricious publication, distribution, and designation patterns are the disgrace of Congress.

Some examples of committee prints will serve to illustrate their quixotic nature and the fact that librarians need to be vigilant when dealing with them:

Considerations in Formulation of National Energy Policy [Prepared by Congressional Research Service] at request of Henry M. Jackson, Chairman, Interior and Insular Affairs Committee, Senate, pursuant to national fuels and energy policy study, 1971. (Y 4.In 8/13:92-4).

Conquest of Cancer [Prepared for subcommittee on Health, Senate Labor and Public Welfare Committee], 1971. (Y 4.L 11/2:C 16/4).

Housing for the Elderly: A Status Report [Prepared for Use of the Senate Banking, Housing and Urban Affairs Committee], 1973. (Y 4.Ag 4:H 81/4; *$0.15).

Drug Use in America: Problem in Perspective: Second Report of the National Commission on Marihuana and Drug Abuse (Mar. 1973. 93-1).

Impeachment: Selected Materials (Oct. 9, 1973. 93-1; *$4.40).

House of Representatives Exclusion, Censure and Expulsion Cases from 1789 to 1973 [Prepared for Use of the Joint Committee on Congressional Operations] (1973; 93-1).

The first two citations were selected at random from the *Monthly Catalog*; the remaining entries were found in *CIS/Index*. None were depository items, although the *CIS/Index* listings might eventually become available on deposit. Two of the prints were placed on sale through the Superintendent.[21] The last three citations did not carry a classification notation at the time of entry. The *Monthly Catalog*, which indexes prints later than *CIS/Index*, will assign a classification and at that time may indicate depository distribution. But the process is patently inadequate.

Reports and Documents

The next section of this chapter will provide an analysis of the *reports* and *documents* that comprise the famous Serial Set. However, some recurring publications of general reference value are issued in this Congressional series. Many librarians choose to separate these publications from their Serial number order in the bound set and have them classed in the general reference collection.

Reports and *documents* are designated by Congress, session, and number, although they are numbered consecutively through a Congress. Some are issued in bound form only; others appear first in unbound form and later are incorporated into the bound Serial volumes. What follows is a partial list of publications issued in this series that are of more than routine importance.

House Manual

The full title of the publication is *Constitution, Jefferson's Manual, and Rules of the House of Representatives* (92-2: H. doc. 384; Item 1029), and it is revised every other year for a new Congress. The reason for the lengthy title is that the parliamentary practice of the House emanates from four sources: the Constitution, *Jefferson's Manual*, the rules adopted by the House itself from the beginning of its existence, and decisions of the Chairman of the Committee of the Whole. In the years from 1797 to 1801 Thomas Jefferson, then Vice President of the United States and President of the Senate, prepared the notable work that has come to be known as *Jefferson's Manual*. This *oeuvre* contributed significantly to House procedures, and many provisions of *Jefferson's Manual* still govern the body.

The rulings of the Speakers of the House and of the Chairmen of the Committee of the Whole are to the rules of the House what the decisions of the courts are to the statutes. Prior decisions of the House have been embodied in the works of Hinds and Cannon, and new editions of these precedents are compiled periodically.[22] The *Manual* thus is the annotated rules, with a detailed subject index. An appendix labeled "Miscellaneous" contains an explanation of the franking privilege members enjoy, and provisions from Title II of the Legislative Reorganization Act of 1946, as amended, and Titles II, III, and IV of the Legislative Reorganization Act of 1970.

Senate Manual

At the commencement of each new Congress, the Senate Committee on Rules and Administration prepares and issues a revised edition of that body's procedures, the full title of which is *Senate Manual, Containing the Standing Rules, Orders, Laws, and Resolutions Affecting the Business of the United States Senate; Jefferson's Manual; Declaration of Independence; Articles of Confederation; Constitution of the United States, etc.* (93-1: S. doc. 1; Item 1048).

Like the House *Manual*, the Senate version embodies the most important rules, regulations, statutes, and other materials relating to the operation and organization of the Senate. Again, the value of the Senate *Manual* lies in its gloss on the procedures governing this body. Both House and Senate *Manuals* are issued in the bound Serial Set edition, and both are sold by the Superintendent of Documents.

Biographical Directory of the American Congress

Earlier editions of this compilation have been issued under different names since 1859. Biographical collections covering the years 1774 to 1949 and 1774 to 1961 were issued as House *documents*. The latest updating covers the years 1774 to 1971 (92-1: S. doc. 8; Item 995-G) and was issued as a Senate *document*. It includes almost 11,000 short biographies of members of the House and Senate for those years, as well as high officers of the executive branch. This edition also contains biographies of Presidents who were not members of Congress. The *Biographical Directory* is updated by the annual *Official Congressional Directory*.

Reports to Be Made to Congress

Rule III, Clause 2 of the House *Manual* requires the Clerk of the House of Representatives to compile a list of reports "which it is the duty of any officer or Department to make to Congress, referring to the act of resolution and page of the volume of the laws or Journal in which it may be contained, and placing under the name of each officer the list of reports required of him to be made." Pursuant to this rule, *Reports to Be Made to Congress* (92-2: H. doc. 221; Item 996) is issued to each member at the commencement of every session of Congress.

A source to be used in conjunction with the *Monthly Catalog* and the *Numerical Lists and Schedule of Volumes*, the *document* gives a brief explanation of the nature, statutory authority, and periodicity of the report; an index provides reference to the citations.

U.S. Contributions to International Organizations

Issued annually as a letter transmitted from the Secretary of State to the Congress, *Contributions* (92-2: H. doc. 377) covers the extent and disposition of contributions the United States has made to international organizations. Tabular data show the scale of assessments, pledges, and contributions of member nations of the United Nations and its specialized agencies. A chart showing U.S. contributions from 1946 to the present is included.

The Annotated Constitution

Of reference value is the *Constitution of the United States of America, Analysis and Interpretation* (92-2: S. doc. 82 [12980-7]; Item 995-G). Annotated to the leading cases, the *Constitution Annotated* (its popular title) includes citations to both federal and state court decisions and other commentaries. Virtually an encyclopedic gloss on the Constitution, it contains tables showing acts of Congress held to be unconstitutional, with their case citations.

In 1970, PL 91-589 was enacted directing the Librarian of Congress to prepare a revised edition of the work. The statute also directed biennial pocket supplements and complete revisions every decade. Preparation of the volumes and the supplements are the responsibility of the American Law Division of the Library's Congressional Research Service.

Executive Reports and Documents

Executive reports and documents are a Senate series only, and they are not depository items. Carried on Readex Microprint, indexed in the *Monthly Catalog* and abstracted in *CIS/Index*, they are classed in Y 1 and designated by Congress and session.

Senate Executive Reports are a *numbered* series that deal chiefly with publications reflecting the Senate's advice and consent to ratification of treaties and to confirmation of presidential nominations of high officials in the executive and judiciary. Examples of Senate Executive Reports include the Judiciary Committee's recommendation of George Harrold Carswell for Supreme Court

Justice (Y 1.91/2:rp. 14); the Banking, Housing and Urban Affairs Committee's favorable report on William J. Casey to be a member of the Securities and Exchange Commission (Y 1.92/1:rp. 4); the Committee on Rules and Administration recommending confirmation of Gerald R. Ford to be Vice President of the United States (Y 1.93/1:rp. 26); the report on the nomination of Henry Kissinger to be Secretary of State by the Foreign Relations Committee (Y 1.93/1:rp. 15); and that Committee's report consenting to ratification of the Patent Cooperation Treaty (Y 1.93/1:rp. 20).

Senate Executive Documents are a *lettered* series that seem to relate exclusively to presidential messages transmitted to the Senate Foreign Relations Committee requesting advice and consent to ratification of treaties, protocols and other agreements in the conduct of foreign policy. An example is the June 1973 extradition treaty with Italy involving narcotic offenses, psychotropic drugs and aircraft hijacking (Y 1.93/1:M).

A *Journal of Executive Proceedings of the Senate* is issued sessionally, but it is an elusive document. Although it is indexed in the *Monthly Catalog*, the number printed is restricted by law to 50 copies. It is classed and designated by volume number; for example, the *Journal* of the 91st Congress, 1st session was assigned the notation Y 1.3/4:112 and printed for official use only.

Memorial Addresses

Eulogies delivered in the House or Senate upon the death of a member or former member are classed in Y 7.1, fittingly the omega in the Superintendent's classification scheme.[23] Libraries subscribing to Item 1005 receive these addresses in bound volumes with the Y 7.1 classification; the class notation uses the Cutter table based on the name of the deceased member.

Memorial addresses are often made available for sale by the Superintendent. Such was the volume of tributes to Robert F. Kennedy (Y 7.1:K 386; *$4.75) cited in the March 1969 issue of the *Monthly Catalog*.

When Presidents or presidential appointees who have held high office in the executive or judiciary are memorialized, the compilations of tributes are issued in the Congressional series. Sometimes duplication occurs inadvertently, but an attempt is made to preserve the distinction. Obviously, a judgmental decision must be exercised in the case of persons who have enjoyed distinguished careers both in the Congress and in other governmental positions.

Some examples will illustrate the pattern. Memorial services in Congress for General Eisenhower were issued as 91-1: H. doc. 195 [12852-9]. Eisenhower, of course, never served in the Congress. However, tributes in eulogy of John F. Kennedy, who served in the House and Senate before becoming President, appeared as 88-2: S. doc. 59 [12624]. Tributes to James F. Byrnes, who served in both houses and on the Supreme Court, was a state governor, and held office in the federal executive, appeared as 92-2: S. doc. 77 [12980-6]. On the other hand, Edward Kennedy's brief tribute to his brother Robert (delivered at St. Patrick's Cathedral on June 8, 1968) was ordered to be printed under S. Res. 304. In this case the address was issued in slip form and later incorporated into the bound set [13938].

Normally compilations in the Congressional series by-pass the unbound House or Senate *documents* series (Item 996) and are sent to libraries in "Serial Set binding" (Item 995-G). Because of this pattern, depository libraries that wish to ensure receipt of all forms should subscribe to Items 1005, 996, and 995-G.

THE SERIAL SET

Einstein once remarked that he could happily contemplate the nature of light for the rest of his days. One might ascribe the same amount of time to the Congressional series known as the Serial Set, though with perhaps less happy contemplation. The odd pattern of distribution of memorial addresses noted above is but one instance of the difficulty of fully comprehending the mysteries of this legendary series. Schmeckebier and Eastin present a thorough account of the historical changes the Serial Set has undergone.[24] This discussion will be concerned with the present use and control of the publications that comprise the series. The composition of the Serial Set is deceptively simple: it consists of two categories of congressional publications—House and Senate *reports*, and House and Senate *documents*.

Reports

For the House and Senate both, this series consists of 1) miscellaneous reports on public bills; 2) miscellaneous reports on private bills; and 3) special reports. The first two designations constitute the vast majority of *reports*. All *reports* are designated by Congress, session, and individual numbers. The numerical designation extends through a Congress, but the citation includes the session to avoid error.

The *reports on public bills* are easily understood. A bill or resolution is studied after it is assigned to the appropriate congressional committee. Amendments may be proposed in committee. Indeed, the bill may be extensively revised and rewritten. The committee may hold hearings on the bill. Because hearings are published separately, only occasionally will the committee report contain testimony of witnesses. If the committee votes to report the bill favorably to the House or Senate, one of the members of the committee is assigned the task of writing the report, which describes the purpose and scope of the bill. The report is a section-by-section analysis of the bill, including (for bills or joint resolutions of a public character directly or indirectly appropriating money) a cost estimate likely to be incurred in implementing its provisions. Thus reports on public bills are of great significance in the process, for they establish legislative intent, and they are used by the courts and the executive departments and agencies as a source of information regarding the purpose and meaning of the law.

Private bills are studied in committee in the same manner as public bills, and *reports on private bills* are, likewise, an analysis of purpose and intent.

Special reports are usually pursuant to a simple resolution in each chamber directing a committee to make an investigation or study a matter of public interest. Generally, the category of "special reports" distinguishes the investigatory function of congressional committees from their legislative function.[25]

Examples of special reports include the following:

Investigation of Metropolitan Police Department Recruitment (90-1: H. rp. 12)

Report of Special Study Mission to Near East (90-1: H. rp. 172)

Migratory Farm Labor Problem (90-1: S. rp. 71)

Criminal Laws and Procedures (90-1: S. rp. 166)

Special Problems of the Rural Aging (93-1: H. rp. 103)

Special reports of the House Committee on Government Operations, primarily a study committee of the Congress, are often grouped sessionally in a bound volume of the Serial Set. Sometimes a committee will publish its preliminary analysis in the *Congressional Record*, or as a committee print, before final issuance in the *reports* series, but this pattern is unfortunately inconsistent.

Documents

The House and Senate *documents* series, like the *reports*, signifies a delimited number of categories. Up to this point, the word "documents" has been used in a generic sense, synonomous with "publications" or "materials." For Serial Set publications, the word assumes a specificity not applied in common parlance.

House and Senate *documents*, like *reports*, are designated by Congress, session, and individual numbers, and the numbering extends through a Congress. *Documents* include a wide variety of materials. At first blush, the series seems like a potpourri whose ingredients are chosen without rhyme or reason. Upon inspection, however, the patterns reveal a rough order. The series falls into three main categories of publications: 1) materials that originate in Congress; 2) materials that originate in executive departments and independent agencies; and 3) materials that originate outside the federal establishment whose national incorporation requires a report to the Congress.

Materials originating in the Congress include the *House Manual, Senate Manual, Biographical Directory of the American Congress, How Our Laws Are Made*, and the like. The Congress, by concurrent or simple resolution, orders printing of these materials as House or Senate *documents*. Publications believed to be of interest to the general public are printed in sufficient amounts so that wider distribution can be made by the Congress or so that the publication can be sold through the Superintendent.

Materials from agencies of the federal government include a) presidential messages, including vetoes; and b) reports by departments and agencies as required by law. Examples of these publications include:

Vetoing H. J. Res. 542, A Joint Resolution Concerning the War Powers of Congress and the President, Message from the President (93-1: H. doc. 171)

Nominating Gerald R. Ford to Be Vice President of the U.S., Message of the President (93-1: H. doc. 165)[26]

Annual Report of Atomic Energy Commission, 1966 (90-1: S. doc. 4)

The third subdivision in the *documents* series is the most peculiar. Organizations outside the government that are required by law to submit annual reports to Congress include corporations, foundations, societies, symphony orchestras, commissions, councils, leagues, and associations. They are listed sessionally in *Reports to Be Made to Congress*, itself issued as a House document. Generally, the reports are required to set forth the scope of financial audit, documentation of the body's assets and liabilities, income and expenses for the reporting period. The reports may also include the activities and achievements of the institution. Those that are ordered to be printed in the *documents* series include:

American Legion Proceedings
Boy Scouts of America
Girl Scouts of the U.S.A.
United Spanish War Veterans
Daughters of the American Revolution

Most of the prominent annual reports in this category by-pass the slip form of the document and are published only in Serial Set binding.

Availability

A few House and Senate *reports* and *documents* are placed on sale through the Superintendent. In the *Monthly Catalog* they are indicated by number in the main entry under the heading "Congress." In *CIS/Index*, availability is noted in the Summary Section. Those *reports* and *documents* not placed on sale may be obtained from the House or Senate Document Room, Capitol; from the issuing unit; or from one's Congressman.[27]

Indexing

Reports are indexed in many places. As soon as a bill has been reported out of a committee, it is assigned a report number. Beginning with the 91st Congress the report number contains a prefix-designator that indicates the session of the Congress. One may then use the index to the *Congressional Record*, the *House Calendars*, *Digest of Public General Bills*, the *Monthly Catalog*, the journals of the House and Senate, and several other sources, including *CIS/Index*. For *documents* the *Monthly Catalog* and *CIS/Index* are the easiest tools to use. For both *reports* and *documents* and for access to the bound Serial Set volumes, there is the indispensable *Numerical Lists and Schedule of Volumes*.

Numerical Lists

This key to the Serial Set represents an abrupt shift in provenance. The *Numerical Lists and Schedule of Volumes* (GP 3.7/2; Item 553) are issued by the Public Documents Department and compiled under the direction of the Superintendent of Documents. They are also available for sale by SUDOCS and arrive in depository libraries almost two years after the session of Congress covered. Slim, unprepossessing pamphlets of 50 or so pages, they bridge the gap between the numerical assignments of individual *reports* and *documents* and their final appearance in Serial Set binding.

Unbound copies of *reports* and *documents* are received in depository libraries under the following Items:

Reports on Public Bills (including "Special Reports")	1008-A
Reports on Private Bills	1008-B
Documents	996

When issued they receive an individual number as noted in the preceding pages. During each session the *reports* and *documents* are accumulated into bound volumes and assigned a serial number. Some *reports* and *documents* are never issued in unbound form but directly appear in the bound Serial Set. Nevertheless, these publications are assigned an individual number as well as a serial number. The *Monthly Catalog* indicates this pattern as follows:

a) Under the heading CONGRESS, *Senate documents*, entry 17120, is found:

> 77. Memorial addresses and other tributes in Congress of United States on life and contributions of James F. Byrnes, 92d Congress, 2d session. 1972. . . . ‡ (Sent to depository libraries in Serial set binding.)

b) Under the heading CONGRESS, *Congressional serial set*, entry 16849, is found:

> no. 77, 92d Congress, 2d session, Memorial addresses and other tributes in Congress of United States on life and contributions of James F. Byrnes
> [Serial 12980-6].   ● Item 995-G

This tells us that 92-2: S. doc. 77 would never appear in unbound form under Item 996, but would appear under Item 995-G (Miscellaneous *documents*, bound) as Serial 12980-6. If the Byrnes memorial compilation had been sent in unbound form (Item 996), however, it still would have been incorporated into the bound Serial Set. Because of the delay in issuance of the bound volumes, research libraries should subscribe to all Items that cover both the bound and unbound *documents* and *reports*.

Use of the *Numerical Lists and Schedule of Volumes* makes this kind of *Monthly Catalog* searching unnecessary. But the *Numerical Lists* have no subject or title approach. One must know the individual report or document number to translate to the bound Serial volumes. The title of this publication literally identifies its two-part organization, as follows:

Part 1, the "Numerical Lists" (Figure 32), gives all House and Senate *reports* and *documents* by individual number, title, and a volume/serial designation. The serial number is followed by subdivisions numbered -1, -2, -3, etc., so that groupings of like categories all have the same base serial number.

Part 2, the "Schedule of Volumes" (Figure 33), shows the individual *reports* and *documents* included in each bound volume. The "Date of Receipt" column is a handy place for librarians to note the bound issues that have been received and to discard all issues received in slip form. Grouping bound volumes into Miscellaneous Reports on Public Bills and Miscellaneous Reports on Private Bills was begun with the 84th Congress; grouping of Special Reports commenced with the 88th Congress.

House and Senate *documents* are grouped in a "Miscellaneous" category and the base serial number is also subdivided. Other *documents*, issued in Serial Set binding only, are listed by title in the "Schedule of Volumes." Some of these are not labelled "Miscellaneous" but are available under that Item (995-G). Still others are available under other Items. The peculiar nature of these categories becomes academic if the user knows the *report* or *document* number; the *Numerical Lists* will get one to the Serial Set.[28]

Duplication

In every issue of the "Schedule of Volumes" section of the *Numerical Lists* there are titles of publications preceded by the following note:

> The documents listed below originated in Executive departments and agencies. They were furnished to depository libraries and international exchanges at the time of printing in the format used by the departments and agencies. They will not be furnished as Congressional documents nor in the volumes as indicated hereby.

This qualification applies only to the House and Senate *documents* series. Over the years, as the list published in *Reports to Be Made to Congress* indicates, the annual reports of departments, bureaus, independent, and regulatory agencies—as well as the non-governmental societies and corporations—have been a requirement of law.[29] Moreover, many reports must be submitted through the President from administrative units under his direct control (in the Executive Office) or from departments, agencies, and selected boards, committees, and councils. When ordered to be printed as a House or Senate *document*, these

Figure 32

NUMERICAL LISTS

NUMERICAL LISTS

Of the Reports and Documents of the 92d Congress, 1st Session

SENATE REPORTS

Figure 33

SCHEDULE OF VOLUMES

SCHEDULE OF VOLUMES

Of the Reports and Documents of the 92d Congress, 1st Session

Note.—For explanation regarding the distribution, etc., of the bound set of Congressional documents and reports listed below see the Preface.

SENATE REPORTS

			Serial no.	Date of receipt
Vol.	1–1.	Nos. 1–34, 36–41, 43–45, 47–48, 50–62, 70–73, 75–107, 109–110, 123–126, 129–130, 132–133, 136–144: **Miscellaneous reports on public bills. I**	12929–1	
Vol.	1–2.	Nos. 145–158, 161–162, 178–207, 217, 219–225, 227, 229–254: **Miscellaneous reports on public bills. II**	12929–2	
Vol.	1–3.	Nos. 255–273, 275–279, 281–282, 284, 290–297, 301–302, 304, 307–345, 349–359: **Miscellaneous reports on public bills. III**	12929–3	
Vol.	1–4.	Nos. 361–378, 380–417, 419–432, 434–437: **Miscellaneous reports on public bills. IV**	12929–4	
Vol.	1–5.	Nos. 438–439, 441–449, 451–453, 485–500, 502–503, 506–507, 509–523: **Miscellaneous reports on public bills. V**	12929–5	
Vol.	1–6.	Nos. 525–534, 537–558, 560–590: **Miscellaneous reports on public bills. VI**	12929–6	
Vol.	2.	Nos. 63–69, 108, 112–122, 127–128, 131, 159–160, 163–174, 208–216, 218 226, 228, 274, 280, 285–289, 298–300, 303, 305–306, 347–348, 379, 454–484, 504, 508, 559: **Miscellaneous reports on private bills**	12930	
Vol.	3–1.	Nos. 35, 42, 46, 49, 74, 111, 134–135, 175–177, 283, 360, 418, 433, 440, 450, 501, 505, 524, 535–536: **Special reports**	12931–1	
Vol.	3–2.	No. 346: Education amendments of 1971	12931–2	

HOUSE REPORTS

Note.—No. 93 is blank

Vol.	1–1.	Nos. 1–10, 12–13, 15–68, 81–84, 92, 94–103, 115–119, 121–128, 130–136, 143–166, 168–170, 176–183, 186–187, 194–195, 197–202: **Miscellaneous reports on public bills. I**	12932–1	
Vol.	1–2.	Nos. 203–230, 232–249, 255–283, 288–290, 296–297, 299–315, 317–324: **Miscellaneous reports on public bills. II**	12932–2	
Vol.	1–3.	Nos. 325–341, 345–348, 350–442, 451–459: **Miscellaneous reports on public bills. III**	12932–3	

reports are assigned an individual number and eventually a serial number for binding.

In 1922 libraries were permitted to receive on deposit only those series they wished, provided they selected the Item in advance of distribution. Departments and bureaus would then send their reports to subscribing libraries *without* the individual document numbers on the title page and *without* the serial number designation. This form of distribution was called the "departmental edition." The "congressional edition" was distributed only to the Senate and House libraries, the Library of Congress, the National Archives, and the Office of the Superintendent of Documents. The latter was thus able to note which materials were to be sent to depository libraries in the appropriate edition and so indicate this in the *Monthly Catalog* and in the "Schedule of Volumes."

Two examples will suffice. Congress has regularly been issuing the annual report of the Librarian of Congress in the congressional edition. But just as regularly the report has gone to depository libraries in the "departmental edition." The "Schedule of Volumes" section of the *Numerical Lists* shows, for the 90th Congress, 1st session, LC's annual report as targeted for libraries in the departmental format:

> Vol. 10. No. 5: Annual report of Librarian
> of Congress, 1966. 12774

This means that the Senate or House libraries, for example, would have received this report as 90-1: H. doc. 5 and shelved it with their complete Serial Set in bound volume 12774. On the other hand, depository libraries would have received this report as LC 1.1: 966 *only if they subscribed to Item 785.*

The *Monthly Catalog* handles it in this way: under a title heading in a typical MC index two entry numbers are given. Turning to both, one finds:

> 16789 Statistical abstract of United States, 1972. . . .
>   Also issued as H. doc. 257, 92d Congress.

> 16940 257 Statistical abstract of United States,
>   1972 . . . . *Available in departmental
>   edition, cloth, $5.50, C56.243:972,
>   and sent to depositories in that form.
>   See Entry no. 16789.

For this publication, the House and Senate libraries would have received 92-1: H. doc. 257 in the congressional edition. Later a Serial Set number would have been assigned. Depository libraries, however, are alerted that this publication was sent to them only in the departmental edition (C56.243:972; Item 150).

Although these and many other publications are issued in both editions, there is no absolute guarantee that this is an immutable practice. The *Statistical Abstract* is one of a group of materials that are not reports at all, but that are important series like the *Minerals Yearbook* and the *Yearbook of Agriculture*. When Congress has wanted a certain number of copies of a publication printed for its use, a law has been passed authorizing the printing. This has resulted in the duplication of issuance. The important point is that only by examining those House and Senate *documents* segregated in the "Schedule of Volumes" section of the *Numerical Lists* sessionally can a library account for the missing serial numbers in the bound volumes of their Serial Set.

Regional depository libraries, of course, will receive the entire Congressional series in its various forms. Selective depositories that wish the full run of the Serial Set will have to be aware of the following patterns:[30]

Table 3

TYPES OF MATERIALS IN THE SERIAL SET

DESCRIPTION	ITEM NO.
Unbound H & S Reports	
On public bills and special reports	1008-A
On private bills	1008-B
Bound H & S Reports	
On public bills and special reports	1007-A
On private bills	1007-B
Unbound H & S Documents	
"Miscellaneous" documents	996
Bound H & S Documents	
"Miscellaneous" documents	995-G
and	
American Legion, Proceedings of National Convention	995-I
Appropriations, Budget Estimates	995-E
Boy Scouts of America and Girl Scouts of U.S.A., Annual Reports	995-P
Daughters of American Revolution, Annual Report of National Society	995-B
Disabled American Veterans, National Report	995-J
House Manual	1029
Secretary of Senate, Report	995-M

Table 3 (cont'd)

DESCRIPTION (cont'd)	ITEM NO.
Senate Manual	1048
United Spanish War Veterans, Proceedings of National Encampment	995-K
Veterans of Foreign Wars of U.S., Proceedings of National Convention	995-L
Veterans of World War I of U.S., Proceedings of National Convention	995-Q

For the rest, one must consult the "Schedule of Volumes" to determine those *documents* issued in the "departmental edition"; one then hopes that the Items under which the publications are issued have been subscribed to. If departmental publications are not depository issuances, the *Monthly Catalog* will show the appropriate distribution pattern.

THE LEGISLATIVE PROCESS

Many are the ways in which legislation originates. Contrary to the view of popular civics, the executive branch rather than the Congress is responsible for the significant legislative proposals submitted. Legislative ideas may come as well from interest groups or individual citizens. Sometimes congressional committees consider proposals that have not been formally introduced. The committee then formulates its own bill, which is introduced by the chairman; this is the customary method for revenue and appropriation bills.

Representatives and Senators, of course, propose legislation too. But whatever the origin, *introduction* of legislation can be made only by a member of Congress. In cases where the legislation originates in the executive, it is transmitted to Congress by message or letter; this is published as a House or Senate *document*, while the accompanying legislation is introduced by a sympathetic member.

Bills and joint resolutions are the legislative vehicles, and they may be introduced in either chamber. Of the thousands of pieces of legislation introduced every Congress, relatively few are ever reported out of committee. And fewer still become law.

Stages of a Bill

The voyage of a bill through Congress begins when it is introduced by a member. In the House, legislation may be sponsored by up to 25 members; the Senate permits unlimited multiple sponsoring. The bill's title is entered in the *Journal* and printed in the *Congressional Record*. It is assigned a number by the

Clerk of the House and referred to the appropriate committee that exercises jurisdiction over like measures. The first printing is known as the "introduced print"; an example of this printing is reproduced in the section that discussed bills and resolutions (Figure 28, page 104).

The committee to which the bill is referred may refuse to consider it, report it unfavorably, rewrite it entirely, or report it favorably with or without amendments. Assuming that the bill is to be considered, it is placed on the committee's calendar, and often it is assigned to a subcommittee of the committee; hearings are scheduled.

After deliberation, the committee is ready to recommend to the full House or Senate the merits of the legislation. If the committee votes to report the bill favorably, a report must be written and a new bill, called a "reported print" is ordered to be printed.

In our example, note that H. R. 8629 in its "reported print" form has the calendar number and the committee report number on the bill. The date of the "introduced print" is given, along with the name of the bill's sponsor and the date of report out of committee (Figure 34).

As we noted in our discussion of the Serial Set, the committee *report* is significant in establishing legislative intent. In our next example, note that amendments are set forth at the beginning; following the amendments are the purpose and scope of the bill, with detailed reasons for recommendation of approval. The name of the committee member assigned to write the report is given, as are the bill number and the name of the committee. The report's proper citation for this measure of legislation is 90-1 : H. rp. 509 (Figure 35, page 128).

As it happened, our exemplary bill was considered in the House and passed that chamber as amended. H. R. 8629 was then sent to the Senate for its consideration. The bill has undergone two more printings, is now technically called "an act," and must pass the scrutiny of a Senate committee having jurisdiction over apposite measures. To this end, the Senate committee also publishes a *report*. Note the calendar number, name of member authorized to write the report and the bill number. The proper citation for this report is 90-1 : S. rp. 609 (Figure 36, page 129).

It often happens, especially with important legislation, that the House and Senate versions of the measure differ. The vehicle for resolving differences between the two chambers is known as the *conference*. Managers, or conferees, are appointed for each body, and they attempt to hammer out a compromise that both chambers can agree to. A *conference report* is written and carries the imprint of the chamber where the legislation originated, the citation in this case being 90-1 : H. rp. 987 (Figure 37, page 130). Only when the bill has been agreed to in identical form by both bodies can it be enrolled for presentation to the President, who vetoes or signs it into law.

Figure 34

BILL: REPORTED PRINT

Union Calendar No. 182

90TH CONGRESS
1ST SESSION

H. R. 8629

[Report No. 509]

IN THE HOUSE OF REPRESENTATIVES

APRIL 17, 1967

Mr. CELLER introduced the following bill; which was referred to the Committee on the Judiciary

JULY 25, 1967

Reported with an amendment, committed to the Committee of the Whole House on the State of the Union, and ordered to be printed

[Omit the part struck through and insert the part printed in italic]

A BILL

To amend the Act of July 4, 1966 (Public Law 89-491).

1   *Be it enacted by the Senate and House of Representa-*

2 *tives of the United States of America in Congress assembled,*

3 That the Act of July 4, 1966 (80 Stat. 259), is hereby

4 amended as follows:

5   1. By adding in section 2 (b) (3) the words "the

6 Secretary of Commerce," after the words, "the Secretary

7 of Defense,".

8   2. By deleting in section 3 (d) the words "two years

9 after the date of the enactment of this Act," and inserting

10 in lieu thereof "July 4, 1969.".

Figure 35

HOUSE COMMITTEE REPORT

90TH CONGRESS	HOUSE OF REPRESENTATIVES	REPORT
1st Session		No. 509

AMERICAN REVOLUTION BICENTENNIAL COMMISSION

JULY 25, 1967.—Committed to the Committee of the Whole House on the State of the Union and ordered to be printed

Mr. ROGERS of Colorado, from the Committee on the Judiciary, submitted the following

REPORT

[To accompany H.R. 8629]

The Committee on the Judiciary, to whom was referred the bill (H.R. 8629) to amend the act of July 4, 1966 (Public Law 89–491), having considered the same, report favorably thereon with an amendment and recommend that the bill do pass.

The amendment is as follows:

On page 2, strike lines 3 through 5 and insert in lieu thereof the following:

"SEC. 7. (a) There is authorized to be appropriated not to exceed $450,000 for the period through fiscal year 1969."

EXPLANATION OF AMENDMENT

The purpose of the amendment is to limit the authorization for appropriations to $450,000 during the period through fiscal year 1969.

PURPOSE OF THE BILL

The purpose of H.R. 8629 is threefold: First, it would add the Secretary of Commerce as an ex officio member of the Commission; second, it would extend the date on which the Commission shall report to the President by 1 year—from July 4, 1968, to July 4, 1969; third, it would authorize the appropriation of public funds to finance the work of the Commission.

STATEMENT

Public Law 89–491, approved July 4, 1966, established the American Revolution Bicentennial Commission to commemorate the American

[Rule XIII of the Rules of the House now require the report to contain an estimate of the costs involved in the reported bill except as to certain committees. Rule XI also requires that when a record vote is taken, on a bill being reported by a committee, the report shall include the result of that vote]

*First page only.

Figure 36

SENATE COMMITTEE REPORT

Calendar No. 592

90TH CONGRESS }	SENATE	{	REPORT
1st Session }		{	No. 609

EXTENDING THE AMERICAN REVOLUTION BICENTENNIAL COMMISSION

OCTOBER 11 (legislative day, OCTOBER 10), 1967.—Ordered to be printed

Mr. DIRKSEN, from the Committee on the Judiciary, submitted the following

REPORT

[To accompany H.R. 8629]

The Committee on the Judiciary, to which was referred the bill (H.R. 8629) to amend the act of July 4, 1966 (Public Law 89–491), having considered the same, reports favorably thereon with an amendment and recommends that the bill as amended do pass.

AMENDMENT

On page 2, after line 4, insert the following:

4. By deleting in section 2(b)(1) the word "Four" and inserting in lieu thereof the word "Six"; and by deleting in section 2(b)(2) the word "Four" and inserting in lieu thereof the word "Six".

PURPOSE OF AMENDMENT

The purpose of the amendment is to increase the Senate membership on the Commission from four members to six members, and to increase the House of Representatives membership on the Commission from four members to six members.

PURPOSE

The purpose of the proposed legislation, as amended, is fourfold: First, it would add the Secretary of Commerce as an exofficio member of the Commission; second, it would extend the date on which the

[With certain exceptions,the Legislative Reorganization Act of 1970, requires the report to contain an estimate of the costs involved in the bill]

*First page only.

Figure 37

CONFERENCE COMMITTEE REPORT

90TH CONGRESS 1st Session	HOUSE OF REPRESENTATIVES	REPORT No. 987

AMERICAN REVOLUTION BICENTENNIAL COMMISSION

NOVEMBER 28, 1967.—Ordered to be printed

Mr. ROGERS of Colorado, from the committee of conference, submitted the following

CONFERENCE REPORT

[To accompany H.R. 8629]

The committee of conference on the disagreeing votes of the two Houses on the amendment of the Senate to the bill (H.R. 8629) to amend the act of July 4, 1966 (Public Law 89–491), having met, after full and free conference, have agreed to recommend and do recommend to their respective Houses as follows:

That the Senate recede from its amendment.

BYRON G. ROGERS,
BASIL WHITENER,
ANDREW JACOBS, Jr.,
RICHARD H. POFF,
CHARLES E. WIGGINS,
Managers on the Part of the House.
EVERETT M. DIRKSEN,
JOHN L. McCLELLAN,
Managers on the Part of the Senate.

Stages of a Law

Provenance for the first official publication of the law shifts from Congress to the Office of the Federal Register, General Services Administration. Known as the "slip law," it takes the form of an unbound pamphlet, printed by photoelectric offset process from the enrolled bill signed by the President. At the Office of the Federal Register it is assigned a Public Law number; these numbers run in sequence, starting anew at the beginning of each Congress. In our example, the act has become Public Law 90-187 (Figure 38).

Figure 38

SLIP LAW WITH LEGISLATIVE HISTORY

Public Law 90-187
90th Congress, H. R. 8629
December 12, 1967

An Act

81 STAT. 567

To amend the Act of July 4, 1966 (Public Law 89-491).

Be it enacted by the Senate and House of Representatives of the United States of America in Congress assembled, That the Act of July 4, 1966 (80 Stat. 259), is hereby amended as follows:

1. By adding in section 2(b)(3) the words "the Secretary of Commerce," after the words, "the Secretary of Defense,".

2. By deleting in section 3(d) the words "two years after the date of the enactment of this Act," and inserting in lieu thereof "July 4, 1969.".

3. By deleting section 7(a) and inserting in lieu thereof the following:

"SEC. 7. (a) There is authorized to be appropriated not to exceed $450,000 for the period through fiscal year 1969."

Approved December 12, 1967.

American Revolution Bicentennial Commission.

Appropriation.

LEGISLATIVE HISTORY:

HOUSE REPORTS: No. 509 (Comm. on the Judiciary) and No. 987 (Comm. of Conference).
SENATE REPORT No. 609 (Comm. on the Judiciary).
CONGRESSIONAL RECORD, Vol. 113 (1967):
    Aug. 7: Considered and passed House.
    Oct. 12: Considered and passed Senate, amended.
    Nov. 28: Senate agreed to conference report.
    Nov. 29: House agreed to conference report.

The Superintendent has assigned GS 4.110 as the class number covering slip laws; Item 575 insures their receipt by depository libraries. The *Monthly Catalog* affords a subject approach to the slip laws, although they are listed under the entry "Congress" rather than "Federal Register Office." Private Laws, too, are indexed by name of petitioner in the *Monthly Catalog* and are listed under the entry "Congress—Laws," but only Public Laws are made available for sale by the Superintendent, either at a sessional subscription price or separately.

The Office of the Federal Register provides marginal editorial notes citing laws or treaties mentioned in the text. Note in our example the useful guide to the "legislative history" of the process at the end of the slip law, following the approval date. A more complete "legislative history" of a bill's voyage through Congress might include any hearings or committee prints pursuant to the measure, as well as any presidential statements.

A chronological arrangement of the slip laws in bound volumes is published as the *Statutes at Large*. Compilation and indexing are the responsibility of the General Services Administration; the Office of the Federal Register issues the *Statutes at Large* (GS 4.111; Item 576) by volumes, in sessional arrangement. When the appropriate volume arrives in one's library, the slip laws covered in that compilation may be discarded.

Like the slip law, the version that appears in the *Statutes at Large* includes the bill number and the date of enactment into law. The "legislative history" found on the slip law is now published in tabular form in the *Statutes*, providing the user with a handy reference to the bill, reports, and dates of consideration and passage. This "Guide to Legislative History of Bills Enacted Into Public Law" first appeared in the *Statutes at Large* in 1963 (Figure 39).

Finally substantive laws are consolidated and codified. They appear in the *United States Code*, which is issued in a completely revised edition every six years with annual supplements between revisions. Title and section numbers are given in the citation, along with the edition date or supplement number.

In addition to the rearranged text of statutes, the *United States Code* has an extensive subject index, a table of acts by popular name, and tables of statutes included or repealed and of *Code* titles revised in later editions. Two commercial publications produce unofficial, annotated editions of the *Code*: *United States Code Annotated* (U.S.C.A.), a West Publishing Company venture, and *Federal Code Annotated* (F.C.A.), published by Lawyers Co-operative Publishing Company (see Chapter 11). Both editions follow the same title and section numbering employed in the *United States Code*, but feature annotations of court decisions, references to opinions of the Attorneys General of the United States, and editorial notes and analytical discussions on specific statutes or provisions. U.S.C.A. and F.C.A. are supplemented by annual pocket parts and special pamphlets during the year, thus providing a recency that the official edition lacks.

The reader is encouraged to supplement this sketch of the legislative process by consulting the more detailed *How Our Laws Are Made* and other legislative guides.[31]

Figure 39

GUIDE TO LEGISLATIVE HISTORY IN STATUTES AT LARGE

GUIDE TO LEGISLATIVE HISTORY OF BILLS ENACTED INTO PUBLIC LAW—Continued

NOTE: Companion bills are in parentheses

Public Law No.	Date approved (1967)	81 Stat.	Bill No.	Report No. and Committee reporting — House	Report No. and Committee reporting — Senate	Dates of consideration and passage (Congressional Record, Vol. 113 (1967)) — House	Dates of consideration and passage — Senate
90-160	Nov. 28	517	S. J. Res. 26	646 Judiciary	241 Judiciary	May 25	May 18; Nov. 17
90-161	Nov. 28	518	H. R. 8632		752 Judiciary	Oct. 2	Nov. 16
90-162	Nov. 28	518	H. J. Res. 936			Nov. 28	Nov. 28
90-163	Nov. 29	518	H. R. 169	344 Merchant Marine and Fisheries	791 Commerce	June 19	Nov. 20
90-164	Nov. 29	519	H. R. 168	342 Merchant Marine and Fisheries	787 Commerce	June 19	Nov. 20
90-165	Nov. 29	519	H. R. 1006	347 Merchant Marine and Fisheries	788 Commerce	June 19	Nov. 20
90-166	Nov. 29	519	S. 2428	928 Armed Services	741 Armed Services	Nov. 20	Nov. 13
90-167	Nov. 29	520	H. R. 3351	345 Armed Services [Conference]	789 Commerce	Nov. 20	Nov. 20
90-168	Dec. 1	521	H. R. 2	13 Banking and Currency; 925 Interstate and Foreign Commerce; 762, 562 [Conference]	732 Armed Services	Feb. 20; Nov. 15	Nov. 8, 16
90-169	Dec. 1	526	H. J. Res. 859	954 Agriculture; 716 [Conference]	725 Labor and Public Welfare	Nov. 21; Sept. 20; Nov. 21	Nov. 22; Nov. 6, 21
90-170	Dec. 4	527	H. R. 6430		793 Agriculture and Forestry	Oct. 20, 23	Nov. 20
90-171	Dec. 4	531	H. R. 10442	898 District of Columbia	340 District of Columbia	Nov. 20	June 13
90-172	Dec. 4	532	S. 764	899 District of Columbia	583 District of Columbia	Nov. 20	Oct. 10
90-173	Dec. 4	532	S. 770	538 Interstate and Foreign Commerce	724 District of Columbia	Sept. 19, 20; Nov. 21	Nov. 6, 21
90-174	Dec. 5	533	H. R. 6418		Labor and Public Welfare	Nov. 21	
90-175	Dec. 5	542	S. 1031	974 [Conference]	223 Foreign Relations	Nov. 21	May 15
90-176	Dec. 6	542	H. R. 2529	807 Foreign Affairs; 115 District of Columbia	803 District of Columbia	Mar. 13	Nov. 27
90-177	Dec. 6	544	S. 706	918 Merchant Marine and Fisheries	472 Commerce	Nov. 20	Aug. 4
90-178	Dec. 8	544	H. R. 8582	378 District of Columbia	802 District of Columbia	June 26	Nov. 27
90-179	Dec. 8	545	H. R. 12910	710 Armed Services	748 Armed Services	Oct. 2; Nov. 20	Nov. 16; Nov. 13, 14, 21
90-180	Dec. 8	550	H. R. 13600	799 Appropriations; 975 [Conference]	742 Appropriations	Oct. 24; Nov. 21	
90-181	Dec. 8	553	S. 2514 (H. R. 12010)	948 Judiciary	720 Public Works	Nov. 20	Nov. 6, 28
90-182	Dec. 8	559	H. R. 2154	272 Interior and Insular Affairs	816 Interior and Insular Affairs	June 5	Nov. 30
90-183	Dec. 10	559	S. 2211 (H. R. 13369)	923 Merchant Marine and Fisheries	717 Commerce	Nov. 20	Nov. 7, 29
90-184	Dec. 10	560	H. R. 4920	355 Interior and Insular Affairs	817 Interior and Insular Affairs	June 19	Nov. 30
90-185	Dec. 11	560	S. J. Res. 35	912 Interstate and Foreign Commerce	202 Interior and Insular Affairs	Nov. 20	May 4; Dec. 1
90-186	Dec. 12	566	S. 343	811 Public Works; 509 Judiciary; 987 [Conference]	82 Public Works	Dec. 4	Apr. 4
90-187	Dec. 12	567	H. R. 8629		609 Judiciary	Aug. 7; Nov. 20	Oct. 12; Nov. 28

OTHER GUIDES TO LEGISLATION

Newspapers, magazines and newsletters—and, of course, the strident voices on the airwaves—carry information of current legislation and its status in the Congress. These sources are largely fragmentary; if the user needs only to know how one's Representative or Senator voted on a given measure this week, a local newspaper will usually provide the answer. However, there are a number of information sources that will furnish greater detail. In addition to the official sources noted above, a library may purchase commercial guides and indexes to the legislative process. Some of the more interesting guides follow.

Congressional Index

A publication of Commerce Clearing House (CCH), a Chicago-based commercial reporting service, *Congressional Index* is popular with many librarians for its recency and ease of use in tracing the status of legislation. All public bills and resolutions are listed and indexed; their progress is reported by looseleaf updating from introduction of the measure to final disposition.

A "Subject Index" refers one to the bill number; as the session progresses, the main subject index is supplemented by a "Current Subject Index," and reference to both is necessary. The "Index by Authors" section lists bills by sponsor and co-sponsor, with reference to subject and bill number. This section too is supplemented by a "Current Index by Authors." Congressional action on proposals initiated by the executive branch—reorganization plans, treaties, nominations—has its own subject index. And yet another section indexes measures that have been approved or vetoed, by bill number and Public Law number, with a subject and author approach.

Identical or very similar bills, as noted, may be introduced in both chambers to expedite their consideration or to please the constituents back home. House measures that are in this relationship to Senate bills are listed, by Senate bill numbers, in the "Companion Bills" section. A cross-reference tabulation is given to Senate measures similar to House introductions in the "Companion Bills—Identical House Bills" section.

Bills are listed by date of introduction and numerical designation. In a section called "Bills Divisions," the number of each measure is followed by a descriptive title, the name of the sponsor, a summary of the bill's provisions, and the committee to which it was referred. Further action on a measure is reported in the "Status of Bills Divisions." Private bills are listed only by number. Separate divisions obtain for joint resolutions, concurrent resolutions, and simple resolutions.

Of great value are the "Status of Senate and House Bills Divisions," which provide a record of all actions taken by Congress and the President on all public measures. As the session progresses, "Current Status Tables" must be used to supplement the main listings. Action on each bill is cumulated in chronological order; status of the resolutions is also reported. If a bill or resolution does not appear in a status table, it means the measure is still in the committee to which it was referred.

All roll call and recorded teller votes on legislation are listed in the "Voting Records Divisions." In each case the record shows how the majority of each political party voted and notes the names of members who did not follow party lines. Other useful reference features include a list of members of both chambers, with biographical data; and all permanent committees *and their subcommittees.* Committee assignments of individual members of Congress are given in their biographies. A record of the public hearings held by all committees on subjects not identified by bill numbers is arranged alphabetically by committee names in these sections; each entry indicates the subject matter, the date the hearings began, and the date the transcript of the hearings became available. The dates for public hearings on subjects identified by bill numbers are found in the "Status of Bills Divisions." As *reports* of investigations and studies by committees and subcommittees are submitted, they are listed under the *report* number assigned when submitted; information includes the subject of the *report* and the date of its submission.

Subscribers receive two reports a week while the Congress is in session. A "Report Letter" contains summaries of legislative highlights of the preceding week, and a list showing which measures were acted upon during the week. Also, a list of "Roll Call Votes" indicates which of these measures put members on the record. Subscribers also receive a special Friday newsletter entitled "The Week in Congress."[32]

United States Code Congressional and Administrative News

Known as *Cong. News* and published monthly by West Publishing Company, this excellent service cumulates information on the status of legislation. The full text of Public Laws signed during the reporting period is included. *Cong. News* features ten tables, seven of them serving as guides to the legislative process, the other three involving presidential and agency materials. Table 1 lists Public Laws by number with page references to the appropriate monthly issues of *Cong. News.* Table 2 features a list of Public Laws with reference to title and section of the *United States Code* and the *United States Code Annotated* affected. Table 3 references pages in *Cong. News* that give information on *U.S.C.* and *U.S.C.A.* sections new, amended, and repealed, arranged by title and section. Table 4 is a "legislative history" of measures, similar to the history given in the *Statutes at Large,* and arranged by Public Law number. Table 5 lists bills and joint resolutions enacted, arranged by bill number. Tables 6, 7, and 8 treat of administrative regulations, proclamations, and executive orders. Table 9, "Major Bills Pending," is an alphabetical status listing by title of measure, with reference to bill number, dates of "reported" and "passed" in House and Senate, whether sent to conference, and Public Law number and date of approval. Table 10 is an alphabetical listing of acts by popular name. All tables cumulate with each issue of *Cong. News,* making use easy. Rounding out each issue is a "Cumulative (Subject) Index."

Congressional Quarterly, Inc.

This Washington-based commercial firm issues a host of useful publications. *CQ Weekly Report*, the most current and perhaps the best of Congressional Quarterly's stable of services, analyzes congressional and political activity for the week. A status table of major legislation shows the more significant bills of the session and their current place in the process. At the end of a session, the *Weekly Report* presents a summary of major legislation passed and not passed, arranged by broad subject areas. On major public bills, the weekly issues include subject matter of the measure; sponsors; what happened in committee, including hearings; floor action (debate, amendments, voting); and results of conferences. A table showing roll-call votes (taken from the *Congressional Record*) for all members during the reporting period, with a brief abstract of the measure, is an extremely useful feature of the *Weekly Report*. Measures approved indicate Public Law number and date signed. Quarterly indexes by names and subjects cumulate throughout the year.

CQ Almanac is published annually; over 1,600 pages long, it distills, reorganizes and cross-indexes the full year in Congress. However, the *Weekly Report* should *not* be discarded even if one purchases the *Almanac*. *CQ Guide to Current American Government* is issued semi-annually and includes analysis and summaries of major issues for the six-month period. *Congressional Roll Call* annually analyzes House and Senate votes for a session. A significant feature reports the vote of every individual Representative and Senator for each roll call, including a concise description of each bill, thus pulling together the listings in the *Weekly Report*.

Larger, more ambitious CQ compilations include *Congress and the Nation, 1945-1964* with supplements covering four-year periods. It is an encyclopedic chronicle of congressional activity. *Guide to the Congress of the United States* (1971) is also a treasure trove of analytic and factual information.[33] Libraries with documents collections cannot afford to ignore the catalog announcements published by Congressional Quarterly, for the assiduous compilers of the many CQ services seem to astonish the world yearly with yet another reporting service that bids to become an instant classic of reference value.

National Journal

The weekly *National Journal* (Center for Political Research, Washington, D.C.) offers systematic coverage of significant topics that shape federal policy. In each issue there is a section called "Weekly Briefing," a checklist of important actions of the President, the departments and agencies, Congress, and the Judiciary. This feature includes "Vote Charts" for roll-call votes of all Representatives and Senators on measures during that week; taken from the *Congressional Record*, the tally does not include quorum calls. Cumulative indexes include personal names, private firms and associations, government agencies (including congressional committees), a geographic index, and a subject index.

Congressional Monitor

The *Congressional Monitor* (Monitor, Inc., Washington, D.C.) is published Monday through Friday each day Congress is in session. Each issue gives House, Senate, and joint committee action scheduled for the day, with a list of witnesses appearing at the several hearings. Future House, Senate, and joint committee action is projected for the week ahead. House and Senate floor action for the previous day and the reporting day are briefly summarized. Subscribers are sent a *Weekly Legislative Status Report*, compiled every Friday at the end of the legislative day. Bills are arranged in 25 numbered categories of "particular interest to *Monitor* subscribers" (Agriculture, Consumer Protection, Education, Energy, etc.), and an index by bill number gives the category number to which the bill applies. The categories are arranged by bill number with reference to name of the committee (subcommittee) to which the bill has been assigned, and its status to date including Public Law number. The Friday Report cumulates every week. Companion bill numbers are carried in the index, providing a cross reference for those bills that have been incorporated or that are of parallel interest.

Finally, those who want immediate information can place a phone call to the House or Senate Democratic or Republican cloakroom, where a recording will announce up-to-the-minute legislative developments. The information during the day is given by bill number, and toward the end of the day there is a recording that summarizes the day's activities.

The above selective list demonstrates that there is no lack of publications designed in whole or in part to provide current information on legislation. Some libraries subscribe to all of the publications, government and private, mentioned in this chapter—and more. Many libraries, however, find that practice both unnecessary and too expensive.

TRACING LEGISLATION: A SUMMARY

Current

Public Bills and Resolutions

The bi-weekly *Congressional Record* Index consists of two sections. The "Index to Proceedings" section is not cumulative, but when a bill is introduced it can be found under the subject or the name of the sponsor. The "History of Bills and Resolutions" section lists that bill when it is introduced and referred to committee. However, this section is cumulative, so that once the bill number is known, page references to the *Congressional Record* can be found without a need to refer to earlier fortnightly indexes. Arrangement of the "History of Bills and Resolutions" section is by bill number, referencing title and latest current status as of the two-week reporting period covered by the index.

The *Congressional Index* (Commerce Clearing House) is perhaps easier to use than the *Congressional Record* Index. Bills are indexed by subject and author (sponsor). There is also a section that lists bills by number and date of introduction. In the "Bills Divisions"—including the three types of resolutions—the number of the measure is followed by the title, sponsor's name, summary of bill's provisions, and committee to which referred. *Congressional Index*, with its semi-weekly reporting, gains a recency advantage over other legislative guides, save only for the *House Calendars*.

Calendars of the United States House of Representatives and History of Legislation are printed daily while Congress is in session, but the subject index appears only in the Monday issue. Moreover, the legislative history of the bill begins when it has been reported out of committee and placed on one of the five calendars used by the House for its legislative procedures. Because they are cumulative (remember to save the Monday index issue until the following Monday), the *House Calendars* are easy to use in tracing legislation at this entry point. An "Index Key and History of Bill" section, arranged by bill and resolution number, cumulates all bills and resolutions from committee report through Public Law number and approval date. The *House Calendars* include Senate actions, so that there is need for only this one document.

Although it appears "in five or more cumulative issues with bi-weekly supplementation as may be needed," the *Digest of Public General Bills and Resolutions* does not generally afford the recency of the above sources. However, it is an excellent resource for the status of legislation. There is a sponsor index, a subject index, a specific-title index, and an identical bill index, all of which give access to the main entries, which are bills and resolutions arranged by number with summaries (digests) of the measures.

CIS/Index, a monthly, has a separate index that lists bills and resolutions by number with reference to the internal alphameric notation scheme used by *CIS/Index*. The notation gets the user to the "Summary Section," where action is abstracted with regard to hearings, reports, and committee prints pursuant to the measure. Bills indexed in the monthly issues refer to action noted for the reporting period only, but the quarterly indexes cover bills and resolutions for a three-month reporting period.

Hearings

The most useful sources for looking up current published hearings are *CIS/Index* and the *Monthly Catalog*. The former is by far the superior tool because it abstracts the contents of the hearings and the testimony of witnesses. Access through the "Index of Subjects and Names" is by subject, names of witnesses, names of organizations represented by witnesses, and names of subcommittees. The *Monthly Catalog*, though less detailed, is considerably cheaper to purchase. Hearings are indexed in the MC by title, committee, and subject.[34]

Committee Prints

Whether prints are pursuant to a bill or resolution in the form of background information for the committee, or in the nature of a report or study peripheral to or even unrelated to specific legislation, they are indexed in *CIS/Index* and in the *Monthly Catalog* just as hearings are.

Reports

The "History of Bills and Resolutions" section of the *Congressional Record* Index notes the committee *report* by number, including conference reports. CCH's *Congressional Index* includes *reports* in its "Current Status" tables. The *House Calendars* provide access to *reports* by bill number in their "Numerical Order of Bills and Resolutions" section, referencing the *report* number and date reported, and in the five calendar tables by both *report* number and bill number. The *Digest of Public General Bills and Resolutions*, Part I, lists measures receiving action by Public Law number or bill number, with reference to *report* number and date reported. *CIS/Index* abstracts *reports* and, in addition to the access points described above in connection with bills and resolutions, has a separate index by House and Senate *report* numbers for the monthly reporting period that refers the user to the "Summary Section." The *Monthly Catalog* indexes *reports* by subject, title, and name of committee. *U.S. Code Congressional and Administrative News* has status tables arranged by Public Law number and bill number, both of which reference committee *reports*.

Floor Action

After a bill is reported back to the chamber where it originated, it is placed on the calendar. If precedence for debate is not granted by a special rule, debate on the measure awaits the call of the calendar. The edited transcript of members' remarks in debate on the measure is indexed in the *Congressional Record*. Because the "History of Bills and Resolutions" section of the *Record* cumulates, reference to all pages in the *Record* where discussion of the measure was printed permits the user to refer back to the appropriate issues.

Bills may be voted on frequently before they are finally approved or rejected. Voting on roll call measures, including amendments to a measure, is cited in the *Record*, and this information is repeated in *Congressional Index, CQ Weekly Report*, and *National Journal*.[35]

Conference Reports

If debate in the two chambers results in disagreement on the provisions of a bill or resolution, House and Senate conferees undertake the job of harmonizing conflicting versions of the measure. All of the sources mentioned in the section on *Reports* above may be used to gain access to the conference report number and date. It is safe to say that at this point knowledge of the bill or resolution number will most easily permit the tracing of its passage through the legislative process. The only thing to remember is what tools provide entry at what stages.

Final Congressional Action

After a bill has been passed by both chambers, it is prepared (an "enrolled" bill) for signing by the Speaker of the House and the President of the Senate. Then it is sent to the White House to await presidential action. The *Congressional Record* Index ("History of Bills and Resolutions" section) includes the examination and signing of the measure and the formality of presentation to the President, referencing the appropriate *Record* pages.

Presidential Approval

Reference to the first stage of an approved measure—the "slip law"—is noted in several places. The *Congressional Record* ("History of Bills and Resolutions" section) gives the Public Law number, referencing the page in the *Record*. *Congressional Index* in its "Current Status" tables carries the legislative process through to the end. Part II of the *Digest of Public General Bills and Resolutions* contains a numerical listing of all enactments indicating Public Law number. The *House Calendars* contain a table, "Public Laws and Resolutions," which is arranged numerically with reference to bill or resolution number. *United States Code Congressional and Administrative News* (Table 1) contains a cumulative list of Public Laws by number with page references to *Cong. News*, where the text of new laws signed during the monthly reporting period is printed. Table 4 of *Cong. News* ("Legislative History") is arranged by Public Law number. *CIS/Index*, in its monthly issues, stops short of the Public Law designation, but *CIS/Annual* takes up that slack. Public Laws are indexed by subject in the *Monthly Catalog*; reference to Private Laws appears in the subject index of the *Monthly Catalog* by name of petitioner.

Presidential Veto

If a bill is vetoed and returned to Congress, it is noted in the *Congressional Record*. The "Index to Proceedings" has a heading "President of the United States," under which messages to Congress, including vetoes, are listed. As we noted in our analysis of the Serial Set, presidential messages such as vetoes are issued as House or Senate *documents*, depending upon the chamber which introduced the vetoed legislation. As such, they are indexed by title and subject in the *Monthly Catalog*. In *CIS/Index* an abstract of the veto message is given in the "Summary Section." The "Index Section" includes access to vetoes by subject and by the form heading "Presidential Vetoes."

Retrospective

Most of the above sources of current legislation, either as they cumulate into a final issue for the session or as their periodic issues are superseded by an annual or sessional volume, serve as retrospective guides to the legislative process. The following is a list of sources that are relatively easy to use if one is tracing legislation that is a year or more old. No attempt will be made to include all the early retrospective guides and indexes discussed in Chapter 5.

Bill to Law

The bound *Congressional Record* has an index volume; as in the fortnightly indexes, access is by subject, name, and bill number. A cautionary note: the bi-weekly indexes cannot be used for the bound *Record*, nor can the sessional index be used for the daily *Record* because, as we noted earlier, the two have different pagination.

The final issue of the *Daily Digest* may be saved. It contains a comprehensive status table for the session, entitled "History of Bills Enacted Into Public Law" (Figure 40). Note that the information provided differs somewhat from that given in the "Guide to Legislative History" of the *Statutes at Large* (Figure 39, page 133), but the former table has a relative recency advantage. Preceding this "History of Bills" is a table arranged by Senate and House bill and resolution number, referencing the Public Law number. Following the table is a subject index to the *Daily Digest*. Bill numbers are affixed to the subject references, which are further subdivided by action on the measures, including presidential communications. Accordingly, the subject approach is itself an account of the status and history of each bill and resolution.

Because of its cumulative feature, the final edition of the *House Calendar* summarizes legislative action. The looseleaf updating service that *Congressional Index* provides serves the same retrospective purpose. The House and Senate *Journals* have a "History of Bills and Resolutions" section; printed at the close of a session, the *Journals* are easy to use if one does not require debate information. Subject, sponsor, and title approaches, in addition to bill number, provide access to legislative action through the *Journals*. The *Legislative Calendar* issued by each congressional committee provides detailed access of measures referred to that committee. Status and action information cumulates for an entire Congress.

Hearings and committee prints pursuant to earlier legislation are indexed by subject, committee, and bill number in the *Cumulative Index of Congressional Committee Hearings* and its supplements. House and Senate *documents* and *reports* are listed by number in the *Numerical Lists and Schedule of Volumes*, the key to the Serial Set. A convenient index to roll call votes for the session is included in the annual *Congressional Roll Call*, published by Congressional Quarterly, Inc.

Figure 40

CONGRESSIONAL RECORD: LEGISLATIVE HISTORY

HISTORY OF BILLS ENACTED INTO PUBLIC LAW (92D CONG., 1ST SESS.)

(Cross-reference of bill number to public law number may be found on pp. D 1432)

Title	Bill No.	Date introduced	Committee House	Committee Senate	Date reported House	Date reported Senate	Report No. House	Report No. Senate	Page of passage House	Page of passage Senate	Date of passage House	Date of passage Senate	Public Law Date approved	Public Law No.
To extend the time for proclamation of marketing quotas for burley tobacco for the 3 marketing years beginning October 1, 1971.	S.J. Res 44 (H.J. Res 365)	Feb. 18	Agr	Agr	Feb. 25	Feb. 24	92-16	92-20	H 882	S 1884	Feb. 25	Feb. 24	Mar. 1	92-1
Extending from March 10 until April 1, 1971, date which Joint Economic Committee may file its report on President's Economic Report.	S.J. Res. 31	Feb. 9	GO						H 882	S 1150	Feb. 25	Feb. 9	Mar. 5	92-2
Authorizing the President to proclaim the second week of March of 1971 as "Volunteers of America Week".	H.J. Res. 337	Feb. 17							H 1144	S 2500	Mar. 3	Mar. 4	Mar. 8	92-3
Making supplemental appropriations for the Department of Labor for fiscal year 1971.	H.J. Res. 465	Mar. 15	App	App	Mar. 15	Mar. 16	92-40	92-36	H 1586	S 3326	Mar. 16	Mar. 16	Mar. 17	92-4
Increasing from $395 billion to $430 billion the ceiling on the public debt limit, and providing a 10-percent increase in social security benefits.	H.R. 4690	Feb. 22	WM	Fin	Feb. 22	Mar. 9	92-13	92-28	H 1174	S 3181	Mar. 3	Mar. 12	Mar. 17	92-5
Authorizing the President to designate the week beginning March 21, 1971, as "National Week of Concern for Prisoners of War/Missing in Action".	H.J. Res. 16 (S.J. Res. 10)	Jan. 22		Jud		Mar. 4		92-25	H 1143	S 2519	Mar. 3	Mar. 5	Mar. 19	92-6
Extending from March 30 until June 30, 1971, continuing appropriations for the Department of Transportation.	H.J. Res. 468	Mar. 15	App	App	Mar. 15	Mar. 19	92-41	92-40	H 1749	S 3869	Mar. 18	Mar. 24	Mar. 30	92-7
To extend until June 1, 1971, certain provisions of law relating to interest rates and cost-of-living stabilization.	S.J. Res. 55 (H.R. 4246)	Feb. 24	BC	BHUA	Mar. 5	Mar. 2	92-36	92-24	H 1392	S 2399	Mar. 10	Mar. 4	Mar. 31	92-8
Providing a 2-year extension of the interest equalization tax.	H.R. 5432	Mar. 3	WM	Fin	Mar. 3	Mar. 30	92-35	92-47	H 1399	S 4156	Mar. 10	Mar. 30	Apr. 1	92-9
To provide poundage quotas for the burley tobacco price-support program.	S. 789	Feb. 11	Agr	Agr	Mar. 31	Mar. 24	92-98	92-45	H 2332	S 4033	Apr. 1	Mar. 29	Apr. 14	92-10
Making urgent supplemental appropriations for fiscal year 1971.	H.J. Res. 567	Apr. 22	App	App	Apr. 22	Apr. 23	92-144	92-77	H 2900	S 5543	Apr. 22	Apr. 23	Apr. 30	92-11
To create a rural telephone bank to provide supplemental financing for telephone borrowers.	S. 70 (H.R. 7)	Jan. 25	Agr	Agr	Feb. 22	Feb. 25	92-12	92-21	H 1963	S 2226	Mar. 24	Mar. 1	May 7	92-12
Increasing authorizations for the Commission on Marihuana and Drug Abuse.	H.R. 5674	Mar. 8	IFC		Apr. 7		92-121		H 3145	S 6152	Apr. 28	May 4	May 14	92-13
To authorize the U.S. Postal Service to receive $2 fee for execution of a passport application.	S. 531	Feb. 2	FA	FR	Apr. 27	Feb. 9	92-123	92-2	H 3449	S 1299	May 4	Feb. 11	May 14	92-14
Extending certain laws relating to payment of interest on time and savings deposits and to economic stabilization.	H.R. 4246 (S.J. Res. 55)	Feb. 10	BC	BHUA BHUA	Mar. 5	Apr. 29 Mar. 2	92-36	92-89 92-24	H 1392	S 6133 S 2399	Mar. 10	May 3 Mar. 4	May 18	92-15
Increasing from $2.2 billion to $3.1 billion the ceiling on authorizations for Small Business Administration loan programs.	S. 1260 (H.R. 4604)	Mar. 16	BC	BHUA	Apr. 27	Apr. 29	92-152	92-90	H 3497	S 6132	May 5	May 3	May 18	92-16

After presidential approval, the slip laws are published chronologically in the *Statutes at Large*, whose index and "Legislative History" provide retrospective access to congressional action on enacted measures. The *United States Code*, where the law makes its final appearance, usefully cites both Public Law number and volume and page in the *Statutes*.

West Publishing Company's *United States Code Congressional and Administrative News* issues bound volumes, or one may use the final monthly cumulation for tracing legislative measures. The *Digest of Public General Bills and Resolutions* cumulates in a final edition at the conclusion of the session. Digests of the legislation and Part I, "Status of Measures Receiving Action," make this a fine retrospective source. The *Monthly Catalog*, of course, indexes hearings, prints, committee reports, and public and private laws.

Finally, *CIS/Annual* not only cumulates the information on bills, hearings, prints, and reports contained in the monthly issues of *CIS/Index* but expands bibliographic coverage to include tracing from bill to law. *CIS/Annual* is able to provide a guide to multi-volume hearings issued by Congress during the year, whereas the monthly issues perforce included those hearings piecemeal. Moreover, abstracts in the annual include the Library of Congress card number and the *Monthly Catalog* entry number. Legislative histories of all recently enacted Public Laws are included. The Public Law number is used in this section as the CIS accession number. Bibliographic data include citation to the *Statutes at Large* and subject of the short title of the law. The official title of the law is followed by an abstract of its provisions; the bill number and related measures; its development (if appropriate) back through previous Congresses citing *CIS/Annual* volumes to 1970 (the year CIS began publishing its monthly and annual service); and reference to hearings, prints, reports, and dates of consideration and passage in the *Congressional Record*. *CIS/Annual* even provides citations to the *Weekly Compilation of Presidential Documents* for presidential messages pursuant to the legislation. This section is afforded access by subject (of either the act or one of its significant parts), name or title, bill number, and Public Law number.

* * *

Large research libraries will probably have all of the above sources. But what of the smaller, less affluent depository library? Every government publication listed in this summary, except the *Legislative Calendars* of the several committees, is available on deposit. In the author's judgment, the only commercial publications worth purchasing if funds are tight are *CIS/Index* and its *Annual*.[36] To be sure, it is easier to use *Congressional Index* than the *Congressional Record* Index, but one can manage without the former.

CIS/Index and *CIS/Annual*, because of their abstracting virtues, offer significantly puissant reference capabilities in conjunction with the government guides and indexes. Hopefully, smaller institutions will find funds for all the worthwhile commercial ventures that provide access to the maze of congressional materials. But it is comforting to know that the librarian can nevertheless render excellent reference service with those government guides and their textual sources that are available through the free depository system.

REFERENCES

1.   No publications of the Botanic Garden and Cost Accounting Board have been listed in the *Monthly Catalog* for over two decades. Since 1965 the semi-annual reports of the Architect of the Capitol have been published in the Senate *document* series, as required by PL 88-454, August 20, 1964.

2.   *Price List 83, Library of Congress*, included in-print materials of interest issued by the Library.

3.   *Presidential Inaugurations, a Selected List of References* (LC 2.2: P 92/3/year) serves as a guide to information on inaugural ceremonies and festivities from 1789 to the present. *Botswana, Lesotho, and Swaziland: A Guide to Official Publications, 1868-1968* (LC 2.8: B65) is an example of the bibliographic service the compilers in the Division so ably perform.

4.   For example, *Motion Pictures, 1960-69* (LC 3.8: M 85/960-69) was made available from the Superintendent in 1973 for $8.00.

5.   The Legislative Reorganization Act of 1970 directs the CRS, upon request, to advise and assist all congressional committees in analyzing and evaluating legislative proposals and to provide whatever other research and analytical services the committees consider appropriate. Any member can direct the Service to provide him or her with a concise memorandum of the purpose, effect, and relevant legislative history of any measure scheduled for hearings.

6.   A succinct, annotated list of Library of Congress publications of more than routine interest is found in the 1970/71 edition of the *U.S. Government Organization Manual*, pp. 702-703.

7.   Because the President, for example, is required by Article II, Section 3, of the Constitution to communicate with Congress, presidential messages are published by the Congress (in the *documents* series) whereas they indeed "issue" from the Oval Office.

8.   *Congressional Record* (daily edition), 92/2: 118/84, H 4951.

9.   The National Congressional Analysis Corporation, a Washington, D.C., based firm, publishes a *Daily Index and Guide to the Congressional Record*, which is delivered to subscribers on the same day the *Record* is issued. It provides a summary, a topical index, and a status report on pending legislation. Most libraries find it sufficient to await the bi-weekly *Congressional Record Index*.

10.   The bound *Record* is designated by Congress and session, with individual book numbers made up of volume and part. For example, 92d Congress, 2d session, volume 100, part 2 is classed X.92/2: 100/pt.2. The daily *Record*, though each issue designates both volume and number, when classed and designated notes only Congress, session, and number, e.g., X/a. 92/2: 84. The *Journals* are designated simply by Congress and session, e.g., XJH: 92-2; XJS: 92-2.

11.   92-2: H. doc. 384, p. 26.

12.   The *Journals* once appeared in the Serial Set, but this practice was discontinued at the end of the 82d Congress.

13.   Rule XIII of the House provides that the *Union Calendar* be used for measures "raising revenue, general appropriations bills, and bills of a public character directly or indirectly appropriating money or property." Placed on the

House Calendar are "all bills of a public character not raising revenue nor directly or indirectly appropriating money or property."

14. Greenwood Press (Westport, Connecticut) is issuing on microfiche all congressional hearings from the earliest, based upon the *Index of Congressional Committee Hearings*; a *Witness Index* to the hearings for the years 1839 to 1966 contains approximately 600,000 cards on microfiche keyed alphabetically by name of witness to the microfiche edition of the hearings.

15. An excellent discussion of private bills is found in *Guide to the Congress of the United States* (Washington: Congressional Quarterly, Inc., 1971), pp. 329-52.

16. 92-2: H. doc. 384, pp. 569-73. See also *How Our Laws Are Made* (92-2: H. doc. 323), a House Judiciary classic, frequently revised, that discusses in detail the passage of a bill through both chambers, with accompanying specimen pages.

17. A bill or resolution designated a "star print" means a printing that has been corrected. The "corrected print" is identified on the bill with a star and "star prints" are so indicated on the Daily Depository Shipping List. For a useful discussion of some of the problems involved in the several printings of a bill, see John H. Thaxter, "Printing of Congressional Bills," *Library Resources and Technical Services* 7: 237-43 (Summer 1963).

18. Tables include revised titles, revised statutes, executive orders, proclamations, and reorganization plans (see Chapter 7). A useful publication of the House Judiciary Committee is *How to Find U.S. Statutes and U.S. Code Citations*, a committee print (2d rev. ed., 1971), a guide that bridges citations between the *Statutes at Large* and the *United States Code*.

19. The *Congressional Staff Directory*, a commercially published venture that has been issued annually since 1959, is in some ways superior to its government counterpart. The *Staff Directory*, for example, gives not only committee but *subcommittee* assignments, an important source curiously absent from the *Congressional Directory*.

20. Hearings are also designated by other devices. For example, the Watergate hearings were conducted in phases, and the issuing notation reads: Y 4.P 92/4: P 92/phase 1/bk. 4, etc. (Presidential Campaign Activities of 1972, S. Res. 60: Watergate and Related Activities; Item 1009A).

21. *Impeachment: Selected Materials* is a significant compilation of materials on the constitutional and procedural bases for impeachment of civil officers; it contains excerpts from the founding fathers and from constitutional scholars like Raoul Berger of Harvard. Unprecedented demand for this publication, following newspaper accounts of its availability, forced the House Judiciary Committee to order extra copies printed and to place the document on sale through the Superintendent. If offered on deposit, it would be available to libraries subscribing to Item 1020.

22. Hinds and Cannon were former Parliamentarians of the House. *Hinds' Precedents of the House of Representatives* contains five volumes and three index volumes. *Cannon's Procedure in the House of Representatives* updates Hinds.

23. Classes Y 5 and Y 6 are reserved in the scheme for Contested Elections and Impeachments, respectively.

24.   Schmeckebier, pp. 109-116; 124-29; 150-66.

25.   The category of special reports also includes pro forma activities of the Congress. For example, 91-2: S. rp. 1134 was the *report* accompanying S. Res. 452 ordering the printing of the 71st *Annual Report of the Daughters of the American Revolution.* The DAR *Annual Report* was then issued as 91-2: S. doc. 102; thus both the committee report and the *Annual Report* became part of the Serial Set, a procedure in this instance that has been followed since 1889.

26.   Interestingly, the committee action on the nomination was issued in the Senate as an *Executive Report* (Y 1.93/1: rp. 26); the House, which has no executive series, issued its confirmation in ordinary *report* form.

27.   For example, the *Annual Report to Congress, Boy Scouts of America*, is generally a sales item and is advertised in the *Selected U.S. Government Publications*. But when it is issued in the *documents* series, it is bound in one volume with the *Annual Report of the Girl Scouts* and sent to libraries under depository Item 995-P.

28.   The word "miscellaneous" loses meaning when one finds, in the 90th Congress, 1st session, all three categories of *documents* labelled the same. Listed as "miscellaneous" are 1) S. doc. 60, Summary of legislative record and digest of major accomplishments, 90th Congress, 1st session; 2) H. doc. 1, President Johnson's State of the Union address; and 3) H. doc. 10, annual report of the Gorgas Memorial Laboratory.

29.   Including agencies of Congress, such as the reports of the Librarian of Congress and Architect of the Capitol.

30.   This pattern of distribution is published on the final page of each current revision of the *List of Classes of United States Government Publications Available for Selection by Depository Libraries* (GP 3.24: year).

31.   Floyd M. Reddick, Parliamentarian of the Senate, has prepared *Enactment of a Law: Procedural Steps in the Legislative Process* (1967). Issued as a Senate *document*, it traces the legislative process from Senate to House. *How to Find U.S. Statutes and U.S. Code Citations* (see reference 18) was prepared by Dorothy Muse of the Office of the Federal Register. Voluminous legislative histories are occasionally published as committee prints, for example, *Enactments By the 91st Congress Concerning Education and Training* (91-2; Committee Print, Senate Committee on Labor and Public Welfare, August 1970). Prepared by the Congressional Research Service, these extensive histories include related presidential recommendations, legislative histories of the several bills that competed for the final version, and digests of enactments.

32.   CCH publishes *Congressional Legislative Reporting Service*, which keeps subscribers in daily contact with action on public bills and resolutions on a selective subject basis. Included in this service are full-text copies of bills, committee reports, and laws.

33.   CQ's *Guide to the Congress of the United States*, for example, includes among its many features a "Glossary of Congressional Terms" and an essay on the legislative process, with specimens; while it is not as detailed as Fischer's *How Our Laws Are Made*, it is easier to read. Semi-annual issues of *Current American Government* have also included these two reference aids.

34.   The "Daily Digest" section of the daily *Congressional Record* gives information on hearings in progress, with names of witnesses, and projections of

committee meetings one week ahead. But the *Record* is useless for finding bibliographic data on published hearings. *Congressional Index* indicates the date the transcript of the hearings becomes available.

35.   For example, *Congressional Index* publishes all roll call and recorded teller votes in its "Voting Records Divisions."

36.   Congressional Information Service has a sliding scale for various types of institutions. The 1974 "package" for *CIS/Index* and the *Annual* was well under $300.

7

PUBLICATIONS OF THE PRESIDENCY

The administration of government, in its largest sense, comprehends all the operations of the body politic, whether legislative, executive, or judiciary; but in its most usual, and perhaps its most precise signification, it is limited to executive details, and falls peculiarly within the province of the executive department.

—The Federalist, LXXII (Hamilton)

INTRODUCTION

Article II of the Constitution states that "the executive power shall be vested in a President of the United States" who is charged "to take care that the laws be faithfully executed." The brevity of this constitutional injunction belies the complexity of the administrative task.

Inherent in any large administrative unit is a line and staff organization. When Jefferson was President, the entire federal government consisted of just over 2,000 persons—from the despised tax collectors to the marshalls of movie and television immortality—while today there are that many units of federal administration. These agencies are organized in the familiar pyramid; each has its own hierarchial structure. Orders theoretically flow from the President, as the chief executive, to the department head, and down to the lesser units—bureaus, agencies, offices—where the work of government is carried out and where most of the publications of government are produced.

Of the over 2½ million civil servants, only a small percentage are presidential appointees. The control and direction of the vast administrative machinery in practice must be delegated by the President. However, the

President has a staff whose job it is to advise and assist him in managing national affairs, and over this group the President has a large measure of control. Indeed, Presidents often choose their staff on the basis of loyalty first and competence second.

Presidential control abides in what has come to be known as the White House Office; this inner locus of power extends outward to what is called the Executive Office of the President, a complex of administrative units that reports directly to the President and whose officers are appointed by the President largely without the advice and consent of the Senate. In his staff organization the President enjoys great flexibility. Moreover, Presidents have used their staff to execute responsibilities of greater moment than the corresponding duties of the Cabinet.

When we speak of publications of the presidency, we must abandon in part the principle of provenance. While the White House Office and the Executive Office of the President are issuing agencies for presidential documents, so are the Office of the Federal Register and the Department of State. Moreover, several kinds of presidential publications are sent from the White House to Congress and are ordered to be published as specific Congressional series. As we saw in Chapter 6, the relationship between executive and congressional authority is circular and not always discrete.

Owing to this pattern of multiple provenance in the issuance of publications related to presidential decision and action, there is much duplication of materials. The multiplicity is sometimes confusing, but, when sorted out, it is manageable if not uniform.

THE WHITE HOUSE OFFICE

Publications of the so-called inner circle of presidential control and authority have been assigned the rubric "President of the United States" and carry a Pr notation in the SUDOCS classification scheme. The number following the letters Pr indicates the ordinal chronology of persons who have held the office, thus, Johnson 36, Nixon 37, Ford 38, etc.[1] Only a few Items are available in this category for subscription by depository libraries, but two of these are very important.

Special committees and commissions (Pr 3-.8; Item 851-J) covers reports issued by ad hoc committees and commissions established by executive order. Materials issued under this classification are not to be confused with those in the Y 3 category (commissions, committees, and boards), which subsume publications of units established by act of Congress or under authority of an act of Congress. Issuing units under Y 3 are not specifically designated in the executive branch nor as independent agencies. When the controversial *Report of the Commission on Obscenity and Pornography* was published, it was given a Y 3.0b 7:1/970 notation. In this case, although the President appointed the members of the commission, the commission was brought into being by PL 90-100, and the report was made to the President from the commission. Technically, therefore, the Y 3 category is not properly part of presidential publications.[2]

Economic Report of the President (Pr 3-.9; Item 848) consists of the President's economic report to Congress and the Annual Report of the Council of Economic Advisers, an agency in the Executive Office of the President. In 1947 and 1948 the Council's report was issued separately. Now combined, the materials cover the previous year's economic developments, with an analysis and indication of trends in major economic issues and recommendations for policy action. Appendixes relate to legislation, and statistical tables include figures on income, employment, and production.

In 1973 the *International Economic Report of the President* was issued for the first time. The report (Pr 37.8: In 8/3/R29/2) examined the commitment of U.S. dollars abroad and the economic needs of the United States in relation to the rest of the world. The report included chapters on a trade program for a changing world, U.S. economic relations with communist countries, aid to underdeveloped countries, and world monetary reform. Numerous graphs and charts were included.

EXECUTIVE OFFICE OF THE PRESIDENT

The administrative structure of the Executive Office of the President is shaped by executive order or legislation. The several units that comprise the Executive Office are under greater presidential control than is the civil service in the line organization. Indeed, members of the White House Office often double as officers in the several agencies within the Executive Office.

Specifically, the Executive Office was created under authority of the Reorganization Act of 1939 (53 *Stat.* 561); various agencies were transferred to this office by the President's Reorganization Plans I and II, effective July 1, 1939. The structure was initially fleshed out by Executive Order 8248 (September 8, 1939), and subsequent legislation permitted creation of new units or a reordering of existing agencies.

The duties assigned to the several administrative units within the Executive Office are broad and varied. In terms of national policy some of these units exercise enormous power, while others have less impact on our lives. The following is an attempt to indicate some of the prominent publications that emanate from the Executive Office. The letters assigned by SUDOCS to this classification area are "PrEx," followed by the appropriate numbers assigned to the subordinate bureaus and agencies.

Office of Management and Budget

A strong case can be made that this agency is the most important arm of executive power and intent in the presidency. Article II, Section 3 of the Constitution requires that the President "shall from time to time give to the Congress Information of the State of the Union, and recommend to their consideration such measures as he shall judge necessary and expedient." Furthermore, presidential initiative was expanded in the Budget and Accounting Act of 1921, which imposed on the President the duty to submit to Congress a plan of proposed expenditures for the executive agencies, including their financing. But a budget is not merely a mass of figures; it is a blueprint of public policy.

When the Congress specifically passed this duty to the chief executive, it acquiesced to presidential initiative in substantive policy measures. Unlike the statements in campaign rhetoric, the budget is an indication of exactly where the President is willing to spend funds. Almost a year in advance of the fiscal year (July 1–June 30), the Office of Management and Budget (OMB) begins securing from the departments and agencies requests for review. When the budget is finally submitted, the Congress is, of course, not required to accept it. But it is an authoritative statement of executive intent.

For many years the agency was known as the Bureau of the Budget. When first created by the 1921 Act, it was located in the Treasury Department, although under the President's immediate direction. The 1939 Reorganization Act transferred it to the Executive Office. By Reorganization Plan 2 of 1970 the Bureau was redesignated (Executive Order 11541, July 1, 1970) and its mission was delegated to the director of the newly renamed Office of Management and Budget. The several functions of the Office demonstrate the power and scope of this unit, and the chief publications of the agency symbolize the importance of its duties.

The Budget of the United States Government (PrEx 2.8; Item 853) is now published in two sections. The first contains the President's budget message and summarizes the recommended taxes and new obligational authority for the current and forthcoming fiscal years. It is accompanied by a separately published *Appendix* (PrEx 2.8:year/App.), a huge tome that amounts to a virtual line item identification. Item 853 also includes a separately published budget for the District of Columbia.

The Budget in Brief (PrEx 2.8/2; Item 855-A) is a summary in non-technical language designed to provide the layman with accurate, condensed information. It includes excerpts from the President's budget message, charts, descriptive material, and historical tables.

Special Analyses, Budget of the United States (PrEx 2.8/5; Item 855-B) contains facts and figures on special aspects of the President's recommendations, such as the impact of the budget on the economy, financial information on selected social program areas, trends in state aid, and the like. Included in this publication are many charts and statistics.

In addition to the preparation and submission of the budget, the director of the Office of Management and Budget is enjoined "to plan and promote the improvement, development, and coordination of Federal and other statistical services." To this end, OMB issues three important documents that bear upon the statistical functions of the government.

Federal Statistical Directory (PrEx 2.10; Item 853-A) is designed to serve as a guide to facilitate communication among governmental agencies. It is a list of professional and technical personnel associated with statistical and related activities of federal agencies, arranged by department with subdivisions and a name index.

Statistical Services of the United States Government is available under Item 854, General Publications of the Executive Office (PrEx 2.2:St 2/year).

This basic reference tool has three parts. Part I describes the federal establishment's statistical system. Part II briefly presents descriptions of the chief economic and social statistical series collected by government agencies. Part III states briefly the statistical responsibilities of each agency and lists its principal statistical publications. An appendix contains a chart of the federal statistical system.

Standard Metropolitan Statistical Areas (PrEx 2.2:M56; Item 854), issued irregularly, indicates the criteria for creating boundaries to establish these areas for statistical purposes. Cities of 50,000 population or more are defined in terms of county units that reflect the economic integration of the metropolitan area.

Other Domestic Agencies

The significance of agencies within the Executive Office waxes and wanes from crisis to crisis. In recent years the Cost of Living Council and the Federal Energy Office have been established to administer programs in response to domestic catastrophes. Although the Cost of Living Council was placed in the *U.S. Government Manual* as an independent entity under the Economic Stabilization Program, its publications have been assigned a PrEx 17 notation (Item 857-L-1). Rules promulgated by authority of the Council were published in Title 6, Chapter I of the *Code of Federal Regulations*.[3]

Other domestic units in the Executive Office which issue a variety of documents include the Office of Economic Opportunity (PrEx 10; Item 857-H), National Clearinghouse for Drug Abuse Information (PrEx 13; Item 831-C), the Council on Environmental Quality (PrEx 14; Item 856-E) and the Office of Consumer Affairs (PrEx 16; Item 857-I).

Central Intelligence Agency

The National Security Council functions under the National Security Act of 1947 (61 *Stat*. 496) to advise the President on the integration of domestic, foreign, and military policies relating to national security. Within the Council lurks the Central Intelligence Agency (CIA), also created by the 1947 Act, and charged with coordinating the intelligence activities of the several government departments and agencies in the interest of national security.

Maps and Atlases

An irregular series, this category's first issuance was the *People's Republic of China Atlas*. It contains a number of standard regional and thematic charts, maps and photographs, and a rousing poem by Chang Chih-min, "Personalities of the Commune," in which the people are admonished to wage agricultural war against the good earth. Classed under PrEx 3.10/4 (the China atlas carries a C44/3 Cutter), CIA maps and atlases have been assigned Item 856-A-1 by the Superintendent.

A number of general reference maps have since been issued under this Item, cartographic endeavors for countries as disparate as Ecuador and Yemen. Each multicolor relief map in this series (PrEx 3.10/4; Item 856-A-1) indicates road and railway networks, seaports, airfields, and urban areas. Additional inset maps provide information about population density, vegetation, land use, economic activity, and ethnic groups.

Foreign Broadcast Information Service

This agency within the Executive Office is not mentioned in the *U.S. Government Manual* index, although it is reported to be under the aegis of the CIA.[4] Nevertheless, the unit is duly acknowledged in the *List of Classes* and issues two important reference services.

Broadcasting Stations of the World (PrEx 7.9; Item 856-B)

This was published biennially prior to 1965, and has been issued in parts since 1952. Now an annual, *Stations* appears in four volumes. Listing all known radio broadcasting and television stations except those in the United States on domestic channels, the volumes include AM stations by country and city, AM stations by frequency, stations according to call letters and name of station or slogan, and FM and television stations.

FBIS Daily Reports

These are distributed five days a week and offer news developments from mainland China, Eastern Europe, and the Soviet Union. These have been monitored from foreign radio broadcasts, foreign news agency transmissions, and newspapers and periodicals published within the preceding 48 to 72 hours. The *FBIS Daily Reports* are available in three volumes. Volume 1 contains major releases of the New China News Agency and Peking Radio, with featured materials from *Red Flag* and *People's Daily*. Volume 2 covers speeches and editorials from radio broadcasts and major East Europe publications like *Neues Deutschland* and *Komunist*. Volume 3 reports from the Soviet Union and includes commentaries from Moscow Radio and *Pravda* and *Izvestia*.

Although the *FBIS Daily Reports* series has been assigned the notation PrEx 7.10, it is available only through NTIS on an annual subscription basis.

OFFICE OF THE FEDERAL REGISTER

The General Services Administration is a so-called independent agency which was established in 1949 to act as a giant records and property management corporation for the federal government. Indeed, as the *U.S. Government Manual* admits, the General Services Administration (GSA) "might well be termed a conglomerate." The agency consists of five operating services and three support activities. One of its subdivisions is the National Archives and Records Service.

The National Archives and Records Service (NARS) performs functions relating to the management, preservation, and disposition of the records of government, and it is in the National Archives Building that the public may view historic exhibits like the Declaration of Independence, the Constitution, and the Bill of Rights.[5]

The responsibilities of NARS are many and include supervision of the Presidential Libraries Program. But the function that concerns us is located in the subunit of NARS called the Office of the Federal Register, for it is this agency that issues several important publications relating to presidential activities.[6]

Federal Register

Statutory law prescribes general intent; Congress delegates to the executive and the departments and agencies the job of detailed administration. Administrative law has legal effect and, indeed, the corpus of regulations and rules governing the manifold activities of individuals and institutions has an immediacy and specificity not found in statutory law.

The machinery for publishing administrative rulings having the force of law was established by an act of July 26, 1935. Known as the Federal Register Act, it created the *Federal Register* to contain all executive orders, proclamations, and other edicts of the President, as well as the rules and regulations of the executive departments and agencies and the independent establishments. Pursuant to the Federal Register Act as amended, other publications that contain presidential materials have been authorized. Together they comprise significant publications for libraries. The Superintendent has assigned to this issuing unit the notation GS 4 and has given depository status to the series.

Issued under the notation GS 4.107 (Item 573) the *Federal Register* is quite possibly the most important publication issued by the federal government. It is certainly the most boring. The *Register* changed its cover design in 1971, to make its visual impact only slightly less depressing, and instituted a section called "Highlights of This Issue." In 1973 a change in policy required that entries have an "explanatory preamble" describing the material in layman's terms. The *Federal Register* is published Monday through Friday, although the Monday issue is mailed to subscribers on the preceding Saturday morning.

Presidential materials published in the *Federal Register* include the following.

Executive Orders

A presidential action legally expressed is rendered in print and given legitimacy in the form of an Executive Order or a Proclamation. The former has "never been defined by law or regulation," thus "in a general sense every act of the President authorizing or directing that an act be performed is an executive order."[7]

Authority for executive orders is claimed by a President in virtue of his office, in his role as Commander in Chief of the Armed Forces, under the Constitution, or under existing legislation; indeed, a President may cite two or more of these authorities as justification. Executive orders cover a variety of matters. Most relate to the conduct of government business or to the organization of executive departments, but their significance varies; for example, Roosevelt in 1933 created most of the emergency agencies by executive order. On the other hand, EO 6420 authorized the appointment of a charwoman in a local post office.[8]

Proclamations

The occasion for this form is usually one of more general and widespread interest than executive orders. Yet some proclamations have legal effect (for example, amending the tariff schedules of the United States relative to the importation of agricultural commodities—Proclamation No. 3884), while others do not have the force of law. In this latter category, we find the many presidential designations of a ceremonial or celebratory nature: National Day of Prayer, Mothers Day, Thanksgiving, Youth Appreciation Week. Authority for proclamations is claimed by a President in virtue of his office, under existing legislation, or in response to a congressional joint resolution.

Other Presidential Documents

Rulings other than proclamations and executive orders include *Memoranda*, usually from the President to the heads of his departments and agencies; *Directives*, designating matters such as assignments for officials of agencies; *Letters*, such as instructions to chiefs of American diplomatic missions; and *Reorganization Plans*, by which a President under prior congressional authority has the right to make changes in the structure of agencies.

Executive orders, proclamations and other presidential documents appear in the first section of the *Register* (Figures 41 and 42). The subject index (published monthly, quarterly, and annually) lists them under the heading "Presidential Documents" divided by category with an inverted title approach. No useful listing in the *Monthly Catalog* is given. Proclamations, for example, are noted in the MC only by reference to the appropriate citation in the *Statutes at Large*.

Code of Federal Regulations

Section 11 of the Federal Register Act of 1935 provided for a compilation of all documents still in force by each executive agency, to be published as a supplement to the *Federal Register*. But further study indicated a need for a

Figure 41

EXECUTIVE ORDER: FEDERAL REGISTER

presidential documents

Title 3—The President

EXECUTIVE ORDER 11788

Providing for the Orderly Termination of Economic Stabilization Activities

The authority contained in the Economic Stabilization Act of 1970, as amended, to impose a system of mandatory wage and price controls expired at midnight on April 30, 1974. Executive Order No. 11781 of May 1, 1974, provided for an orderly transition from mandatory controls, for the continuation of enforcement procedures under the Economic Stabilization Act of 1970, as amended, with respect to acts committed prior to May 1, 1974, for the continuation of the Cost of Living Council, and the continuation of monitoring and other functions of the Council for the period May 1, 1974, through June 30, 1974. However, the orderly termination of the Economic Stabilization Program will require several more months of follow-up activities. The Economic Stabilization Act of 1970, as amended, permits the maintenance of authority to take appropriate action with respect to any action or pending proceedings, civil or criminal, not finally determined on April 30, 1974, or with respect to matters before the Council that relate to wages paid for work performed prior to May 1, 1974, and prices charged prior to May 1, 1974. In order to meet these requirements and to assure the proper disposition of the files, records, data, and other financial and administrative matters relating to the Economic Stabilization Act, I am, by this Order, delegating to the Secretary of the Treasury such Presidential authority as may remain under the Economic Stabilization Act of 1970, as amended, and assigning to him the responsibility for taking such action as may be necessary and appropriate to achieve the limited objectives described above.

NOW, THEREFORE, by virtue of the authority vested in me by the Constitution and Statutes of the United States, including the Economic Stabilization Act of 1970 (P.L. 91–379, 84 Stat. 799) as amended, and as President of the United States of America, it is hereby ordered as follows:

SECTION 1. The Cost of Living Council, established by Section 2 of Executive Order No. 11615 of August 15, 1971, and continued by Executive Order No. 11627 of October 15, 1971, Executive Order No. 11640 of January 26, 1972, Executive Order No. 11695 of January 11, 1973, Executive Order No. 11730 of July 18, 1973, and Executive Order No. 11781 of May 1, 1974, is hereby abolished.

Figure 42

PROCLAMATION: FEDERAL REGISTER

presidential documents

Title 3—The President

PROCLAMATION 4297

Father's Day, 1974

By the President of the United States of America

A Proclamation

For many Americans, Father's Day is best celebrated by showering the male head of the household with carefully chosen gifts.

These gifts are symbolic, of course, of the year-round love and gratitude which children feel for both of their parents. From their fathers frequently come the strength and stability which children of all ages need in order to grow up to be constructive, confident men and women. Fathers offer guiding hands for children to pass successfully through the difficulties and awkwardness of youth. And fathers bring harmony and balance to life in the home.

Nineteen seventy-four is an especially poignant time to celebrate Father's Day, since this year no young American soldiers are being sent to fight anywhere in the world. A nation at peace: this is the legacy that all fathers want to leave their children and is ultimately the greatest gift of all on Father's Day.

NOW, THEREFORE, I, RICHARD NIXON, President of the United States of America, in accordance with a joint resolution of Congress approved April 24, 1972, do hereby request that June 16, 1974 be observed as Father's Day. I direct Government officials to display the flag of the United States on all Government buildings, and I urge all citizens to display the flag at their homes and other suitable places on that day.

IN WITNESS WHEREOF, I have hereunto set my hand this seventh day of June, in the year of our Lord nineteen hundred seventy-four, and of the independence of the United States of America the one hundred ninety-eighth.

Richard Nixon

[FR Doc.74–13520 Filed 6–7–74:4:01 pm]

codification rather than a mere compilation. Out of this need the appropriate section of the act was amended in 1937, and the *Code of Federal Regulations* (GS 4.108; Item 572) was created, its first edition assembled as of June 1, 1938.

The *Federal Register* stands to the *Code of Federal Regulations* (CFR) as the *Statutes at Large* stand to the *United States Code*. Indeed, the CFR is composed of 50 titles, many of which correspond to those in the *United States Code*. Whereas the *Statutes* and the *United States Code* contain that body of law passed by the Congress and signed by the President, the *Federal Register* and the CFR are the embodiment of administrative law generally pursuant to legislative enactments.

Title 3, The President

The several kinds of presidential documents published in the *Federal Register* are set aside for inclusion in this title of the CFR. Prior to the creation of the *Register* and the CFR, executive orders and proclamations were issued in separate form.[9] These publications began appearing in the CFR with Proclamation 2287 and EO 7906 of June 6, 1938. Compilations of Title 3, however, have gone back to 1936 and include those publications that appeared in the *Register* before the CFR was created.

The 1972 compilation of presidential documents was given a new designation and called "Title 3A." Now known as "The President, Appendix," Title 3A contains the text of proclamations, executive orders, and other presidential documents just as did the earlier editions of Title 3 since 1938. Accordingly, Title 3, which is still called "The President," is manifestly different in content. The 1973 revision of Title 3 indicates the following changes: Chapters I to III were "Reserved," their contents having been transferred to Title 3A; Chapter IV is a codified text of selected presidential proclamations and executive orders; and Chapter V deals with the Executive Office of the President.

Title 3A has an interfiled subject/government author/title index, with headings like "Days of Observance" for a list of proclamations. Other tables and guides that relate to the CFR are carried in a separate volume entitled "Finding Aids," which is revised annually. Table II in this volume is titled "Parallel Tables of Presidential Documents" and contains proclamations and executive orders included or cited in the CFR.[10]

Title 3 has been issued annually with five-year compilations and a 1936-1965 volume of cumulated indexes and tables. Thus current Title 3 (now Title 3A) annual editions *cannot* be discarded until a larger cumulation is prepared and distributed. The other titles in the CFR do not have this peculiar feature and may be discarded when a revised issue arrives.

Statutes at Large

As indicated in Chapter 6, the *Statutes at Large* (GS 4.111; Item 576) is primarily a compilation of public and private laws; however, it does include presidential materials. A list of proclamations by number is given for the congressional session, referencing the page number of the *Statutes* volume where the full text is published. Another list shows presidential documents amended, repealed, or otherwise affected by provisions of Public Laws. Entitled "Tables of Laws Affected," the list includes executive orders, proclamations, and reorganization plans. Like proclamations, the text of reorganization plans is published. Occasionally, executive orders are required by law to be printed as an appendix to a specific statute, but there is no separate compilation of the text of executive orders in the *Statutes*.[11] Each volume of the *Statutes* has a subject index that refers the user to the published proclamations and reorganization plans.

Weekly Compilation of Presidential Documents

The *Weekly Compilation* (GS 4.114; Item 577-A) is called a "special edition" or supplement of the *Federal Register*; it did not begin publication until August 2, 1965. It is perhaps the single most useful collection of presidential activities in the public record.

Issued each Monday for the week ending the previous Saturday, the *Weekly Compilation* includes the text of proclamations and executive orders, addresses and remarks, appointments, letters, nominations submitted to the Senate, acts approved by the President, checklists of White House press releases, messages to Congress, and announcements of resignations and retirements. Excluded from the *Weekly Compilation* are lists of promotions of members of the uniformed services, nominations to the Service Academies, and nominations of Foreign Service officers. A useful feature of this periodical is a continuing cumulative index for each issue. Other index cumulations include a quarterly, plus semi-annual and annual subject indexes that are separately issued.

Public Papers of the Presidents

Annual volumes of the *Public Papers* (GS 4.113; Item 574-A) have been issued since 1957 in response to a recommendation of the National Historical Publications Commission. Until then, there had been no systematic publication of presidential papers. Many presidential documents could be found only in mimeographed White House releases or as reported in the press. The Commission thus recommended the establishment of an official series, which was incorporated in regulations issued pursuant to Section 6 of the Federal Register Act as amended. While contemporaneous compilations were mandated, provision was also made for a retrospective collection.[12]

It is advisable not to discard the *Weekly Compilation* upon receipt of the *Public Papers*, for the series is edited. Most of the public messages and statements, however, are included in the annual volumes. Materials are presented in chronological order with a subject index. White House releases not included in the main portion of the text, reports of presidential task forces, awards of Congressional Medals of Honor and of Presidential Unit Citations, presidential reports to Congress—these items are located in the several appendixes at the end of the volumes.

United States Government Manual

Like all reference sources, this tool changes in substance and format with its various editions. The *Manual* (GS 4.109; Item 577) is not as useful as it could be; nevertheless, it contains information not found elsewhere and it is indispensable to libraries.[13] It is issued annually. The 1973/74 edition dropped the word "Organization" from the title, an unfortunate decision based, according to the compilers, on "a continuing attempt to direct the *Manual* to the general public rather than to the specialist in government."

The *Manual* does not contain presidential documents, but its section on the executive branch summarizes the duties and functions of the agencies. Congressional or executive authority for each agency's establishment is cited, and the prominent publications are listed for some of the more important units. Appendix A is a list of "Executive Agencies and Functions of the Federal Government Abolished, Transferred, or Terminated Subsequent to March 4, 1933." The *Manual* contains a separate name and subject index.

Of course, the *Manual* includes much more; it is the official handbook of the federal establishment. It describes the purposes and programs of most government agencies and contains a number of useful reference features. It should be in the reference collection of every library.[14]

DEPARTMENT OF STATE

The Constitution vests in the President command of two major instruments of foreign policy, the armed services and the diplomatic corps. Although Presidents can and do rely heavily on their staff for foreign policy implementation, the duly constituted line organization has the machinery in place for the administration of foreign relations.

The Department of State is the oldest executive body of the U.S. government. Its predecessors had limited functions and little real power until the creation, in 1781, of a separate Department of Foreign Affairs. In 1789, following the election of Washington, the Department was reconstituted, its name was changed to Department of State, and with Jefferson as the first Secretary of State its functions were expanded to make it the most important of the government offices within the executive establishment.[15]

State Department publications are many and varied, but a few materials issued by State are directly and specifically presidential in nature. The President, of course, as chief executive is responsible for the decisions and activities of the eleven departments and their agencies, including State; but the treaty and agreement powers of the President, as they are made manifest by action, constitute a major category of President-related publications.

Department of State Bulletin

This periodical (S 1.3; Item 864) is the official weekly record of United States foreign policy. A significant portion of each issue is devoted to presidential activities in the area of foreign affairs. Presidential documents included are addresses, remarks, and statements excerpted from TV and radio; correspondence and memoranda; exchanges of greetings with officials of foreign countries; joint communiques, remarks and exchanges of letters; messages and reports to Congress on foreign policy; news conferences where foreign affairs are discussed; and proclamations as they relate to aspects of world affairs. The index to the weekly issues lists these materials under "Presidential Documents"; in the semi-annual indexes citations to the materials are found under the name of the President. In the last section of each *Bulletin* is found information on two important instruments by which foreign policy is recorded, notification of treaty action, and announcement of executive agreements reached.

Treaties

A President's authority in the treaty-making process is set forth in Article II, Section 2 of the Constitution: "He shall have power, by and with the advice and consent of the Senate, to make treaties, provided two thirds of the Senators present concur." A summary of current treaty action is found in the final pages of each weekly *Bulletin*.

Agreements

In recent decades, "executive agreement" accounted for more than five times as many arrangements with foreign governments than did the treaty route. An agreement has been defined as "an international arrangement made by the Executive without the advice and consent of the Senate.... Such agreements usually consist of an exchange of notes between the Secretary of State and the head of the diplomatic mission of a foreign power or between the chief diplomatic officer of the United States in a foreign country and the head of the Foreign Office.... Not every interchange of notes constitutes an executive agreement. One essential element to bring the paper within the classification is that each government binds itself to take or not to take a specified action."[16]

Agreements can be made by the President pursuant to or in accordance with existing legislation or a treaty, subject to congressional approval or implementation, or under and in accordance with the President's constitutional powers. Like treaties, agreements are summarized in the *Bulletin*; information includes title, place and date signed, date entered into force, and reference to the full text (TIAS number).

Treaties in Force

This annual volume (S 9.14; Item 900-A) is a list of treaties and agreements to which the United States has become a party and which are in force as of the date of compilation. *Treaties in Force* and the weekly updating provided in the *Department of State Bulletin* may be used as current guides to the international arrangements entered into by the United States.

Treaties and Other International Acts

Known by the acronym TIAS (S 9.10; Item 899), this series is issued in unbound (slip) form and includes the *text* of agreements and treaties. In using the term "treaties" the government either defines it in its narrow sense (Article II, Section 2 of the Constitution) or in a broad sense to indicate any official international arrangement variously called convention, protocol, charter, constitution, agreement, etc. In this latter sense the TIAS series includes the generic scope of arrangements. The series is numbered consecutively and, in addition to its reference in the *Department of State Bulletin*, is indexed in the *Monthly Catalog* by subject and key word of title.

United States Treaties and
Other International Agreements

Just as public laws are bound together chronologically in the *Statutes*, so the TIAS series is collected into *United States Treaties* (S 9.12; Item 899-A). The text of treaties and agreements that were proclaimed during a calendar year constitutes this final series compilation. A subject index is provided, and the treaties and agreements published are printed in the language or languages of the original. Because the *Statutes* ceased printing treaties in 1949, Volume 1 of *United States Treaties* (UST) began in 1950.[17]

Note in our example (Figure 43) that the text is preceded by a succinct "history." For citing the unbound series, only the number is needed; the proper citation for its bound form indicates volume and page (e.g., TIAS 6503; 19 *UST* 5018). Item 899-A also insures receipt of the multi-volume *Treaties and Other International Agreements of the United States of America, 1776-1949.*[18]

CONGRESSIONAL SERIES

A final major category that includes a substantial number of publications associated with the presidency is the category of Congress itself. As our discussion of the Serial Set in Chapter 6 demonstrated, a peculiarity of Congress as an issuing agency is that many so-called congressional publications do not originate in that body. For example, some of the materials reviewed in this chapter are assigned to the House or Senate *documents* series but are sent to depository libraries in their "departmental edition": *Economic Report of the*

Figure 43

UNITED STATES TREATIES AND
OTHER INTERNATIONAL AGREEMENTS

UNION OF SOVIET SOCIALIST REPUBLICS

Consular Convention and Protocol

Signed at Moscow June 1, 1964;
Ratification advised by the Senate of the United States of America
March 16, 1967;
Ratified by the President of the United States of America March 31,
1967;
Ratified by the Union of Soviet Socialist Republics April 26, 1968;
Ratifications exchanged at Washington June 13, 1968;
Proclaimed by the President of the United States of America
June 13, 1968;
Entered into force July 13, 1968.

———

By THE PRESIDENT OF THE UNITED STATES OF AMERICA

A PROCLAMATION

WHEREAS a consular convention between the Government of the
United States of America and the Government of the Union of Soviet
Socialist Republics, together with a protocol relating thereto, was
signed at Moscow on June 1, 1964;

WHEREAS the originals of the convention and protocol, in the English and Russian languages, are word for word as follows:

President, Budget, etc. In the annual *Reports to Be Made to Congress* mentioned in Chapter 6, over five pages are devoted to a listing of reports the President is required to submit to Congress.

Congressional Record

The index entry for actions of the chief executive is "President of the United States" and there is also a subject approach. The kinds of presidential materials printed in the *Record* include proclamations, executive orders, addresses, messages (including vetoes), statements, and the like. Because a member can request that virtually anything be printed in the *Record*, it is reasonable to assume that at one time or other any presidential document may appear in its pages.

House and Senate Journals

Presidential materials in the *Journals* include addresses (for example, the State of the Union address), communications to the Congress (for instance, urging that certain legislation be passed), messages (*documents*) from the President transmitting legislation, and veto messages (published in the *Journal* of the chamber where the bill originated). The quadrennial inaugural address of a President is customarily printed in the Senate *Journal*. The index entry in the House *Journal* for presidential materials is "President"; in the *Journal* of the Senate, "President of the United States."

Serial Set

Presidential messages, reorganization plans, addresses, etc., are among the materials sent by a President to Congress and published in the House or Senate *documents* series (see Chapter 6).

Senate Executive Documents

Issued in a lettered series, Senate Executive Documents are not depository items, but they are indexed in the *Monthly Catalog* (thus available on Readex) and abstracted in *CIS/Index*. Unlike Senate Executive Reports (see Chapter 6), the Executive Documents series appears to be confined to messages from the President transmitting the text of treaties and other international agreements to the Senate Foreign Relations Committee. The Committee meets in executive (closed) session to consider the message and accompanying papers (which are prepared officially by the Secretary of State). After the Foreign Relations Committee makes its "Executive Report" to the Senate, both document and report are released in limited quantity. For Executive Documents, *CIS/Index* provides maximum bibliographic information (Figure 44).

Figure 44

SENATE EXECUTIVE DOCUMENT: ABSTRACT

S385   Executive Documents
FOREIGN RELATIONS
Committee, Senate

S385–6   **CONVENTION CONCERNING THE PROTECTION OF THE WORLD CULTURAL AND NATURAL HERITAGE, Message from the President.**
Mar. 28, 1973.   93-1.   †
vii + 18 p.   Exec. Doc. F, 93-1.
Y1.93/1:F.

Request for Senate advice and consent to the Convention for the Protection of the World Cultural and Natural Heritage creating international means for identification and protection of natural and cultural areas of outstanding universal value. Convention was negotiated under auspices of UNESCO. Contains Convention text and article-by-article analysis (p. 1-18).

COMMERCIAL GUIDES TO PRESIDENTIAL ACTIONS

Some of the commercial reporting services discussed in Chapter 6 may be used for research in presidential materials. Although their primary value concerns the bibliographic apparatus associated with legislation, there is no need to overlook their other features.

Congressional Index

Commerce Clearing House's *Congressional Index* has a section (called a "Division") which deals with congressional action on proposals generated by the executive branch; materials include presidential nominations, reorganization plans, and treaties. The Division has a subject index.

CQ Weekly Report

Congressional Quarterly's service includes the full text of presidential press conferences, major statements, messages, and speeches.

United States Code Congressional
and Administrative News

Tables 7 and 8 of *Cong. News* list (by number, date, and subject) presidential proclamations and executive orders, respectively. References are to the pages in *Cong. News* that contain the text of these materials.

CIS/Annual

In addition to information provided in the monthly *CIS/Index* issues, the *Annual* cites presidential statements, messages, and other initiatives related to the legislative history of enacted measures. Reference, for example, will be made, if applicable, to the appropriate entry in the *Weekly Compilation of Presidential Documents*.

SUMMARY

The foregoing has been an attempt to categorize the various publications that are generated by the presidency and that issue from the several units responsible for the "provenance" of these materials. Although the duplication of publications that carry the public record of presidential activity may be considered egregiously wasteful, such duplication does provide one clear advantage to libraries and other institutions that require these documents. By the very duplication, information centers small and large, non-depository and depository, indigent or affluent, may participate in the acquisition of at least some of these publications.

It is within the budget of a small library, for example, to subscribe to the *Weekly Compilation of Presidential Documents* or to the *Department of State Bulletin*. Moreover, most of the publications cited are depository items. A selective policy for the several types of libraries should not be difficult to implement. Our tabular summary affords a convenient finding aid for the more important presidential initiatives and their location in government publications (Table 4).

Table 4

CHECKLIST OF MAJOR PRESIDENTIAL PUBLIC ACTIONS

Type of Publication	Location
Addresses and Remarks	Dept. State Bulletin; Cong. Record; Journals; Serial Set; Weekly Comp./Public Papers
Executive Orders	Cong. Record; Fed. Register/CFR; Weekly Comp./Public Papers
Letters	Dept. State Bulletin; Cong. Record; Fed. Register/CFR; Weekly Comp./Public Papers
Messages	Dept. State Bulletin; Cong. Record; Journals; Senate Executive Documents; Serial Set; Weekly Comp./Public Papers
Press Releases	Weekly Comp./Public Papers
Proclamations	Dept. State Bulletin; Cong. Record; Fed. Register/CFR; Statutes at Large; Weekly Comp./Public Papers
Reorganization Plans	Cong. Record; Fed. Register/CFR; Serial Set; Statutes at Large; Public Papers
Treaties and Agreements	Dept. State Bulletin/Treaties in Force (list); TIAS; U.S. Treaties & Other Int. Agreements (text)

REFERENCES

1.   According to a Department of State ruling, Grover Cleveland is counted twice, as the 22nd and the 24th President, because his two terms were not consecutive. A recent publication issued in the General Publications Series of the White House was *Submission of Recorded Presidential Conversations to the Committee on the Judiciary of the House of Representatives by President Richard Nixon*, April 30, 1974 (Pr 37.2:C 76; Item 850).

2.   The most famous report issued under this Item in recent years was the *Report of President's Commission on the Assassination of President John F. Kennedy* (Pr 36.8:K 38/R 29) in one volume and the accompanying *Investigation of Assassination . . . , Hearings before President's Commission* (Pr 36.8:K 38/H 35) in 26 volumes.

3. Apposite examples of the transitory nature of agencies created in reaction to a crisis are the Cost of Living Council, which Congress permitted to expire in 1974, and the Federal Energy Office, which became the Federal Energy Administration in that year.

4. Its predecessor, the Foreign Broadcast Intelligence Service, was established in 1941 to analyze, translate, and report on foreign broadcast programs to interested agencies. It was abolished 60 days after the Japanese armistice.

5. It was noted in Chapter 2 that the major retrospective portion of the library of the Public Documents Department was transferred to the Archives in 1972.

6. As well as a General Publications Series (GS 4.102; Item 574).

7. Schmeckebier, p. 341.

8. Schmeckebier, pp. 340-41.

9. Ibid., pp. 340-45.

10. Title 32A (National Defense, Appendix) of the CFR lists executive orders directly related to the regulations set forth in this title.

11. For example, PL 91-231 (April 15, 1970) required that EO 11524 and 11525 be included following the text of the legislation.

12. For collections of presidential materials, see Schmeckebier, pp. 330-40. As noted in Chapter 6, the Manuscript Division of the Library of Congress issues a Presidents' Papers Index Series (LC 4.7; Item 811-B).

13. The 1973/74 edition of the *Manual* contains a list of Federal Information Centers where citizens may inquire about any aspect of the federal government. Information specialists at these centers perform reference and referral work. An explanation of the program, which began in 1966 and by 1974 boasted 36 locations in major cities, is given in *Illinois Libraries* (April 1974), pp. 282-84.

14. A "Guide to Federal Register Finding Aids" in tabular form was published in 34 *Federal Register* 18785 (November 22, 1969). The "Guide" contains a list of aids and tables for locating agency materials, researching presidential documents, and ferreting out statutory materials. Table 4 is a checklist of materials with their location.

15. According to the *U.S. Government Manual* (1973/74 ed.), the Continental Congress established in 1775 a Committee of Secret Correspondence, with Benjamin Franklin as chairman, to keep in touch "with our friends in Great Britain, Ireland, and other parts of the world." In 1777 it was succeeded by a Committee for Foreign Affairs. Early in its history the Department of State had domestic duties, such as supervising the census, issuing patents, and handling territorial affairs.

16. Schmeckebier, pp. 363-64.

17. Before 1950, the full text of treaties was published in the *Statutes at Large*. At the end of each current volume of the *Statutes*, treaties and agreements expressly affected or otherwise cited by provisions of Public Laws are simply listed.

18. A commercial venture, *UST Cumulative Index, 1950-1970* (New York: Central Book Company, Inc.) provides in four volumes an index to *United States Treaties and Other International Agreements*. The index volumes afford access to the official series by TIAS number, date, country or intergovernmental organization, and subject.

8

DEPARTMENT AND AGENCY PUBLICATIONS

"The President may require the opinion, in writing, of the principal officer in each of the executive departments, upon any subject relating to the duties of their respective offices." This I consider as a mere redundancy in the plan, as the right for which it provides would result of itself from the office.

—*The Federalist*, LXXIV (Hamilton)

The actual conduct of foreign negotiations, the preparatory plans of finance, the application and disbursement of the public moneys in conformity to the general appropriations of the legislature, the arrangement of the army and navy, the directions of the operations of war,—these, and other matters of a like nature, constitute what seems to be most properly understood by the administration of government. The persons, therefore, to whose immediate management these different matters are committed, ought to be considered as the assistants or deputies of the chief magistrate, and on this account, they ought to derive their offices from his appointment, at least from his nomination, and ought to be subject to his superintendence.

—*The Federalist*, LXXII (Hamilton)

INTRODUCTION

There is an old saying around our nation's capital: administrations may come and go, but the bureaucracy endureth forever. While this is an implied comment upon the limitations of presidential power over the departments and agencies that the chief executive titularly heads, it also suggests, misleadingly, a static quality. For in fact the bureaucracy endures while suffering many sea changes. Reorganization of existing entities is a continual process. New agencies, even departments, are created, enjoy their place in the federal sun, and die—sometimes with a bang, often with barely a whimper. The most common pattern of change finds internal modifications at the bureau level—mergers and dissolutions—that affect the lines of issuing authority for publications. Moreover, sporadic bursts of economy, generally more cosmetic than substantive, signal a publication's quick demise. The ongoing sound and fury of government reorganization signify nothing but trouble for the documents librarian.

The preceding chapter noted that the modern presidency tends to rely upon the staff rather than the line. Crucial policy decisions are arrived at with informal meetings of a cabinet head, perhaps a middle-management chief of an agency within the department, and some of the President's staff. A President will often attempt to control his administrative empire by assigning the Cabinet a low institutional profile. Presidential disenchantment with the Cabinet as a body is too well known to belabor.

Indeed, the Cabinet itself is an oddity. Although it has existed since George Washington's administration, it is not mentioned by name in the Constitution. The only allusion to this body is in the 25th Amendment, which states that a Vice President "and a majority of either the principal officers of the executive department or of such other body as Congress may by law provide" may declare a President unable to discharge the powers and duties of his office. While the Senate must consent to a President's appointment of his Cabinet heads, most of the time compliance is a formality. Moreover, although Cabinet rank is prestigious, the Cabinet as a collectivity has only symbolic value, a value that readily disappears in the process of critical decision-making. The secretary of a department is in the awkward position of being at once beholden to a President and to his bureaucratic constituency. Where divided or ambiguous fealty arises, a President can—and does—ignore Cabinet sentiments.

SELECTED PUBLICATIONS OF DEPARTMENTS
AND AGENCIES

There were in 1974 eleven departments in the executive establishment. The old Post Office Department was reorganized as an independent agency in 1970 and emerged with the title United States Postal Service. Ironically, this was its title when it was created under the Continental Congress in 1775, Benjamin Franklin having become its first and most illustrious Postmaster General. It now has a Board of Governors, one of whose members is the Postmaster General.

Over two hundred administrative subunits of the federal executive issue publications available to depository libraries. Within each bureau or agency the individual Items available range widely. Interior's Alaska Power Administration, for example, offers two series under one Item. On the other hand, H.E.W.'s Office of Education alone makes available over sixty Items, which range from one multi-volume directory issued annually to an indefinite number of publications of a serial nature. This amount does not, of course, include the many non-depository materials listed in the *Monthly Catalog* or sold through NTIS.

It would be an exercise in futility even to list all of the kinds of publications that the eleven departments and their several subordinate units issue. Titles within one Item represent a mine of reference riches too great to be extracted in an introductory text. Moreover, any omission, deliberate or inadvertent, would be rightly if not righteously challenged. The needs of users cannot be circumscribed by one person's experience with documents. A slumbering statistic in an obscure series may be for the seeker more important than King Richard's horse.

However, there are agencies whose publications are significant in general reference work; and these materials no librarian ignores without peril. We will note some of these "important" series. For the many documents precluded the author pleads *mea culpa levissima* and begs the reader's indulgence. The following information is arranged in keeping with the principle of provenance.

DEPARTMENT OF AGRICULTURE

Created by act of Congress in 1862, the Department of Agriculture is directed by law to acquire and disseminate useful information on agricultural subjects in the most general and comprehensive sense. The Department has approximately 36 subordinate units, of which over 20 issue publications available to depository libraries. Total employees of the Department number over 100,000.[1]

Office of the Secretary

Surely the famous Yearbook of Agriculture is a worthy reference source to introduce first. Although it is an annual (A 1.10; Item 17), each volume is devoted to one broad subject of interest to the general reader. This monographic concept was begun with the 1936-37 two-volume *Better Plants and Animals* and continues to the present. Individual Yearbooks are extremely popular sales publications of the Superintendent, and a number of Yearbooks are kept in print. Recent titles include *Handbook for the Home* (1973), *Landscape for Living* (1972), *Food for Us All* (1969), and *Outdoors USA* (1967). Each Senator and Representative receives 550 and 400 copies, respectively, of every annual, for distribution to favored constituents.[2]

Prior to 1936 the Yearbook of Agriculture contained a statistical section. This information is now found in the annual *Agricultural Statistics* (A 1.47; Item 1), a compendium of statistical series on acreage, yield, and production of crops; farm resources; livestock production; and the like.

The monthly *Agriculture Decisions* (A 1.58/a; Item 2) makes available decisions of the Secretary of Agriculture under regulatory laws administered in the Department; the December issue contains a cumulative list of decisions reported for the year.

Popular series include Farmers' Bulletins (A 1.9; Item 9) and Home and Garden Bulletins (A 1.77; Item 11). Both series are written in a non-technical, readable style and present useful information on such topics as trout farms, controlling tomato diseases, and building kitchen cabinets for remodeled farm houses.

Forest Service[3]

The annual *Report of the Chief of the Forest Service* (A 13.1; Item 80) contains a section devoted to the various research projects currently being conducted by the Service. These include activities promoting the conservation of the nation's forest lands, almost a third of the total land area of the United States. A statistical supplement is presented in tabular form.

Lists of Publications (A 13.11; Item 85-A) provides basic bibliographic information and has been issued since 1905. *Fire Management* (A 13.32; Item 82) is a quarterly devoted to the techniques of forest fire control. The annual index appears in the October issue. Prior to the Spring 1973 issue, the magazine was titled *Fire Control Notes.*

National Agricultural Library

Beginning with Volume 34 (1970), the monumental *Bibliography of Agriculture* became a commercial venture. Formerly a depository publication (A 17.18; Item 94), the *Bibliography* was begun in 1908 as the "Report of the Librarian." It was issued from 1926 to 1942 as "Agricultural Library Notes"; Volume 1 under the current title began in July 1942. Under its new publisher, Macmillan Information, a subsidiary of Crowell Collier and Macmillan, Inc., it remains a monthly index to the literature of agriculture and the allied sciences received in the National Agricultural Library. The Library still supplies magnetic tapes; CCM has them computer processed, using several vocabulary control mechanisms. Access to the main entry section of the *Bibliography* is by an author and subject index.

Information Office

Since 1841, various lists have appeared covering publications of the Agriculture Department.[4] Presently, the *List of Available Publications of the United States Department of Agriculture* (A 21.9/8; Item 91) appears annually and contains a section on general information, a broad subject approach, and an alphabetical listing of subjects with reference to titles. Although only publications in the departmental series (Office of the Secretary) are listed, information is included on the various periodicals and other series within the department.

Complementing the above is a *Bi-Monthly List of Publications and Motion Pictures* (A 21.6/5; Item 92). Entries are briefly annotated; for the motion pictures, title, sound, color, size in mm., running time, and a description of the film are included.

Soil Conservation Service[5]

The monthly *Soil Conservation* (A 57.9; Item 122) is the official magazine of the Service. It contains eight to twelve short articles per issue covering such subjects as cattle farming, watershed programs, gully control and other Soil Conservation Service activities. Most of the articles are popular, and even the technical articles can be comprehended by the informed layman.

Soil Survey Reports (A 57.38; Item 102) consists of a series of soil maps superimposed on aerial photos. Each report includes a description of the area, productivity estimates, and the like. Each survey is prepared for an area in cooperation with a state or university agricultural experiment station. A *List of Published Soil Surveys* (A 57.38: list; Item 102-A) indicates surveys that have been published, the date of the survey, and whether a survey is out-of-print.

Water Supply Outlook Reports (A 57.46) are published periodically for the western states. The reports contain detailed information on snow survey measurements, streamflow forecasts, etc. They are available from the issuing unit.

Agricultural Research Service

Highly technical series comprise the issuances of this unit, such as the *Index-Catalogue of Medical and Veterinary Zoology* (A 77.219; Item 31) with its supplements, and the monthly *Agricultural Research* (A 77.12; Item 25-A), which consists of technical articles on the results of research projects in livestock management, poultry, crops, fruits and vegetables, and related agricultural areas.

Economic Research Service

Whereas the above agency's research is oriented toward production and consumption, the Economic Research Service conducts programs of research in economics and marketing in both domestic and foreign commerce.

"Situation" reports on a number of areas in the field of agriculture are widely disseminated. Some of the titles include:

Demand and Price Situation (A 93.9/2; Item 21-A), quarterly
Farm Cost Situation (A 93.9/3; Item 42-A), annual
Wheat Situation (A 93.11; Item 21-I), quarterly
Rice Situation (A 93.11/3; Item 21-P), 5 X per year
Fruit Situation (A 93.12/3; Item 21-K), quarterly
Dairy Situation (A 93.13; Item 21-B), 5 X per year
Cotton Situation (A 93.24; Item 21-M), 5 X per year
Tobacco Situation (A 93.25; Item 24-D), quarterly

The reports contain statistical data, special articles, and charts and tables on a wide variety of agricultural indices.

The agency's ERS-Foreign series (A 93.21/2; Item 76-G) consists of individual reports devoted to a single country, usually covering the agricultural situation or trade of that country. Studies are periodically updated. The series is issued irregularly, and in July and August short mid-year reviews appear for regions.

Less formidably technical is the monthly magazine *Farm Index* (A 93.33; Item 42-F), which reports the results of the Service's broad research programs. Articles are grouped according to the special interests of farming, rural life, marketing, consumer news, and the foreign market. They are readable on the layman's level.

DEPARTMENT OF COMMERCE

Designated by act of Congress in 1913, the Department's broad mandate is to foster, serve, and promote the nation's economic development and technological advancement. Commerce has fifteen major subdivisions, while over fifteen issuing units make available publications for deposit.[6] About 35,000 employees serve the activities of the Department.

Office of the Secretary

United States Department of Commerce Publications (C 1.2: P 96; Item 128) originated in 1952 and is supplemented annually. The basic volume is a catalog and index of selected publications of the Department and its predecessors. The annual supplements also serve as a cumulation of the yearly issues of the *Business Service Checklist*.

Business Service Checklist (C 1.24; Item 127) is a weekly guide to new Department publications, including NTIS documents and a list of Census Bureau publications. The newsletter is of great value to librarians as an ordering guide.

Overseas Business Reports (C 1.50; Item 231-B) are irregularly issued and provide information of interest to exporters, importers, investors, manufacturers, and researchers on international trade and world economic conditions. Subseries in the OBR series include basic data on the economy of specific countries, a "how to" report on establishing a business overseas, foreign trade regulations of foreign countries, market factors in individual countries, and the like.

The bi-weekly *Commerce Today* (C 1.58; Item 127-A) superseded *International Commerce* and is a news review of the Department's activities. The issues contain articles on various developments in business and technology, and a section on "New Publications"—brief annotations of documents including NTIS reports on government-sponsored research.

National Bureau of Standards

The *Journal of Research of the National Bureau of Standards* (C 13.22/sections A,B,C) presents papers of interest to scientists in the fields of physics, chemistry, mathematics, and engineering. Issues contain an annotated bibliography of publications compiled by the Bureau, including papers published in outside journals.

Section A: A bi-monthly covering physics and chemistry (Item 246-A) with major emphasis on standards of physical measurement, fundamental constants, and properties of matter.

Section B: A quarterly covering pure and applied mathematics (Item 246-B), including theoretical physics, chemistry, and engineering; the emphasis is on mathematical content or methodology.

Section C: A quarterly presenting the results of studies on engineering and instrumentation, including acoustics, applied mechanics, building research, and cryogenic engineering (Item 246-C).

The Bureau's Monographs are an irregularly issued series (C 13.44; Item 247-A) consisting of contributions to the technical literature too lengthy for publication in the *Journal of Research*.

In the Applied Mathematics series (Item 239) there is the famous *Handbook of Mathematical Functions, with Formulas, Graphs and Tables* (C 13.32:55). Revised periodically, this NBS handbook includes every special function needed by anyone who uses mathematical tables in his work.

Patent Office

The *Official Gazette of the United States Patent Office* has been published weekly since 1872. In 1971 *Patents* and *Trademarks* began separate issues. Both are available to depositories under Item 260.

Official Gazette: Patents (C 21.5) contains an abstract and a selected figure from the drawings for each patent granted during that week, decisions and notices, indexes of patents and patentees, and general information.

Official Gazette: Trademarks (C 21.5/4) contains trademarks, trademark notices, marks published for opposition, trademark registrations issued, and index of registrants.

Index of Patents (C 21.5/2; Item 255), issued in two volumes, is the annual index to the *Official Gazette: Patents*. Volume I is an index of patentees; Volume II lists the classes and subclasses, and includes a listing of libraries receiving the *Official Gazette* and a list of Patent Copy Depository Libraries. These institutions have the *complete* patent specifications, which are merely abstracted in the *Official Gazette*.

Index of Trademarks (C 21.5/3; Item 256) is the annual index to the *Official Gazette: Trademarks*. It is an index of registrants and contains classes and subclasses.

Manual of Classification (C 21.12; Item 258), issued irregularly in looseleaf form, contains an updated list of all the classes and subclasses, including a subject index.

Classification Definitions (C 21.3/2; Item 252) contains the changes in classification of patents as well as *definitions* of new and revised classes and subclasses; also issued irregularly.

The Patent Office has prepared on microfilm lists of the numbers of the patents issued in each of its subclasses. Libraries that purchase the microfilm lists, and subscribe to the above noted manuals and indexes, can assist a patron in a patent search. The patron can then be referred to the Patent Copy Depository Library nearest him, or he may make use of the facilities of the Patent Office.

The Patent Office Search Center in Arlington, Virginia, has available for public use a Search Room where all patents granted since 1836 may be examined. A Record Room is also maintained, where the public may inspect the files of issued patents and supporting records. Persons who cannot come to the Search Room or Record Room may order from the Patent Office copies of lists of original patents or of cross-referenced patents contained in the subclasses comprising the field of research. Depository libraries should also subscribe to Item 254, the Patent Office's General Publications series, for brochures such as *General Information Concerning Patents* and *General Information Concerning Trademarks*, which are revised and updated periodically.

Maritime Administration

Merchant Fleets of the World (C 39.212; Item 236-B) is a semi-annual publication that indicates seagoing steam and motor ships of 1,000 gross tons and over, by type of vessel and country of registration. *Statistical Analysis of World's Merchant Fleets* (C 39.224; Item 237-A) is a biennial publication that gives breakdown by specified tonnage groups. Figures on age, size, speed, and draft are supplied, with summary tables for all types. Data on countries include Argentina, Australia, Brazil, Denmark, Finland, France, Germany, Greece, Sweden, United Kingdom, and the Soviet Union.

National Technical Information Service

Formerly known as the Clearinghouse for Federal Scientific and Technical Information, NTIS has become a central source for the public sale of government-sponsored research, development, and engineering reports and other analyses prepared by federal agencies, their contractors or grantees. The agency is obligated by statute to recover its cost and has become largely self-sustaining. It supplies the public with approximately three million documents and microforms annually. All of the over 100,000 documents currently kept in stock are for sale.

Publications for sale by NTIS are indicated in the *Monthly Catalog* by an "at" sign (@). However, the principal tools for securing citations to literature available through NTIS are *Government Reports Announcements* (GRA) and *Government Reports Index* (GRI), both of which are sent to depository libraries under Item 270. For non-depository institutions, both are available for sale by NTIS.[7]

Government Reports Announcements (C 51.9/3), issued semi-monthly, abstracts published government research, covering close to 60,000 citations annually. The whole text of most of the documents abstracted may be ordered directly from NTIS in paper copy or on microfiche. GRA features a quick-scan format, which includes title, price, and corporate author, with an edge index to subject fields and a report number locator list. Disciplines include the behavioral and social sciences as well as the physical and life sciences.

Government Reports Index (C 51.9), the semi-monthly companion to GRA, is published concurrently. It indexes the GRA abstracts by corporate author, subject, personal author, contract/grant number, and accession/report number (Figures 45 and 46).[8]

Other information services include *Weekly Government Abstracts* (not available on deposit), which consist of new reports in several fields such as transportation, information theory, and urban technology (C 51.9/nos.). The four- to eight-page newsletters selectively abstract reports from more than 60,000 documents received by NTIS. NASA abstracts are included in this reporting service. *NTISearch* provides access by subject to the total NTIS data base. The *NTISearch* information collection covers all federally sponsored research projects completed since 1964; the user can initiate this customized search by phone, where information needs are discussed directly with an information specialist. For more leisurely requirements, NTIS provides a form to be mailed to its offices in Springfield, Virginia.

NTIS offers many packages in both paper copy and on microfiche. We noted in Chapter 7 the *FBIS Daily Reports* service on China, Eastern Europe, and the Soviet Union. Foreign translations through NTIS's Joint Publications Research Service are available on standing order. NTIS distributes *Selected Water*

Figure 45

GOVERNMENT REPORTS ANNOUNCEMENTS: MAIN ENTRY

COM-71-80015-14   PC-GPO/MFS1.45-NTIS
Bureau of the Census, Washington, D.C.
CENSUS OF HOUSING: 1970. CHARAC-
TERISTICS OF SPANISH LANGUAGE
HOUSEHOLDS FOR THE UNITED STATES:
1970.
Supplementary rept.
Jun 73, 16p CENSUS-70-HC(S1)-14
Paper copy available from GPO $0.25 as
C3.224/8:970/14.

Descriptors: *Census, *United States,
*Residential buildings, Tables(Data), Spanish lan-
guage, Income, Value.

The report provides data on the income in 1969 of
families and primary individuals by persons per
room for owner and renter occupied housing units.
All data are for Spanish head of household in the
United States, arranged by persons per room, persons, plumbing facilities, units in structure, year
structure built, household composition, years of
school completed by head, labor force status of
head, occupation of employed head, value, value-
income rent, gross rent, and gross rent as percentage of income. The tables are reprints of table A-
18 from Final Report HC(7)-3, Space Utilization of
the Housing Inventory.

COM-71-80017-7D   PC-GPO/MFS1.45-NTIS
Bureau of the Census, Washington, D.C.
CENSUS OF POPULATION: 1970. SUBJECT RE-
PORTS: GOVERNMENT WORKERS.
Jun 73, 311p CENSUS-70-PC(2)-07D
Paper copy available from GPO $3.20 as
C3.223/10:970/7D:.

Descriptors: *Census, *United States,
*Government employees, Tables(Data),
Socioeconomic status, Employment, Earnings.

The report presents national statistics on the occupation and industry of government workers cross-
classified by selected social and economic characteristics. The data are based on the 1970 Census of
Population. Occupation and industry data for
government workers are cross-classified by one or
more of the following: Race; Spanish origin; age;
sex; years of school completed; detailed and
selected occupation; weeks worked in 1969; wage
and salary earnings in 1969; family income in 1969
of family heads. Two other tables provide data on
the occupation and industry of employed government workers, and a summary of total employed
and government workers employed by race and
Spanish origin. Five appendices included in the report provide general information concerning the
data.

Figure 46

GOVERNMENT REPORTS INDEX: SAMPLE INDEX ENTRIES

Each index is arranged alphanumerically (that is, alphabetical data precedes numerical data). Document titles are included in all indexes except the CONTRACT NUMBER INDEX. The document ACCESSION (ORDER) NUMBER and the COSATI Field/Group location of the report citation in the Government Reports Announcements (GRA) are given on the last line of the entry. Document prices are given in the ACCESSION/REPORT NUMBER INDEX only. A sample entry for each index follows.

CORPORATE AUTHOR
Entries are sequenced by corporate author name, report number, and accession number. The monitor agency number is given following the report title.

> AEROSPACE CORP EL SEGUNDO CALIF LAB OPERATIONS
> TR-0059(6260-20)-1
> Charge-Exchange Cross Sections for Hydrogen and Helium
> Ions Incident on Atomic Hydrogen:1 to 1000keV.
> (SAMSO-TR-70-258)
> AD-709 722   7D

SUBJECT
Entries are sequenced by major subject term, second paired term, and accession number.

> TREES
> Measurement
> A New and Easier Way to Estimate the Quality of Inland
> Douglas-Fir Saw-Timber.
> PB-193 216   2F

PERSONAL AUTHOR
Entries are sequenced by personal author, title of the report, and accession number.

> BOCK, FREDERICK C.
> Optimized Cellulose Membranes for Artificial Kidney
> Dialysis Applications.
> PB-192 898   6L

CONTRACT/GRANT NUMBER
Entries are sequenced by contract or grant number, corporate author, and accession number.

> NASW-2037
> TECHTRAN CORP, GLEN BURNIE, MD.
> N70-30006   3B

ACCESSION/REPORT NUMBER
Entries are sequenced by accession, report, or monitor agency number. DOCUMENT PRICES ARE GIVEN IN THIS INDEX. Order by the accession (order) number given in the last line of the index entry.

> CTC-20
> The Use and 'Testing' of Al, Fe, Ni, Cu, and Pb Secondary
> Gamma-Ray Production Data Sets from the POPOP4 Library
> AD-709 459   20G   PC$3.00 MF$0.95

Resources Abstracts and unclassified Atomic Energy Commission research reports. Selected Categories in Microfiche (SCIM) is a standing-order service which offers microfiche copies of reports in highly selective interest categories. One can even subscribe to *Civil Tax Cases* of the Internal Revenue Service on microfilm. The listing consists of docketed civil tax cases and includes the taxpayer's name, the court, the assigned Chief Council field office, and the filing date of the petition or complaint.[9]

NTIS is directed by statute to price its products and services. In 1973 Lockheed Information Retrieval Service, a unit of the Lockheed Missiles and Space Company of Sunnyvale, California, was awarded a $220,000 contract from NTIS to provide computerized access to some 300,000 government technical reports. Lockheed will find and retrieve bibliographies and technical abstracts on specific subjects for a healthy fee.

That is the rub. Although NTIS perversely prides itself on its cost recovery, self-sustaining capabilities, the service is just one more financial burden for libraries. Like the escalating prices that GPO is now charging for SUDOCS sales publications, NTIS fees have skyrocketed in recent times. Despite the enabling legislation that permits NTIS to recover costs, the policy is clearly not in the public interest.[10]

National Oceanic and Atmospheric Administration

The National Oceanic and Atmospheric Administration (NOAA) is a splendid example of government reorganization. NOAA was created within the Commerce Department in 1970. Its formation brought together the functions of the Environmental Science Services Administration (ESSA);[11] Bureau of Commercial Fisheries, Marine Game Fish Research Program and Marine Minerals Technology Center (formerly of the Interior Department); National Oceanographic Data Center and National Oceanographic Instrumentation Center (formerly administered by the Navy); National Data Buoy Development Project (formerly of the Coast Guard, Transportation Department); National Sea Grant Program (formerly of the National Science Foundation); and elements of the U.S. Lake Survey (formerly of the Army Corps of Engineers).

The quarterly journal *NOAA* (C 55.14; Item 250-E-1) is written to acquaint readers with the policies and programs of the Administration. Other series include NOAA Technical Reports (C 55.13; Item 208-B-7), which present the results of a single research project of scientific or engineering analysis in a single field specialization; Professional Papers (C 55.25; Item 208-B-6), issued irregularly; and Hydrometeorological Reports (C 55.28; Item 275-A), a series devoted to discussions of area rainfall, thunderstorms, hurricanes, and studies of particular river basins.

The *Monthly Weather Review* (formerly C 55.11; Item 277), like the *Bibliography of Agriculture*, is no longer published by the government. Begun in 1872, this excellent periodical contained articles describing original research results in meteorology and related disciplines. It is now published by the American Meteorological Society, another example of an ominous trend in diminished access to public information.[12]

National Weather Service

Publications of the old Weather Bureau (formerly classed in C 30) are now issued by the National Weather Service and the Environmental Data Service, both of which were established within NOAA in 1970. Publications of the National Weather Service include a Weather Service Observing Handbooks series (C 55.109/2; Item 275-E), which prescribe uniform instructions for standard weather observing and reporting techniques; and *Average Monthly Weather Outlook* (C 55.109; Item 275-F), a semi-monthly periodical that gives a summary of average rainfall and temperature for the preceding month and the outlook for the following month.

Environmental Data Service

Of value is the *Climatological Data* series (C 55.214), which unfortunately is not a depository Item but which is available for sale from NOAA. Monthly reports for states and sections include tables of daily and monthly precipitation, wind movements, temperatures, and the like. An annual summary is issued separately for each state, which can be bound together with the monthly issues. Individual sections are distinguished by the number following the shilling mark (e.g., California . . . C 55.214/6).[13]

National Ocean Survey

United States Earthquakes (C 55.417/2; Item 208) provides an annual summary of earthquake activity in the United States and regions that are outside the United States but under its jurisdiction. Recent seismological activities of interest to both general and specialized readers are found in the bi-monthly *Earthquake Information Bulletin* (C 55.611; Item 191-A), issued by NOAA's Environmental Research Laboratories.

The Survey prepares nautical and aeronautical charts, conducts geodetic, oceanographic, and marine geophysical studies, and predicts tides and currents. Concerning this latter function, a series of *Tide Tables* is published (C 55.421; Item 199) that cover the coasts and oceans of the world. *Tidal Current Tables* (C 55.425; Items 190, 191) are issued annually for the Atlantic Coast of North America and for the Pacific Coast of North America and Asia.

Social and Economic Statistics Administration

Creation of this new agency in 1972 affected two former units: the famous Census Bureau was established as a component of SESA, and the former Office of Business Economics was brought within the Administration and renamed the Bureau of Economic Analysis.

Bureau of Economic Analysis

Now issued under this subunit is the important *Survey of Current Business*, a monthly (C 56.109; Item 228) that presents information on trends in industry, the business situation, and the outlook, based on critical economic indicators. Included in the subscription to the *Survey* is the weekly *Business Statistics* (C 56.109/2; Item 229). *Business Conditions Digest* (C 56.111; Item 131-A) presents monthly some 500 economic indicators organized in sections on national income, cyclical indicators, analytical measures, and international comparisons.[14]

Bureau of the Census

Article I, Section 2, of the Constitution provides that "Representatives and direct taxes shall be apportioned among the several States which may be included within this Union, according to their respective numbers. . . . The actual enumeration shall be made within three years after the first meeting of the Congress of the United States, and within every subsequent term of ten years, in such manner as they shall by law direct." Accordingly, within a year after George Washington assumed the office of President, the first census was taken.

The content of the first census was simple; under the Constitution the government had only to determine the number of free and slave persons in each state. As the need for more data increased, the content and operation of census taking changed and became more sophisticated. Quinquennial censuses were fashioned to meet the information needs of government and the private sector. Currently there are ten categories of censuses; data are reported in different time segments so that the operation of the Bureau is a continuous process.

Guides to Information Found in Census Bureau Publications

The Bureau's ceaseless activities result in numerous preliminary reports, advance reports, and special studies before the final volumes are published in each category for the decennial, quinquennial or other reporting periods. Moreover, many federal agencies, as well as the Congress and the Office of the President, use data gathered by the Census Bureau in their own publications. Until the librarian becomes directly conversant with the myriad Census Bureau documents, it is best to proceed through guides that unlock these statistical doors.

Bureau of the Census Catalog (C 56.222; Item 138). Published quarterly, with monthly supplements (C 56.222/2), the *Catalog* cumulates annually. It is an indispensable tool and is divided into two parts. Part I (Publications) is a classified and annotated guide to all publications issued by the Bureau for the reporting period, with geographical and subject indexes provided. Included is a section titled "Selected Publications of Other Agencies," which lists documents of other departmental units that make extensive use of data compiled and furnished by the Bureau. Part II (Data Files and Special Tabulations) provides a listing of materials available at the Census Bureau during the reporting period. Under the heading "Data Files" are listed the large machine-readable files that are available either for sale or for use by the Bureau to prepare special tabulations for individual customers. Also included in Part II are special services provided to customers at cost, such as population estimates and projections, and technical assistance.

   Statistical Abstract of the United States (C 56.243; Item 150). Published annually since 1879, this renowned reference work is a basic guide to the major statistical surveys of the federal government. In addition, the *Statistical Abstract* contains information from private companies and from states and individual regions.

   Following every table, *source notes* refer the user to the issuing unit where more comprehensive data can be found. If the source note indicates "unpublished data," one may write the issuing agency for further information. Every annual issue is revised and refined in an attempt to improve the presentation of data. Appendixes include a guide to statistics sources, a guide to state statistical abstracts, and source agencies and table numbers. A supplement, *USA Statistics in Brief* (C 56.243/2; Item 151) accompanies the *Statistical Abstract* or may be purchased as a separate.

   Pocket Data Book, USA (C 56.243/3; Item 150-A). This biennial supplement to the *Statistical Abstract* is a further condensation of data, usually about one-third the length of the parent volume. It is designed for easy reference use, retains the crucial source notes, and uses color attractively to highlight many charts and key items in the tables.

   Historical Statistics of the United States, Colonial Times to 1957 (C 56.243/2; Item 151). A compilation of over 8,000 statistical series from 1610. A supplement, *Historical Statistics ... Continuation to 1962 and Revisions*, updates the series that are still current in the basic volume and includes series that are complements to, or substitutes for, series discontinued since 1956, including revisions and corrections. Future revisions will appear from time to time. The *Statistical Abstract* contains an appendix that is an index to tables in the *Abstract* in which *Historical Statistics* series appear.

   County and City Data Book (C 56.243/2; Item 151). Issued after each group of major censuses has been taken, this publication is a comprehensive presentation of local area data. It is an indispensable reference source for a variety of economic and social facts on counties, cities, metropolitan areas, urbanized areas, and unincorporated places of 25,000 inhabitants or more in the United States. The *Data Book* includes maps of each state showing counties, SMSA's, and cities of 25,000 or more inhabitants. Subjects covered range from agriculture to employment to retail trade, and there are numerous explanatory notes, source citations, and appendixes.

   Congressional District Data Book (C 56.243/2; Item 151). This supplement provides a statistical picture of each congressional district; data from the major censuses are included. When redistricting occurs, supplements to this source are issued for individual states.

Census Bureau Programs and Publications: Area and Subject Guide (C 3.6/2:P 94; Item 146-A). Issued in 1968, this publication is organized in subject chapters using the headings of the *Bureau of the Census Catalog*. Appendixes include guides to recent Bureau statistics and a list of recent methodological studies. There is a geographical index to this valuable aid.

1970 Census Users' Guide (C 3.6/2:C 33/2; Item 146-A). The two-part *Users' Guide* records salient information on the 1970 Census of Population and Housing. Part I includes a Census Users' Dictionary; in Part II several appendixes describe magnetic tapes that are available for some portions of the 1970 census.[15]

Census Bureau Special Services

In addition to the services involving selected tabulations of Census Bureau data for individual buyers, the National Archives has both original and microfilmed population census schedules for 1850, 1860, and 1870 and microfilm copies only for 1880. Prices and contents for rolls containing positive microfilm copies of the schedules and the index are listed in *Federal Population Censuses, 1790-1890*, which may be obtained upon request from the Publications Sales Branch, National Archives and Records Service, Washington, D.C. 20408. In 1974 the Archives opened its 1900 census records to individuals with a need to know, despite charges that this might violate the privacy of many living Americans. However, this census may be inspected only in person, and photocopying is not permitted.

The Census Bureau maintains a staff of employees in Pittsburg, Kansas. This office maintains population census records for 1880 and later (except for those of 1890, which were almost totally destroyed by fire in 1921), and will be provided at nominal cost to individuals who lack other documents of birth or citizenship. Certain census information, of course, is confidential by law (Title 13, *United States Code*).

Almost all depository libraries subscribe to some of the numerous items under which categories of census information are distributed. Moreover, the Bureau has been furnishing copies of its reports to an additional number of information centers, which have been designated Census Depository Libraries; these were chosen on the basis of population (in the case of a municipal institution) or enrollment (in the case of a college or university library). Census Depository Libraries number over 100; a current listing by state and location may be obtained by writing to the Publications Services Division of the Social and Economic Statistics Administration, Washington, D.C. 20233.[16]

Individuals and institutions may procure the census information that is for sale from the Superintendent, Bureau of the Census, or NTIS on microfiche. The several catalogs, guides, and indexes to Census Bureau publications indicate ordering procedures.[17]

Bureau of Competitive Assessment and Business Policy

Useful is the annual *U.S. Industrial Outlook* (C 57.309; Item 215-L). The report gives information on the energy situation, consumer credit, pollution control costs, and a general summary of anticipated trends. Detailed analysis of over 200 individual manufacturing and non-manufacturing industries are arranged in ten major sections. Each industry statement contains information on recent and projected developments.

Construction Review (C 57.310; Item 219), a monthly, contains articles, tables, legislation news, and construction regulations for this vital industry. The periodical is a sales item from the Superintendent.

DEPARTMENT OF DEFENSE

By progressive stages of euphemism, the War Department became the National Military Establishment, and found its present title by virtue of the National Security Act amendments of 1949. The Department provides for the security of the United States. Within the Office of the Secretary there are thirty subdivisions; and within the Departments of Army, Navy, and Air Force there are a combined total of over fifty subordinate agencies and bureaus. Almost that many administrative units offer publications available to depository libraries. More than one million civilians are employed by Defense, excluding foreign nationals provided by contractual agreement.

Office of the Secretary

The *Annual Report* of DoD (D 1.1; Item 310) includes the annual reports of the Secretaries of Army, Navy, and Air Force, and deals with current operations, new equipment, research and development, manpower, logistics and training. Bibliographies and Lists of Publications (D 1.33; Item 304-D) provides the bibliographic structure. Of the many specialized bibliographies, *Arctic Bibliography* (formerly D 1.22; Item 302-A), which was prepared for DoD under the direction of the Arctic Institute of North America, appeared irregularly from 1953 to 1966 and indexed the scientific literature on the arctic and subarctic regions.[18]

Defense Supply Agency

Directly under the control of the Secretary of Defense, DSA is responsible for providing support to the military services and to federal civil agencies for materiel commodities and items of supply, logistics services, and other support functions. Pursuant to these materiel management activities, the Agency issues *Cataloging Handbooks* (D 7.6/2; Item 314-A) and an *Index of Specifications and Standards* (D 7.14; Item 314-G). Also available from DSA are Bibliographies and Lists of Publications (D 7.16; Item 314-I).

Defense Documentation Center

As one of four service centers administered by DSA, the Defense Documentation Center is responsible for the development, maintenance, and operation of the management information system in the field of scientific and technical information. DDC's technical report services include announcements, bibliographies, and copies of reports furnished to registered DDC users. Those documents that are unclassified and that have no distribution limitations are available to the public through NTIS. For example, *Corporate Author Headings*, a comprehensive listing of corporate body names for better standardization in cataloging, was prepared for the Committee on Scientific and Technical Information (COSATI) by agreement with NTIS and DDC. Although the data were computer-produced by NTIS and photo-composed by the Government Printing Office, the work is available only through NTIS.[19]

National Guard Bureau

The National Guard Bureau was established in 1958 by act of Congress. It is a joint bureau of the Department of the Army and the Department of the Air Force within DoD and its publications are classed in D 12. Two works of reference value are issued by this unit: the *Official Army National Guard Register* (D 12.9; Item 358-A) and the *Air National Guard Register* (D 12.9/2; Item 358-A).

Department of the Army

Numerous documents are issued under the Army Department's Army Regulations series (D 101.9; Item 323), Technical Manuals series (D 101.11; Item 329), Field Manuals series (D 101.20; Item 324), and numbered Pamphlets series (D 101.22; Item 327). Among these series, certain publications have general reference interest. DA Pam 210-1, *United States Army Installations and Major Activities in Continental United States*, contains useful information for dependents traveling to overseas areas as well as important directory information. DA Pams in the 550 series comprise the "Area Handbook" publications on a number of countries. Every library should have these valuable guides, which cover the sociological, political, economic, and military background of the country; extensive bibliographies refer the reader to more detailed information.[20]

Documents librarians receiving the above Items should faithfully screen the publications received. An Army Regulation (55-60, 1968), *Official Table of Distances, Continental United States, Alaska, Hawaii, Canada, Canal Zone, Central America, Mexico and Puerto Rico*, is over 1,200 pages long and offers extensive information on distances between the smaller towns. Field Manual 21-26 (1969) happens to be the fourth revision of a publication titled *Map Reading*, which provides important information for persons engaged in the use of maps, aerial photographs, and related materials. Given the typical separation of the acquisitions and reference functions in library operations, many useful publications like these are doomed to oblivion on the shelves or in the stacks.

Adjutant General's Office

The *Army Register* (D 102.9; Item 332), which goes back to 1813, is currently issued in three volumes. Volume 1 consists of the regular Army active list; Volume 2, Army, NGUS, USAR, and other active lists; and Volume 3, retired lists. The *Register* is also issued in the House *documents* series.

Office of Military History

This Office issues the official, authoritative multi-volume history, *United States Army in World War II* (D 114.7; Item 345). The series is accompanied by a *Master Index, Reader's Guide* (D 114.7/2), which provides analytics to each of the volumes. More recently, the Office has begun a series on our penultimate police action, *United States Army in the Korean War* (D 114.2; Item 344). No college or university library can afford to be without these documents. *Publications of the Office, Chief of Military History* (D 114.10; Item 344-B) provides the bibliographical access.

Department of the Navy

Scientific and technical communication by the Navy includes the interchange of information within the Department, with other components of DoD and other federal agencies, and with private industry and the public subject to distribution limitations. Navy has a Government Industry Data Exchange Program, and the Department continues to make increasing use of the centralized data banks at the Defense Documentation Center in coordinating its research and development program. Among the series available to depository libraries within the Office of the Secretary are Regulations (D 201.11; Item 372), Handbooks, Manuals and Guides (D 201.6/12; Item 370-A), and Navy Procurement Directives (D 201.6/10; Item 373).

Naval Oceanographic Office

Until 1962 this was known as the Hydrographic Office. Among the important publications of this Office are *List of Lights and Fog Signals* (D 203.22; Item 378), a service for mariners; and *Sailing Directions* (as above). The latter series furnishes information that is needed by the navigator but that cannot be shown conveniently on nautical charts. Both are issued irregularly.

Publication number nine in this numbered series is the famous reference tool *American Practical Navigator* (D 203.22: 9; Item 378), a compendium of data on the fundamentals of navigation, piloting and dead reckoning, electronic and celestial navigation, oceanography, weather, and hydrography.

Naval Training Support Command

Before 1972 this was called the Naval Personnel Bureau. Publications include the *Register of Commissioned and Warrant Officers of the Navy and Marine Corps and Reserve Officers on Active Duty* (D 208.12), and its companion volumes, the *Register of Commissioned and Warrant Officers of the United States Naval Reserve* (D 208.12/2) and *Register of Retired Commissioned and Warrant Officers, Regular and Reserve, of the United States Navy and Marine Corps* (D 208.12/3). All are annually issued and all may be subscribed to under Item 405. *All Hands*, a monthly magazine (D 208.3; Item 401), contains articles about the Navy and its operations; it is intended for naval personnel and the general public.

Naval Observatory

Important navigational aids issue from this unit. The *Air Almanac* (D 213.7; Item 393) provides the astronomical data required for air navigation. The *American Ephemeris and Nautical Almanac* (D 213.8; Item 394), issued from one to two years in advance of the data presented, contains information relating to the sun, moon, planets, stars, eclipses, ephemerides, and satellites. The *Nautical Almanac* (D 213.11; Item 395) contains the sections from the *American Ephemeris* that are of use in navigation. The *Air Almanac* appears three times a year; the latter publications are issued annually.

Department of the Air Force

The Office of the Secretary issues the usual General Publications series (D 301.2; Item 424), Air Force Manuals (D 301.7; Item 421), a Pamphlets series (D 301.35; Item 421-A) and its Bibliographies and Lists of Publications (D 301.62/2; Item 424-I). Useful serial publications include the *Air University Library Index to Military Periodicals* (D 301.26/2), available to libraries on an exchange basis; *Air University Review* (D 301.26; Item 422-A), a journal designed to stimulate professional thought concerning aerospace doctrines, strategy, tactics, and related techniques; and *Driver* (D 301.72; Item 423-B), a monthly with popular articles on traffic safety.

Air Adjutant General's Office

Like its Army and Navy counterparts, the *Air Force Register* (D 303.7; Item 426) lists its personnel of officer rank. This *Register* is issued in two volumes, the first containing the active lists, the second containing the retired lists.

Service Academies

The *Catalogue* for West Point (D 109.8; Item 353), Annapolis' *Catalogue of Information* (D 208.109; Item 390-A), and the *Catalog* of the Air Force Academy (D 305.8; Item 425-A) are issued annually. Because the Coast Guard is an agency of the Department of Transportation, its *Catalog of Courses* is classed in TD 5.16 (Item 930-B).

DEPARTMENT OF HEALTH, EDUCATION, AND WELFARE

The Department of Health, Education, and Welfare (HEW) was created in 1953; the legislation abolished HEW's predecessor unit, the Federal Security Agency, and transferred all its functions to the new Department. This mammoth administrative bureau is involved in the lives of more Americans than any other federal agency; its several large subdivisions literally advise, regulate, and otherwise play a role in the activities of citizens from the womb to the tomb. Employing over 100,000 persons, the Department administers a budget of over 70 billion dollars.

Office of the Secretary

The *Annual Report* (HE 1.1; Item 444) is submitted by the Secretary of HEW to the President and the Congress for the fiscal year. A *Catalog* of HEW publications (HE 1.18/3; Item 444-B) is issued quarterly with an annual volume. A *Grants Administration Manual* (HE 1.6/7; Item 445-A) is issued irregularly; its purpose is to provide guidelines on the fiscal and administrative aspects of grant management to all granting units within HEW.

Social Security Administration

To carry out its task of providing social security and medicare benefits, the Social Security Administration (SSA) employs some 9,000 record-keeping personnel and operates the world's largest computer installation under one roof to keep track of 100 million active work histories on magnetic tape and microfilm.

The monthly *Social Security Bulletin* (HE 3.3; Item 523) is the official periodical of the Administration and reports current data on the operations of SSA and the results of research and analysis pertaining to the social security program. The *Bulletin* has an annual *Statistical Supplement* (HE 3.3/3; Item 523), which cumulates the monthly data. A bi-monthly digest, *Social Security Rulings on Old-Age, Survivors, and Disability Insurance* (HE 3.44; Item 523-A) contains interpretations and decisions of the Administration, court cases of particular significance, changes in Title II of the Social Security Act and related legislation, and news of general interest. SSA rulings and decisions are cumulated annually in *Social Security Rulings, Cumulative Bulletin* (HE 3.44/2; Item 523-A).

Office of Education

The Office of Education (OE) dispenses about 7 percent of the total United States expenditure (at all levels of government and the private sector) for education, and its operations and publications cover virtually every area and level of formal educational activities.

An important reference tool, *Education Directory* (HE 5.25; Item 460), is issued annually in several parts, covering state governments, public school systems, higher education, etc. Peculiarly, these parts of the *Directory* are issued under various other Item numbers. For example, the 1971-72 Part 2 section (Public School Systems) was available to libraries under Item 460 *and* Item 460-A-20. Consequently, libraries subscribing to all subseries under Item 460 will theoretically end up with two sets of the *Directory*.

American Education (HE 5.75; Item 455-B) is a lively, interesting journal which is issued 10 times a year. It replaced two OE magazines, *School Life* and *Higher Education*. The periodical covers preschool to adult education, new research and demonstration projects, major education legislation, and articles on contemporary problems in education. It is directed to a general as well as a pedagogical audience.

OE issues many useful publications under a number of series, including Elementary and Secondary Education, Higher Education, and Vocational Education. Within these broad groupings are many specific divisions. The Superintendent's notation for these series employed a mnemonic device by which one could identify the division with a minimum of bibliographic information. Thus, publications on Library Science were grouped in OE numbers 15,000 to 15,999 with the alphameric agency class HE 5.215 (Item 460-A-15). Similarly, Teacher Education—a division of the Higher Education grouping—had been assigned the numbers 58,000 to 58,999, with the class HE 5.258 (Item 460-A-58). In 1971 this notation was abandoned, which eliminated this useful mnemonic artifact, and a Department-wide system of publication numbering was initiated. Thus, the publication *Library Statistics of Colleges and Universities, Analytic Report*, formerly HE 5.215:15031, is now classed in HE 5.92/7(year).

In addition to the large number of publications generated by OE itself, the Educational Resources Information Center (ERIC) forms a nationwide information system; established by OE, it is designed to serve and advance American education at all levels. ERIC's basic objective is to provide ideas and information on current activities as developed through research reports, articles, theoretical papers, program descriptions, published and unpublished conference papers, newsletters, curriculum guides, and the like. To publicize the existence and availability of these studies, ERIC Central in the Office of Education provides policy, guidance, training funds, and general services to some sixteen clearinghouses throughout the country in its network.[21]

The vehicle that ERIC uses to announce these studies is the monthly *Resources in Education* (HE 18.10; Item 466-A). This abstracting service, sold through SUDOCS, abstracts and indexes the results of OE-sponsored research and other kinds of research that tend to bypass the primary journals. Workers in all fields of education, including librarians, are encouraged to submit studies to the appropriate clearinghouse so that they may be processed into the ERIC system. *Resources in Education* (RIE) contains separate subject, author, and institution indexes, while an accession number section provides a cross-reference from the ERIC clearinghouse number to the document (ED) number for the abstract summaries. Semi-annual and annual indexes are not included as part of the monthly SUDOCS subscription but are sold separately.[22]

Leasco Systems and Research Corporation, under contract with OE, offers (in microfiche or hard copy) the full text of most publications abstracted in RIE; a number of libraries now house full ERIC collections on microfiche. Leasco processes the material for Linotron printing; like NTIS publications, ERIC materials largely stand outside the depository system, except those publications that clearly are defined as "government documents." Thus the *Monthly Catalog* will occasionally list ERIC publications.

Macmillan Information of New York publishes a *Thesaurus of ERIC Descriptors*, a structured vocabulary of several thousand educational terms used to index and enter documents into the system. Macmillan also publishes a monthly companion to *Resources in Education*. Entitled *Current Index to Journals in Education* (CIJE), the service indexes over 230 English language journals in the field of education and related literature (including library science). RIE, CIJE, and the H. W. Wilson Company's more modest *Education Index* provide libraries and users with bibliographic access to a vast amount of literature on education.

Social and Rehabilitation Service

Organized in 1967, the Social and Rehabilitation Service administers the federal programs that provide the many necessary services to families in need, the disabled, children and youth, and the aged and aging. In 1974 the Service began issuing a new monthly entitled *Social and Rehabilitation Record* (HE 17.27; Item 532-A-13). The new periodical replaced three discontinued journals, *Rehabilitation Record* (HE 17.109), *Mental Retardation Abstracts* (HE 17.113), and *Human Needs* (HE 17.26). The latter had been in existence only since 1972, having replaced the useful bi-monthly *Welfare in Review* (HE 17.9). *Social and Rehabilitation Record* is available for sale through SUDOCS.

Within the Social and Rehabilitation Service is the Administration on Aging, which issues a popular monthly for senior citizens appropriately titled *Aging* (HE 17.309; Item 444-A). Presented in succinct and readable fashion, its articles cover accounts of senior citizen centers, news of social security developments, low-cost meals for the elderly, and congressional hearings on the problems of aging. A useful section on publications contains annotations of government documents as well as of commercial monographs and magazines of interest to the elderly.

Public Health Service

This major unit of HEW has undergone significant reorganization during the period from 1968 to 1974. In 1973 the Secretary of HEW announced a budget-trimming exercise in which almost 300 publications were terminated within fiscal year 1974. These included internal newsletters distributed to HEW employees, external periodicals subscribed to by individuals and libraries, and "single issuance publications"—reports and monographs developed for external, public dissemination which had been revised and updated over a period of several years. The majority of documents within these categories issued from units within the Public Health Service, particularly the Health Services Administration, Food and Drug Administration, and National Institutes of Health. A predictable result of these zealous reorganizational activities has been the reclassifying of a number of issuing authors. One can only hope that the following useful reference series shall not be eliminated in order to save a few pennies.

Where to Write for Birth and Death Records, United States and Outlying Statistics (HE 20.2002:B 53) is an important source of information for those who must verify these vital statistics for official purposes. Companion brochures, all of which are revised periodically, include *Where to Write for Marriage Records* (HE 20.2002:M 34); *Where to Write for Divorce Records* (HE 20.2002:D 64); and *Where to Write for Birth and Death Records of U.S. Citizens Who Were Born or Died Outside of the United States and Birth Certifications for Alien Children Adopted by U.S. Citizens* (HE 20.2002:B 53). All provide addresses of offices in states and territories where one must make inquiries, and all are available to libraries under Item 483-T-1.

If sources listed in these booklets do not result in the appropriate information, the National Archives may be of assistance. Although it has very few *original* records of birth, marriage, and death, the Archives has records of adoptions for the District of Columbia, 1907 to 1937, and guardianship papers from 1802 to 1878. Furthermore, it has records of births at Army camps, posts, and stations from 1884 to 1912, and some files through 1935 of births registered at American foreign-service offices, of children of American citizens residing abroad.

Current vital statistics are published in the *Monthly Vital Statistics Report* (HE 20.2209; Item 508-B). These provisional statistics on births, marriages, divorces, and death cumulate in the definitive *Vital Statistics of the United States* (HE 20.2212; Item 510), which is usually published in two volumes and contains extensive data on marriage, divorce, natality, fetal mortality, and mortality.

The monumental *Index Medicus* is issued from the National Library of Medicine. Its first form is that of a monthly (HE 20.3612; Item 508-E); part of the January issue contains medical subject headings, which may be purchased from SUDOCS separately but which comes to depository subscribers. The *Cumulated Index Medicus* (HE 20.3612/3) is available under the same Item and is the annual compilation of citations of journal articles from the world's periodical biomedical literature indexed in the monthly issues. The *Abridged Index Medicus* (HE 20.3612/2; Item 508-E-1) is a monthly list based on articles from approximately 100 English language journals; it is designed for the information needs of the individual practitioner and libraries of small hospitals and clinics. It, too, cumulates annually and is entitled *Cumulated Abridged Index Medicus* (HE 20.3612/2-2; Item 508-E-1). The *Monthly Bibliography of Medical Reviews* (HE 20.3610; Item 508-F) is designed to provide guidance to the latest reviews in the journal literature of biomedicine. However, this service is part of the monthly *Index Medicus*; libraries electing to receive Item 508-E need not subscribe to the *Monthly Bibliography*.

Another important bureau within the Public Health Service is the Food and Drug Administration, HEW's regulatory arm. The Administration (FDA) investigates the safety and effectiveness of new products from food and drug firms; its activities are directed toward protecting the public health of the nation.

FDA Consumer (HE 20.4010; Item 475-H) was formerly titled *FDA Papers*. Sold through SUDOCS, it is a monthly that contains information written for consumers about FDA's regulatory and scientific decisions and about the safe use of products regulated by the Administration. The *National Drug Code Directory* (HE 20.4012; Item 475-N) has been issued irregularly and contains descriptions of over 20,000 prescription and over-the-counter pharmaceutical products.

Office of Child Development

The Office of Child Development is considered a specialized unit which functions administratively under the Office of the Secretary of HEW. *Children Today* (HE 21.9/2; Item 449) was formerly titled *Children*; it is issued from the Office bi-monthly. It tells of federal, state, and local services for children, child development, health and welfare laws, and other news pertinent to child welfare. The Office of Child Development absorbed the functions of the venerable Children's Bureau by departmental reorganization in 1969. Of the numbered publications of the Bureau, perhaps the most famous is *Infant Care* (HE 21.110; Item 453).

DEPARTMENT OF HOUSING AND URBAN DEVELOPMENT

Established by act of Congress in 1965, the Department assists in providing for development of the nation's communities and metropolitan areas. Major subdivisions of HUD include community planning and development, housing production and mortgage credit, and federal disaster assistance. Seven issuing units offer publications to depository libraries; the Department employs almost 20,000 persons.

Office of the Secretary

The *Annual Report* (HH 1.1; Item 581) includes reports of the subordinate agencies within HUD. It reviews housing, home financing, and urban renewal activities for the year: selected housing and community facilities, housing market trends and characteristics, and the like, with statistical data compiled from government and other sources on housing production and costs. HUD issues a Housing and Planning Reference series (HH 1.23/3; Item 582-D) consisting of a selected list of publications and an index of articles on housing and planning acquired or noted in the libraries of HUD and the Federal Home Loan Bank Board. This bi-monthly can be used to supplement HUD's Bibliographies and Lists of Publications series (HH 1.23; Item 581-D).

The monthly *Housing and Urban Development Trends* (HH 1.14), available from HUD, consists of statistical data from various agencies on housing production, construction costs, home financing, and public housing. *HUD Challenge* (HH 1.36; Item 582-K) is a monthly sold by SUDOCS; it serves as a clearinghouse for the exchange of ideas and programs among HUD staff throughout the country. The field operations of the Department are carried out through a number of regional and area offices, and the magazine provides a forum for the discussion of official HUD policies and projects.

HUD Research (No. 1, February 1974) is a newsletter of interest to various groups working in the fields of housing and urban affairs. The report highlights the results of some of the research programs sponsored by HUD's Office of Policy Development and Research, which plans and coordinates all the major research efforts of the Department. The first issue was devoted to HUD's role in helping to solve the energy crisis.

HUD's general publications series includes a number of useful materials. For example, the *Registry of Minority Contractors and Housing Professionals* (HH 1.2: M 66/vols.; Item 582) is a multi-volume listing of contractors and housing professionals in selected cities. The *Registry* is divided into ten volumes corresponding to HUD's regional areas. Part one of each volume lists, by metropolitan areas, names of contractors and professionals with directory information. Part two provides additional background information on each of the businesses listed in part one.

The *Statistical Yearbook* (HH 1.38; Item 582-M) provides an annual summary of the Department's activities and operations, including characteristics of the properties, projects, and communities assisted under HUD programs.

DEPARTMENT OF THE INTERIOR

Created by act of Congress in 1849, Interior's duties over the years have changed from that of general housekeeper for the federal government to that of custodian of the nation's natural resources. Consisting of fourteen major subdivisions, Interior is comprised of eight regional field committees that promote the development and execution of natural resource programs for the Department. Interior's payroll numbers over 68,000 employees.

Office of the Secretary

The Department assigns to its several subordinate units the responsibility of preparing and issuing their annual reports.[23] However, the Conservation Yearbooks series, begun in 1965, has essentially taken the place of the Department's annual report. Like the Yearbook of Agriculture, these handsome, attractively illustrated monographs have different titles each year. Issued under the same notation and Item (I 1.95; Item 601-A), they have, for the most part, been kept in print for sale by the Superintendent; they appear from time to time in the *Selected U.S. Government Publications* and are listed in the 1973/74 edition of the *United States Government Manual*. The first Yearbook was titled *Quest for Quality*, followed by *The Population Challenge* (1966), *The Third Wave* (1967), *Man . . . An Endangered Species?*, etc.

Geological Survey

Price List 15, Geology, noted in-print publications of this agency, whose objectives are to perform surveys and research covering topography, geology, and the mineral and water resources of the United States and to publish data relative to these activities.

The Survey publishes maps of the National Topographic Map Series covering the United States and its outlying areas. The unit of survey is a quadrangle bounded by parallels of latitude and meridians of longitude. Topographic maps represent relief by brown contour lines, and each map is named for some town or natural feature in the area represented. In addition to publishing all standard quadrangle maps of United States area, the Survey issues separate index maps. All topographic maps must be obtained from the Geological Survey; they are not sold by SUDOCS nor are they ordinary depository items.[24]

The National Atlas of the United States (I 19.2: N 21a; Item 621), published in 1970, was the first national atlas this country produced. Prepared by the Survey with the cooperation of more than 80 government agencies and many commercial and university cartographic services, *The National Atlas* is a multi-purpose atlas for general reference, covering physical, economic, socio-cultural, and historical characteristics, with subject and place name indexes.

Publications of the Geological Survey (I 19.14; Item 623) is an annual bibliography arranged by types of publications, with author, subject, geographic area, and geological survey research indexes. Unfortunately, the Survey no longer issues some useful publications it once made available through depository channels. *Geophysical Abstracts* (formerly I 19.43; Item 621-A) was issued monthly from 1929 through December 1971. It contained abstracts of literature relative to the physics of the solid earth, physical methods, geological problems, and geophysical exploration. Monthly issues were indexed by author with annual cumulative author and subject indexes. Another publication that ceased with the December 1971 issue was *Abstracts of North American Geology* (formerly I 19.54; Item 619-A). This monthly began in 1966 and contained abstracts of technical papers and books—as well as map citations—covering the geology of

North America (including Greenland, the West Indies, Hawaii, Guam, and other island possessions of the United States).

Still available on deposit are the Survey's Bulletins series (I 19.3; Item 620), technical papers on all phases of geology and allied disciplines; Water Supply Papers (I 19.13; Item 625), technical papers on various aspects of hydrogeology; and Professional Papers (I 19.16; Item 624), a series of technical reports on many aspects of geological activity. The *Journal of Research* began publication in January 1973. Issued six times a year (I 19.61; Item 619-D), the periodical contains papers written by members of the Survey and their professional colleagues on various subjects in geology, hydrology, topography, and related earth sciences. Issues also contain a listing and brief annotation of recently released Geological Survey publications. A subject index is issued annually. The *Journal* supersedes the short-papers chapter in the former *Geological Survey Research*, which was an annual review issued as part of the Professional Papers series.

Bureau of Indian Affairs

This controversial agency, attacked by cultural anthropologists as well as members of the Indian community, issues several series that libraries find useful to obtain. Few, however, are available on deposit.

The *Progress Report from the Commissioner of Indian Affairs* (I 20.1; Item 626-A) serves as the annual report of programs pursuant to the agency's objectives. Libraries should subscribe to the General Publications (I 20.2; Item 627) series, as well as the Indians of [Various States] series, irregularly issued pamphlets treating of Indians of the several areas (I 20.51; Item 627-A).

Journals issued by or under the aegis of the Bureau include *Indian Leader* (I 20.39), *Indian School Journal* (I 20.41), and the monthly *Indian Record* (I 20.55). All are available from the Bureau only, and only the *Record* is a depository item (627-B).

Bureau of Reclamation

The purpose of this agency is to stabilize and promote the growth of local and regional economies through optimum development of water and related land resources throughout the 17 contiguous western states. *Reclamation Era* (I 27.5; Item 663) is published quarterly by the Bureau and sold by SUDOCS. About six articles per issue discuss subjects like irrigation, crops, pasturing and land recovery; the articles are written simply and are understandable at the high school level. *Reclamation Safety News* (I 27.18) issues from the regional office in Denver, Colorado, and reports safety performance information concerning reclamation projects.

Bureau of Mines

Of significant reference value is the four-volume *Minerals Yearbook* (I 28.37; Item 639), an annual review of the mineral industries of the United States and foreign countries. Volumes 1 and 2, "Metals, Minerals and Fuels," contain reviews of the mineral industries, statistical summaries and specific chapters on individual commodities. Volume 3, "Area Reports: Domestic," covers each state and the U.S. possessions. Volume 4, "Area Reports: International," consists of a summary chapter on minerals in the world economy followed by chapters on over 130 countries and areas.

Noteworthy Bureau series include Reports of Investigations (I 28.23; Item 637-A), which are studies describing the principal features and results of minor investigations; Bulletins (I 28.3; Item 636), which are more technical, describing major investigations and reports on large research projects conducted by the Bureau; and Information Circulars (I 28.27; Item 637-A), which contain digests, reviews, abstracts, and discussions of activities and developments in all aspects of the mineral industries.

National Park Service

Libraries subscribing to all Items available under this agency are inundated with the many editions and revisions of leaflets, bulletins, brochures, booklets, and folders on parks, seashores, lakeshores, rivers, military parks, monuments and historic places administered by this, the most benign of government units. Established in the Interior Department in 1916, the goals of the Service can be faulted by few: to so administer the areas under its jurisdiction that the environment is protected and citizens' enjoyment and education are enhanced.

In addition to the several categories of Information Circulars, the Service issues an Historical Handbook series (I 29.58; Item 649), booklets that provide surveys on historical and archeological areas of the National Park Service. Of reference importance are annuals like the *National Register of Historic Places* (I 29.76; Item 648-D) and *National Parks and Landmarks* (I 29.66; Item 646-B).

Board on Geographic Names

Although the *U.S. Government Manual* lists the Geographic Names Board in one of its appendixes, its publishing provenance is within the Department of Interior. The Board was established to provide uniformity in geographic nomenclature and orthography throughout the federal government. To this end, the Board issues *Decisions on Geographic Names in the United States* (I 33.5/2), a quarterly available from the Board. Another useful series sold by SUDOCS is the Board's Gazetteers (I 33.8; Item 617), which appear irregularly. Each volume covers a single country or group of countries. The Gazetteers are the authoritative source of geographic names for official government use. Moreover, they include the more important unapproved names or spellings cross-referenced to the approved ones. Recent titles include *South Vietnam and the South China Sea*, and *Europe and USSR*.

Fish and Wildlife Service

Progressive Fish Culturist (I 49.35; Item 612-B) is a quarterly that contains articles in the field of fish culture, propagation, stream stocking, fish management, and aquatic biology. The index is found in the October issue. A number of the publications of the Service, such as *Fishery Statistics of the United States*—an annual graphic and analytic review of the commercial fisheries scene—have been transferred to the issuing provenance of the National Marine Fisheries Service (NOAA) and are now classed in the C 55.301-99 series.

Bureau of Land Management

The Bureau is responsible for the management of a large acreage of the nation's federal lands and administers the laws pertaining to land use and resources. The annual *Public Land Statistics* (I 53.1/2; Item 633-C) is a compendium of data on acquisitions in the public domain, financial transactions, acreage, range development projects, and the like. Useful to all libraries is the quarterly *Our Public Lands* (I 53.12; Item 633-A), which contains popular articles on subjects such as natural history, erosion, wildfire detection, and minerals exploration. A regular feature, "Public Sale Bulletin Board," gives current information on forthcoming sales of public lands, with a brief description of the site and per-acre prices if appraised.

Ephemeris of the Sun, Polaris and Other Selected Stars with Companion Data and Tables (I 53.8; Item 630) is prepared by the Naval Observatory but issued by the Bureau. Published annually one year in advance of the data covered, it presents astronomical information practiced by engineers at the Bureau.

Bureau of Outdoor Recreation

The Bureau is enjoined to promote and develop programs relating to outdoor recreation and enhance and protect the environment. For federal, state, and local public officials, as well as other interested organizations and individuals, the Bureau issues a looseleaf service entitled *Outdoor Recreation Grants-in-Aid Manual* (I 66.8/2; Item 657-B-3). The *Manual* sets forth policies regarding the use of grant money from the Land and Water Conservation Fund and provides guidance in obtaining federal assistance.

A quarterly, *Outdoor Recreation Action* (I 66.17; Item 657-B-5), reports major federal, state, local, and private initiatives affecting outdoor recreation, natural beauty, and related conservation matters. It is designed to help interested officials and citizens keep abreast of significant developments in this area.

DEPARTMENT OF JUSTICE

The Justice Department was established by act of Congress in 1870. Its chief purposes are to enforce the federal laws and to construe the laws under which other departments operate. It has over 20 divisions and employs 47,000 persons.

Office of the Attorney General

The *Annual Report of the Attorney General* (J 1.1; Item 717-C-1) includes the reports of subordinate bureaus. The Office also issues the *Annual Report of the Law Enforcement Assistance Administration* (J 1.1/2; Item 717-C), which was established in 1968 to assist state and local governments in reducing crime. *Opinions of the Attorney General* (J 1.5/a) are issued as separates and later appear in bound volumes (J 1.5). Both issuances may be subscribed to under Item 718.

Federal Bureau of Investigation

The best known publication of this famous agency is the Uniform Crime Reports for the United States series (J 1.14/7; Item 722). Issued annually as *Crime in the United States*, the data presented are based on police statistics voluntarily contributed by local law enforcement agencies. Over 70 tables present statistics grouped by type of crime, geographic area of crime, race and sex of persons involved, population groups concerned, police employee data, and arrest trends. Although the sample lacks validity and reliability, all libraries should receive this publication. It is usually a SUDOCS sales item.

Bureau of Prisons

Although the Bureau issues no publications that are available on deposit to libraries, it cooperates with the Administrative Office of the United States Courts to publish an outstanding magazine called *Federal Probation* (Ju 10.8). Subtitled *Journal of Correctional Philosophy and Practices*, it attempts to present points of view relating to all phases of preventive and correctional activities in delinquency and crime. The journal appears quarterly, consists of 10 to 12 signed articles by experts in the field of criminal justice, and is printed at the U.S. Penitentiary, Marion, Illinois, by inmates in a rehabilitation program. It may be ordered free by writing the Administrative Office of the United States Courts, which is the issuing unit, at the Supreme Court Building in Washington, D.C.

Immigration and Naturalization Service

The official organ of the Service is the monthly *I & N Reporter* (J 21.10/2). Not a depository Item, it contains articles of interest to members of the Service and to other professionals interested in immigration and naturalization problems. Libraries would be well advised to subscribe to the Federal Textbook on Citizenship series (J 21.9; Item 724) as a reference service to candidates for naturalization to prepare for their citizenship tests. A popular title in this series is *Our Constitution and Government* (J 21.9: C 76/year). Of use to young students as well as to candidates for citizenship, the publication contains simple explanations of the Constitution and government processes, with word definitions, quizzes, and activities.

Drug Enforcement Administration

The Bureau of Narcotics and Dangerous Drugs (BNDD) was created in 1968, when the Bureau of Drug Abuse Control and the Federal Bureau of Narcotics were combined. But the activities of BNDD were taken over in 1973 by the Drug Enforcement Administration, created by Reorganization Plan 2 of 1973. Under the former provenance a bi-monthly with a newsletter format titled *BNDD Bulletin* (J 24.3; Item 968-B) was issued. Addressed to chiefs of police, drug abuse committees, state criminal investigation units, and high school guidance counselors and teachers, it provided information on the activities of the Bureau, including features summarizing new legislation on drug abuse, prevention and control, and news items of arrests following drug activities.

DEPARTMENT OF LABOR

At one time under the Interior Department and later part of the Department of Commerce and Labor, this agency gained full Cabinet rank in 1913 by act of Congress. The purpose of the Department of Labor is to administer and enforce statutes designed to promote the welfare of the wage earners of the nation. The Department has ten regional offices and its subdivisions have numerous regional locations throughout the United States. Labor's labor force numbers about 13,000.

Office of the Secretary

The *Annual Report* of the Secretary (L 1.1; Item 744) has been issued since 1913 and includes reports from the several subordinate bureaus. Bibliographies and Lists of Publications (L 1.34; Item 744-A) includes lists of a miscellaneous nature.

Manpower Administration

The Manpower Administration (MA) encompasses a group of offices and services designed to implement the responsibilities assigned to the Department for the conduct of work-experience and manpower training programs. These programs are directed by the Assistant Secretary of Labor for Manpower and the Deputy Assistant Secretary of Labor for Manpower and Manpower Administrator.

The *Manpower Report of the President and Report on Manpower Requirements, Resources, Utilization and Training* (L 1.42/2; Item 746-C) is an annual in two parts. The first part, consisting of the President's report to Congress on manpower requirements, is relatively brief. The report by the Department itself on the manpower situation is more detailed and is accompanied by an extensive statistical appendix. *Manpower* magazine (L 1.39/9; Item 746-N) is a monthly, sold by SUDOCS, that publishes news and articles pertinent to the field in readable, layman's terms. A useful regular feature is called "Publications," annotated listings of documents issued by the Manpower Administration and the Bureau of Labor Statistics on manpower and related topics.

An *Index to Publications of the Manpower Administration, January 1969 through June 1973* lists (under 54 subject headings) approximately 850 publications, reports, and articles issued by the Manpower Administration since its first full year of centralized operation. The *Index* is available without charge from the Information Office, Manpower Administration, Department of Labor, Washington, D.C.

Bureau of Labor Statistics

The Bureau of Labor Statistics (BLS), like the Bureau of the Census, is a major producer of salient economic primary and general purpose statistics. It is the government's principal fact-finding agency in the field of labor economics; it is specifically concerned with the collection and analysis of data on manpower and labor requirements, labor force, unemployment and employment, hours of work, wages and employee compensation, prices, living conditions, labor-management relations, productivity and technological developments, occupational safety and health, poverty, urban conditions, and international aspects of these subjects.

Large depository libraries should subscribe to all Items offered by BLS. For the non-depository library, the "Guide to Sources" appendix of the *Statistical Abstract of the United States* may serve as a checklist, depending upon the needs of the library's public. Significant if not indispensable publications for libraries include the following titles and series:

BLS Bulletins (L 2.3; Item 768) cover studies on all phases of labor as noted above. A number of sub-series are issued on a recurring basis; they include important directories, guides, handbooks, and, of course, statistical compilations of value in a reference situation. Titles include *Analysis of Work Stoppages*, *Directory of National and International Labor Unions in the United States*,

Handbook of Labor Statistics, *Area Wage Surveys*, and the famous *Occupational Outlook Handbook*. All these series are classed under L 2.3 followed by a Bulletin number. Changes in numbering occur in two ways: for recurring editions of some titles (e.g., *Occupational Outlook Handbook*), the number changes completely (the 1963 edition was assigned number 1375 while the 1972 edition was number 1700). For recurring editions of other titles (e.g., *Employment and Earning Statistics for the United States, 1909-19–*) the 1967 edition was bulletin number 1312-5 while the 1972 edition carried the number 1312-9.

The *Monthly Labor Review* (L 2.6; Item 770) is the official journal of BLS and makes the proud claim of being "the oldest and most authoritative government research journal in the fields of economics and the social sciences." In addition to articles of import and interest, each issue contains several recurring features of note, particularly "Current Labor Statistics," some thirty pages of data on over thirty categories collected by BLS. This excellent magazine is indexed in *Readers' Guide*, *PAIS*, and elsewhere, and should be in the collections of all libraries.

The *Consumer Price Index* (L 2.38/3; Item 768-F) is a household phrase to the public. The data collected for each issue measure average changes in prices of goods and services usually bought by urban wage earners and clerical workers. Prices for items are obtained in urban portions of 39 Standard Metropolitan Statistical Areas (SMSA's) and 17 smaller cities chosen as a sample to represent the universe of urban United States, including Alaska and Hawaii.[25] Most tables in this publication appear later in the *Monthly Labor Review*. Conversely, more recent information is found in the daily *News, U.S. Department of Labor* which, like the *Consumer Price Index*, is free from the Office of Information of the Department. A useful free pamphlet entitled *The Consumer Price Index, A Short Description* may be obtained by writing the Bureau in Washington or any of the regional BLS offices.

Current Wage Developments (L 2.44; Item 768-D) is a monthly available from SUDOCS that presents important developments in the collective bargaining process, with data on selected wage and benefit changes according to industry product. Of great value to business libraries, it is useful for university and public libraries as well.

Employment and Earnings (L 2.41/2; Item 768-B) presents monthly the most current information available on trends and levels of employment, hours of work, earnings, and labor turnover. Each issue contains a three-page written summary of employment and unemployment developments for the preceding month.

Occupational Outlook Quarterly (L 2.70/4; Item 770-A) supplements the information contained in the *Occupational Outlook Handbook*. Each issue contains from six to eleven articles on employment opportunities, including an issue devoted each year to college graduates' prospects in the marketplace. Like the *Monthly Labor Review*, the *Quarterly* should be subscribed to by all libraries.[26]

Finally, the selective subscriber may wish to receive the *Publications of the Bureau* catalog (L 2.34; Item 768-E). Issued semi-annually (January-June and

July-December coverage), the catalog is a classified list of publications; many of the entries are briefly annotated, and ordering information is given.

Women's Bureau

This agency is responsible for formulating standards and policies that shall promote the welfare of wage-earning women, improve their working conditions, and advance their opportunities for professional employment. To this end, the Bureau has 10 regional offices throughout the United States.

Publications of the Women's Bureau are classed in L 36. The Bureau has been a relatively strong participant in the non-GPO publications endeavor of the Superintendent. Useful series include the agency's numbered Bulletins (L 36.103; Item 781), which are irregularly issued popular reports on employment opportunities, working conditions, legislation and welfare, and employment of older women; *Women Workers in [State]* (L 36.114; Item 783-C-1), a series of statistical tables by state on employment, age distribution, marital status, earnings and income, etc.; and the non-GPO *Labor Laws Affecting Women* (L 36.111; Item 782-A), capsule summaries for each state on current labor laws applicable to women.

DEPARTMENT OF STATE

As discussed in Chapter 7, the Department of State is the President's chief instrumentality for implementing foreign policy. The Secretary of State is responsible for the overall direction, coordination, and supervision of U.S. foreign relations and for the interdepartmental activities of the U.S. government overseas. The Department employs 23,000 persons worldwide, including over 10,000 foreign nationals. The Agency for International Development, a major bureau within the State Department, has 11,000 employees.

In addition to the Treaties series discussed in the preceding chapter, State issues a number of useful publications of informational and educational worth. Some of the more widely known and used sources follow.

Office of the Secretary

Foreign Relations of the United States (S 1.1; Item 872). Volumes in this historic series have been published since 1861, but there is now a considerable time-lag between the period the volume covers and the date of publication. Special supplements have been issued from time to time on topics (e.g., *The Paris Peace Conference*) and nations (e.g., *Russia; Japan; China*).

Foreign Service List (S 1.7; Item 873). Issued three times a year, this pamphlet gives directory information for officers including ambassadors; ministers and chiefs of mission; Foreign Service officers; consular agents; officers for the Agency for International Development, the United States Information

Agency, and the Foreign Agricultural Service of the Department of Agriculture; and United States missions to international organizations.

Diplomatic List (S 1.8; Item 865). Issued quarterly, this directory lists foreign diplomats in Washington, D.C., arranged alphabetically by country and in rank order.

Employees of Diplomatic Missions (S 1.8/2; Item 868-C). To complement the *Diplomatic List*, this quarterly lists the lower-ranked employees of the foreign diplomatic presences in Washington.

Foreign Consular Offices in the United States (S 1.69; Item 871). An annual listing of consular offices by state and city. Directory information includes name, rank, jurisdiction of chief officer, and date of recognition.

Biographic Register (S 1.69; Item 863). Also published annually, the *Register* gives brief career biographies of civil service employees of the State Department in the grade of GS-12 and above, including officers of comparable rank in AID, the U.S. Information Agency, and the USDA's Foreign Agricultural Service.

Key Officers of Foreign Service Posts, Guide for Businessmen (S 1.40/2; Item 876-B). A useful compilation of chiefs and deputy chiefs of missions, the senior officers of the political, economic, commercial and consular sections of the post, and the agricultural attache; also included are all embassies, legations, and consulates general.

Background Notes on the Countries of the World (S 1.123; Item 862-B). A subscription service consisting of short, factual pamphlets about various countries and territories, with information on the country's land, people, history, government, economy, and foreign relations. Extremely useful for school libraries.

Basic Language Courses, Foreign Service Institute (S 1.114/2; Item 872-A). These manuals for language study, which range from commonly known European languages to exotic tongues such as Urdu, are useful for the language and literature section of a departmentalized library. They are also available for sale from SUDOCS.

World Strength of Communist Party Organizations (S 1.111; Item 900-B). An annual that provides analytical reviews accompanied by statistical data on world communist parties, with electoral and party membership information. A checklist preceding the regional tabulation gives basic information and references the complete text.

Libraries would do well to subscribe to the various geographic series the State Department publishes, for the monographs within those series contain much that is useful and important to the student of foreign policy. Examples of State Department series include the Inter-American series (S 1.26; Item 877), the East Asian and Pacific series (S 1.38; Item 870), the Near and Middle Eastern series (S 1.86; Item 883), and the African series (S 1.116; Item 862-A). Subscription to Item 875 will enable the library to receive the excellent General Foreign Policy series (S 1.71). A special supplement in this series is the annual *American Foreign Policy, Current Documents* (S 1.71/2), a one-volume compilation of the principal published official papers selected to indicate the scope, goals, and implementation of United States foreign policy.

Laws, Treaties

Earlier Digests of International Law (S 7.12) have been issued by the Department.[27] The most recent in this series, prepared under the direction of Marjorie Whiteman, covers the period from 1940 and is known as the *Whiteman Digest* (S 7.12/2; Item 864-A). It is an official digest of legal materials arranged by categories. Subjects include sovereignty, states' rights and responsibilities, asylum, jurisdiction, diplomatic privileges and immunities, extradition, expropriation of property, and civil strife and war. The *Whiteman Digest* emphasizes the factual and historical settings of cases and incidents and quotes extensively from original sources. It is not a statement of the law, but rather a reference tool to be used in ascertaining the law.

Treaties and other international agreements are classed in S 9 and were covered in Chapter 7.

Agency for International Development

The Agency for International Development (AID) was established within the State Department pursuant to Executive Order 10973 (November 3, 1961) as amended. Its major responsibility is to carry out assistance programs that are designed to help the people of the less developed countries acquire the knowledge and resources essential for growth and development.

AID's annual *Report to Congress on the Foreign Assistance Program* (S 18.1; Item 900-C-3) is prepared by the Agency with the cooperation and participation of both State and Defense. There is a series titled Projects, By Field of Activity and Country (S 18.28; Item 1056-D). *Development Digest* (S 18.33; Item 900-C-6), a quarterly, is a journal of selected excerpts, summaries, and reprints of current materials on economic and social development.

DEPARTMENT OF THE TREASURY

The Treasury Department, along with the Departments of War and State, was established by the first federal Congress in 1789. Its jurisdiction includes formulating tax and fiscal policy and acting as financial agent for the U.S. government. Treasury contains over a dozen subdivisions, and there are as many issuing units for publications sent to depository institutions. The Department employs over 100,000 persons.

Office of the Secretary

The *Annual Report of the Secretary of the Treasury on the State of the Finances* (T 1.1; Item 923) contains a review of fiscal policies and includes the activities of the subordinate units; statistical tables accompany the report. The *Daily Statement of the United States Treasury* (T 1.5; Item 923-A-1) is sold by the Superintendent; it consists of the daily statement and monthly and final fiscal year statements of the receipts and expenditures of the government. This important periodical also shows cash deposits and withdrawals as they affect the account of the Treasurer of the United States, records changes in the public debt, details inter-fund transactions, and gives figures in the U.S. Savings Bonds Program.

The monthly *Treasury Bulletin* (T 1.3; Item 926-A) is a synopsis of Treasury activities, including an account of reported tenders received for various treasury bills; domestic and foreign series are noted, as are Eurodollar series subscriptions. A cumulative table of contents covers the yearly topics of the periodical. The weekly *Customs Bulletin* (T 1.11/3) contains regulations, rulings, decisions, and notices concerning customs and related matters, and decisions of the U.S. Customs Court and the Court of Customs and Patent Appeals. The bound volume of *Bulletins* is available on deposit (T 1.11/4; Item 927).

Bureau of Customs

The Customs Bureau is active in functions that involve traffic in illegal narcotics (in conjunction with the Drug Enforcement Administration), munitions control and pier pilferages (in conjunction with the FBI), hijacking (through the Sky Marshal program), articles in international trade (with the Patent or Copyright Office), environmental protection programs (assisted by the U.S. Coast Guard), and special marking provisions for wool, fur, and textile products (controlled domestically by the Federal Trade Commission). Pursuant to these activities, the Bureau issues a looseleaf subscription service, sold by SUDOCS, entitled *Customs Regulations of the United States* (T 17.9; Item 948-A). The service consists of regulations made and published for the purpose of carrying out laws administered by the Bureau; subscription includes the basic volume plus supplementary service for a two-year period.

Internal Revenue Service

Who among us has not felt the chilling impact of the rules and directives issued by this agency? The Service publishes the useful *Cumulative List [of] Organizations Described in Section 170 (c) of the Internal Revenue Code of 1954* (T 22.2: Or 3; Item 956), which contains information on organizations to which the citizen may contribute on a tax deductible basis. The basic list is updated irregularly by supplements.

The *Internal Revenue Bulletin* (T 22.23; Item 957) is a weekly whose indexes cumulate monthly, quarterly, and semi-annually. The latter, which cover January-June and July-December, are called *Cumulative Bulletins* (T 22.25; Item 960). The weekly is the authoritative instrument through which the Commissioner of Internal Revenue announces official rulings, procedures, regulations, tax decisions, and legislation affecting the Service.

The Service has established a system of looseleaf tax regulations, divided into five individual services. Titled *Internal Revenue Looseleaf Regulations System* (T 22.19/3; Item 961), the services include Income Tax, Estate and Gift

Tax, Employment Tax, Excise Taxes, and Procedure and Administration. They are available from SUDOCS as separates, and generally follow the arrangement of the subchapters and parts in Chapter 1, Title 26 of the *Code of Federal Regulations*.

In addition to the well-known *Your Federal Income Tax* (T 22.44; Item 964-B), all libraries will want to obtain the following tax guides for special groups: *Farmer's Tax Guide*, *A Guide to Federal Estate and Gift Taxation*, *Tax Guide for U.S. Citizens Abroad*, and *Tax Guide for Small Business*. These annual aids are issued in the Handbooks, Manuals, and Guides series (T 22.19/2; Item 956-A) and are sold separately by SUDOCS and in many post offices throughout the country. Additionally, subscription to Item 964-B, the Tax Information series, will secure for libraries many IRS publications on tax guides, instructions, and other aids for individuals in certain categories.

Bureau of the Mint

The agency that produces our coins issues an *Annual Report of the Director of the Mint* (T 28.1; Item 965), which includes a review of the operations of the mints, assay offices, and bullion depositories for the fiscal year; reports on gold, silver, and coinage metals; and the world's monetary stocks of gold, silver, and coins.

Secret Service

The General Publications series (T 34.2; Item 974) includes the useful booklet entitled *Know Your Money*. The brochure tells how to detect counterfeit bills and coins and how to guard against forgery losses. Other categories under Item 974 include *Report to the Public* (T 34.1/2) and the Handbooks, Manuals and Guides series (T 34.8).

DEPARTMENT OF TRANSPORTATION

The most recently created of the eleven departments, Transportation was established by act of Congress in 1966, one year after Housing and Urban Development. The purpose of the Department is to develop national transportation policies and programs conducive to fast, safe, efficient, and convenient transportation at low cost. Employees of the Department number 68,000.

Office of the Secretary

The Department issues an *Annual Report* (TD 1.1; Item 982-C); a General Publications series (TD 1.2; Item 982-C-1); *Regulations of the Office of the Secretary* (TD 1.6/2; Item 982-C-3), which includes the basic manual plus supplementary data; and various reports to Congress on the administration of acts pursuant to highway and traffic vehicle safety.

Federal Highway Administration

Highway Statistics (TD 2.23; Item 265-B) is an annual compendium of statistical data, with appropriate tables, on driver licensing, highway mileage, state highway finance, federal aid, motor fuel, and highway finance data for towns, counties, cities, and other governmental units. *Public Roads* (TD 2.19; Item 268) is a quarterly subtitled "A Journal of Highway Research." Containing two to four signed articles per issue, *Public Roads* treats of technical matters relevant to planning, design, construction, and finance. Some articles are not wholly research oriented; those dealing with personnel management and travel can be appreciated by the informed layman. Regular features include "Digest of Recent Research and Development Results" and "New Publications."

Federal Aviation Administration

Formerly the Federal Aviation Agency, the FAA became part of the Transportation Department in 1967; the Administration has regulatory functions in air commerce, aviation safety, and air traffic control. For libraries specializing in these materials, the Superintendent offers over forty Items under this issuing agency.

The monthly periodical *FAA Aviation News* (TD 4.9; Item 431-A-11), an attractive publication, contains articles devoted to aspects of flight service and aviation in general. Recurring features include accounts of famous flyers or flights, "Pilot Briefs"—news stories of interest to pilots—and news about FAA safety regulations and notices. Airman's Information Manual (TD 4.12; Item 431-C-5) is published in four parts. Part 1, issued quarterly, is entitled *Basic Flight Manual and ATC (Air Traffic Control) Procedures*; Part 2, *Airport Directory*, is published semi-annually; Parts 3 and 3A, *Operational Data* and *Notices to Airmen*, are issued bi-weekly; and Part 4, *Graphic Notices and Supplementary Data*, issued twice a year, concludes the series. Each part may be purchased from SUDOCS as a separate.

United States Civil Aircraft Register (TD 4.18/2; Item 431-F-5) combines in its new title two regular annual reports formerly entitled *Statistical Study of U.S. Civil Aircraft* and *U.S. Active Civil Aircraft by State and County*. The *Register* provides information on civil aircraft such as make, model, manufacturer's serial number, number of engines and the like. The *FAA Statistical Handbook of Civil Aviation* (TD 4.20; Item 431-C-14) contains statistics on airports, federal airways, general aviation, aeronautical production and exports, accidents, and scheduled air carrier operations. The *Handbook* is issued annually.

FAA issues many useful training publications and examinations in its TD 4.8 and TD 4.408 (Flight Standards Service) series. Exams include those for commercial pilot, ground instructor, and flight engineer. Manuals include instrument flying and basic helicopter.

Coast Guard

For many years an agency of the Treasury Department, the Coast Guard was transferred to Transportation in 1967. Useful series include *Boating Statistics* (TD 5.11; Item 941-A), a semi-annual publication containing figures on boat registration, accidents, and related statistics. *Merchant Vessels of the United States* (TD 5.12/2; Item 950), an annual, is kept up to date by a *Monthly Supplement* (TD 5.12; Item 950-B). It includes tabular information on ownership changes in steam, motor, and sail vessels of 100 gross tons and over; changes of names of vessels; documented vessels removed from the Merchant Marine; and changes in gross and net tonnage and home ports for steam, motor, and sail vessels of 500 gross tons and over.

Under Item 942 are issued the annual *Register of Officers and Cadets* and *Register of Reserve Officers* (TD 5.19 and TD 5.19/2).

FEDERAL REGISTER

A number of departments and agencies issue compilations of rules and regulations; the Superintendent designates this category of publications by the number "6." But if users are concerned with recent and in-force administrative legislation, it is appropriate to direct them to the *Federal Register* and the *Code of Federal Regulations* (CFR). Thus, for example, current rulings of the Agricultural Stabilization and Conservation Service would be determined first by consulting the *Federal Register* indexes and then Title 7, Chapters VII and VIII of the CFR. At the same time the librarian should be aware that compilations are issued from time to time in A 82.6 and may be subscribed to under Item 110.

Appendix B of the 1972/73 edition of the *U.S. Government Organization Manual* contains an alphabetical list of assignments in the *Code of Federal Regulations*, so that quick reference can be made from the name of the issuing unit to the appropriate Title and Chapter reference in the CFR. Unfortunately, the 1973/74 edition of the *U.S. Government Manual* eliminated this source. For libraries that lack earlier issues of the *Federal Register*, complete sets from 1936 can be obtained in the microfilm edition, or purchased as separates, from the National Archives and Records Service.

REFERENCES

1.   *Organization of Federal Executive Departments and Agencies* is a useful document. Published as a large chart, it provides a detailed breakdown of the federal establishment with precise data on the number of federal employees by administrative unit. It is issued annually as a committee print by the Senate Committee on Government Operations and sold by the Superintendent.

2.   Until 1936 the *Yearbook* consisted in part of the annual report of the Secretary of Agriculture. Now a separate publication, annual reports (A1.1; Item 6) are available to depository libraries as a non-GPO category.

3.   The reader is by now aware that little uniformity exists in the terminology of government units. They are variously called office, agency, bureau, administration, service, survey, board, council, etc.

4.   For a useful compilation of retrospective lists and indexes of the several departments and their agencies, see Schmeckebier, pp. 37-64.

5.   In 1974 the Secretary of Agriculture consolidated the county field offices of four agencies—including the Soil Conservation Service—into central service centers, in order to effect greater efficiency of operation.

6.   The National Oceanic and Atmospheric Administration (NOAA) itself contains eight issuing subdivisions, including the National Weather Service and the National Ocean Survey.

7.   Free distribution to depositories of GRA and GRI causes a loss of income to NTIS and keeps the cost of these tools high for subscribers. The Director of NTIS thinks that the Service should be severed from government and made a private corporation "with stock issued and the government holding about 40% of it." Under this scheme prices would rise even higher; the putative benefit would be in the realm of better service. See *American Libraries* 5: 285-86 (June 1974).

8.   Item 270 includes quarterly cumulations for *Government Reports Index* (C 51.9/2) and an *Annual Index* (C 51.9/4).

9.   A useful list of NTIS services is found in Catherine Ettlinger's "NTIS: The Nation's Biggest Publisher," *Government Executive* (February 1974), p. 44.

10.   J. G. Coyne, "The National Technical Information Service," *Illinois Libraries* 56: 269-71 (April 1974) presents the Service's official apologia for its practices and philosophy.

11.   ESSA itself was established in 1965 to absorb the Weather Bureau, Coast and Geodetic Survey, and Environmental Data Service, only to be abolished in 1970 with the creation of NOAA.

12.   *Monthly Weather Review* had been published by the government for 101 years. In 1973 subscription through SUDOCS cost $19 per calendar year. When the American Meteorological Society assumed publication, in January 1974, the annual subscription jumped to $60.

13.   The sections represent states, possessions, and groups of states, and the series must be ordered from the National Climatic Center, Federal Building, Asheville, North Carolina 28801.

14.   *Economic Indicators* (Y 4. Ec 7; Item 997) is a monthly prepared by the Council of Economic Advisers for the Congressional Joint Economic Committee; issued by the Committee, it contains much useful information to complement the statistical series issued by the Bureau of Economic Analysis.

15.   See Albert Halcli, "Census Data: From Magnetic Tape to Microfiche," *Illinois Libraries* 56: 279-82 (April 1974).

16.   The Census Depository Library Program is being phased out, owing to the increase in the number of ordinary designated depositories that subscribe to sufficient numbers of Census Bureau publications.

17.   A useful overview of guides and other readings for the librarian working with census materials is found in W. R. Thompson's article, "The Census—How It Can Help You Help the Patron," *Wilson Library Bulletin* 46: 275-79 (November 1972).

18. *Arctic Bibliography* is currently being printed in Canada under the direction of McGill University.

19. DDC's *Technical Abstract Bulletin* (TAB) was given a "confidential" security classification in 1967, and in 1971 that security label was placed on the indexes to TAB, thus removing them from public access.

20. The class notation shows a subdivision to distinguish individual countries following the 550 series of DA Pamphlets (e.g., *Cambodia*, D 101.22: 550-50/3; *Libya*, D 101.22: 550-85/2, etc.).

21. The number of clearinghouses has fluctuated over the years in response to the shifting needs of the educational community. Because of the decentralized nature of American education, a network of clearinghouses seemed more feasible than a monolithic center in Washington, D.C. Field units are hosted by organizations, primarily universities and societies, already prominent in the area of the discipline in which the units would function.

22. RIE is similar to GRA/GRI in its capabilities, except that the abstract section and indexes in RIE appear within one cover. The ERIC Clearinghouse on Library and Information Science (ERIC/CLIS), which was established in 1968, was merged with the clearinghouse on Educational Media and Technology in 1974 to form a new unit called the ERIC Clearinghouse on Information Resources (ERIC/IR).

23. The annual *Reports to Be Made to Congress* indicates that in addition to agency reporting requirements, the Comptrollers of Guam and of the Virgin Islands must report at the close of the fiscal year on the fiscal condition of their territorial governments. Issued by the Department's Office of Territories, these financial reports may be subscribed to under Items 672-A and 671, respectively.

24. See Chapter 3, reference 28.

25. When the BLS announced that it was planning to dismantle its present *Consumer Price Index* in favor of a more broadly based index, Senator William Proxmire introduced S 3361 (April 22, 1974), assuring continuation of the publishing of the index in its present form but not prohibiting BLS from creating and publishing other indexes designed to measure CPI data in other ways.

26. The *Dictionary of Occupational Titles* consists of one volume of title definitions and a second volume, an occupational classification and industry index. The third edition of this valuable work (1965) was issued from the Employment Security Bureau (L 7.2: Oc 1), which was abolished in 1969; its function was transferred to the Manpower Administration. Irregular supplements to the third edition have been issued in the General Publications series of the Training and Employment Service (L 34.2; Item 755).

27. Miscellaneous compilations are summarized in Schmeckebier, pp. 375-78.

9

DOCUMENTS OF INDEPENDENT AND REGULATORY AGENCIES

The rise of administrative bodies probably has been the most significant legal trend of the last century and perhaps more values today are affected by their decisions than by those of all the courts, review of administrative decisions apart. They also have begun to have important consequences on personal rights. . . . They have become a veritable fourth branch of the Government, which has deranged our three-branch legal theories much as the concept of a fourth dimension unsettles our three-dimensional thinking.

Courts have differed in assigning a place to these seemingly necessary bodies in our constitutional system. Administrative agencies have been called quasi-legislative, quasi-executive or quasi-judicial, as the occasion required, in order to validate their functions within the separation-of-powers scheme of the Constitution. The mere retreat to the qualifying "quasi" is implicit with confession that all recognized classifications have broken down, and "quasi" is a smooth cover which we draw over our confusion as we might use a counterpane to conceal a disordered bed.

—Supreme Court Justice Robert H. Jackson,
FTC v. Ruberoid, 343 *U.S.* 470 (1952)

Quis custodiet ipsos custodes?

—Juvenal

INTRODUCTION

In addition to the White House Office, Executive Office of the President, and the departments, there exist within the structure of the executive branch a number of so-called "independent agencies." Owing to that *bête noire* of federal government, imprecise terminology, the phrase is somewhat misleading; independence is at the very least a relative term. The phrase has never been defined by statute, but a satisfactory beginning definition is offered by Burns and Peltason:

> Broadly speaking, all agencies that are not corporations and that do not fall under an executive department (such as Treasury or Interior) are called independent agencies. Many of these agencies, however, are no more independent of the President and Congress than are the executive departments themselves.[1]

Students of government find it convenient to divide the independent establishments into two categories: the regulatory bodies, and the other agencies that exist structurally outside of the formal executive departments. Like the Orwellian pigs in *Animal Farm*, some independent establishments are more independent than others.

Discriminating among these administrative units becomes a matter of academic punctilio. For purposes of studying the publications that issue from the independent agencies, it is sufficient to use the list that appears in the "Contents" section of every edition of the *United States Government Manual*. Although the *Manual* includes government corporations, such as the Tennessee Valley Authority, in its list, it constitutes an official enumeration for our purpose, which is to identify the locus of provenance.

However, it is also useful to identify those independent establishments that perform significant *regulatory* functions. While many of the independent agencies have regulatory activities, discussion of the government as regulator usually centers on the establishments known as the "Big Seven." With their power and authority to affect virtually every segment of national economy, these entities have become something tantamount to a fourth branch of government.

The transition of the American economy from rural to industrial begat regulatory involvement by government. Prior to the Civil War, the United States was more interested in "encouraging exploitation of the nation's resources than in controlling their use."[2] As business, and later labor, grew in power, and as a response to the complexity of the nation's economic intercourse, Congress felt constrained to create administrative units to police and restrict certain interest groups. In a sense the regulatory activities of government are negative—to impose limitations upon institutions, to prevent one interest from interfering with the rights of others.

Regulatory agencies are said to possess quasi-executive, -legislative, and -judicial power. They plan and execute decisions relatively independent of a President's direction. They make administrative law largely independent of Congress, which defers to their putative expertise. And they are empowered to render decisions independent of the courts. Checks and balances, however, are inherent in the mandate of the regulatory bodies. Their degree of independence is circumscribed by a President's appointive power, by Congress's power of the purse, and by the courts' power of judicial review. All this is nicely theoretical; in practice it is not so tidy. No independent establishment can be free from the political dialectic in a democracy.

THE BIG SEVEN

To isolate seven regulatory agencies from among the over fifty independent establishments listed in the *U.S. Government Manual* is *not* to suggest that they alone exercise regulatory functions. Almost all departments and their bureaus have some regulatory duties. The Federal Aviation Administration within the Department of Transportation is charged with regulating air commerce to foster aviation safety. The Food and Drug Administration in HEW exercises surveillance over food, drugs, and cosmetics. Examples can be multiplied. We are considering the *degree* of power, as we are regarding the relative *degree* of independence from the three constitutionally established branches.

Interstate Commerce Commission

The first of the "Big Seven" regulatory establishments, the Interstate Commerce Commission (ICC) came into being through the Interstate Commerce Act of 1887. The Commission was created by Congress to regulate, in the public interest, carriers engaged in transportation in interstate commerce and in foreign commerce to the extent that it takes place within the United States. Surface transportation under the Commission's jurisdiction includes railroads, trucking companies, bus lines, freight forwarders, water carriers, oil pipelines, transportation brokers, and express agencies.

The Commission is made up of eleven members. From among their number, the President designates the chairman. The members elect a vice-chairman annually. The other nine members serve on one of three divisions, which function in an appellate capacity for action on petitions for reconsideration or rehearing of decisions of the divisions or boards of employees. Subsequent legislation has strengthened and broadened the scope of the Commission's authority.

Publications of the ICC follow the regular form of classification for materials of the Commission as a whole, such as annual reports (IC 1.1), general publications (IC 1.2), bulletins (IC 1.3), etc. Thereafter, they are grouped by subject, because the Commission had no subordinate agency and bureau breakdown at the time class notations were assigned. Subject designation takes the form of adding the first three or four letters of the subject word to the main designation of IC 1, as follows:

Symbol	Publications relating to:
IC 1 acco.	Accounts
IC 1 act.	Acts regulating commerce
IC 1 hou.	Hours of service
IC 1 mot.	Motor carriers
IC 1 pip.	Pipe line companies
IC 1 saf.	Safety
IC 1 ste.	Steam roads (Railroads)
IC 1 wat.	Water carriers

Many ICC series are available to depository libraries. *Transport Statistics in the United States* (IC 1.25; Item 699) is released in seven separate sections. The complete set consists of 1) railroads; Parts 2) and 3), which have been consolidated into Part 1); 4) electric railways; 5) carriers by water; 6) oil pipe lines; 7) motor carriers; 8) freight forwarders; and 9) private car lines. *Interstate Commerce Acts Annotated* (IC 1 act. 5/2; Item 676), issued irregularly, include digests of pertinent decisions of the courts and the ICC with the text of, or reference to, general rules and regulations of the Commission.

Federal Trade Commission

The Federal Trade Commission (FTC) was established in 1915 pursuant to the Federal Trade Commission Act of 1914; subsequent acts enlarged the regulatory duties of the Commission. Charged with keeping competition both free and fair, the Commission acts to prevent price-fixing agreements, the dissemination of false or deceptive advertisements, and dishonest packaging and labeling. A chairman and four commissioners function to restrain offenders in the areas under the Commission's jurisdiction. The formal proceedings are similar to those used in courts. Cases may originate through complaint by a consumer or a competitor, or by a federal, state, or municipal agency. Conversely, the Commission may initiate an investigation to determine possible violation of the laws it administers. An adverse decision by the Commission has the force of law unless the respondent petitions an appropriate United States Court of Appeals to review the order.

Some useful publications are issued by the Commission. The *Quarterly Financial Report for Manufacturing Corporations* (FT 1.18; Item 536-A) is prepared jointly by the FTC and the Securities and Exchange Commission; for each calendar quarter, it shows the financial characteristics and operating results for manufacturing corporations. The monthly *Consumer Alert* (FT 1.24/2) is a newsletter that gives popular accounts of current FTC action. *FTC News Summary* (FT 1.19/2) is issued on a semi-monthly pattern and reports current activities of the Commission. Both newsletters are available free from the Commission.

The Commission is relatively responsive to the public. In February 1974, FTC's Chairman announced a broad set of "sunlight" policies, among them a provision to process more expeditiously requests for scrutiny of records under the Freedom of Information Act.

Federal Power Commission

The Federal Power Commission (FPC) operates under the Federal Power Act, as amended, which was originally enacted as the Federal Water Power Act of 1920. Additional responsibilities have been assigned to the Commission by other legislation and executive orders. The FPC regulates the rates and other aspects of interstate wholesale transactions in electric power and natural gas, and prescribes and enforces a uniform system of accounts for regulated electric utilities and natural gas pipeline companies.

Composed of a chairman, vice-chairman, and three commissioners, the FPC issues publications that are primarily of a statistical nature. The annual *National Electric Rate Book* series (FP 1.18; Item 437-A-1 to 437-A-50) consists of individual state rate books showing rates charged by publicly and privately owned electric utilities in communities with a population of 2,500 or more. The monthly *Electric Power Statistics* (FP 1.27; Item 435-E) presents summaries of statistics from reports that electric utilities filed with the Commission on a number of subjects: production of energy and capacity of plants; fuel consumption of electric power plants; electric utility system loads; sales of electric energy; and financial data of private utilities. *Federal Power Commission Reports* (FP 1.20/a) are available from SUDOCS and, although the issues are dated monthly, are received on an irregular basis. Issues contain the formal opinions and accompanying orders of the Commission. This information is cumulated semi-annually in an *Opinions and Decisions* series (FP 1.20; Item 438).

Federal Communications Commission

The Federal Communications Commission (FCC) was created by the Communications Act of 1934; it was assigned additional regulatory jurisdiction under the provisions of the Communications Satellite Act of 1962. FCC regulates interstate and foreign communications in the areas of radio and television broadcasting; telephone, telegraph, and cable television operation; two-way radio and radio operators; and satellite communication. Regulatory functions include overseeing compliance with the fairness doctrine, political broadcasting, and fair competition.

The weekly *Federal Communications Commission Reports, 2d Series* (CC 1.12/2a), sold by SUDOCS, contains all decisions, reports, memorandum opinions, orders, statements of policy, public notices, and all other official pronouncements and acts of the Commission that are or may be of precedential value or public interest. These weekly reports later appear in bound volumes, issued irregularly (CC 1.12/2; Item 284). The annual *Statistics of Communications Common Carriers* (CC 1.35; Item 288) is a compilation of financial and operating data from all common carriers engaged in interstate or foreign communications activities.

Securities and Exchange Commission

The Securities and Exchange Commission (SEC) was created under authority of the Securities Exchange Act of 1934. Its purpose is to provide the fullest possible disclosure to the investing public, and to protect the interests of the public and investors against malpractices in the securities and financial markets. Composed of a chairman and four commissioners, the SEC serves as advisor to United States district courts in connection with reorganization proceedings for debtor corporations in which there is a substantial public interest.

The monthly *Official Summary of Security Transactions and Holdings* (SE 1.9; Item 906-A) includes securities holdings figures showing owners, relationships to issuers, amounts of securities bought or sold by each owner, their individual holdings at the end of the reporting period, and types of securities. The monthly *Statistical Bulletin* (SE 1.20; Item 908-A) contains statistical summaries of new securities, securities sales, common stock prices, stock transactions, and other phases of securities exchange. The *News Digest* (SE 1.25/12; Item 908-B) is a daily report of SEC announcements, decisions, orders, rules and rule proposals, current reports and applications filed, and litigation developments. *SEC Docket* (SE 1.29; Item 908-C) is a weekly compilation of the full texts of SEC releases under various acts. Also included are the full texts of Accounting series, Corporate Reorganizations, and Litigation Releases.

National Labor Relations Board

The duties of the National Labor Relations Board (NLRB), which was created by the National Labor Relations Act of 1935 (Wagner Act), were expanded by the Taft-Hartley Act of 1947 and the Landrum-Griffin Act of 1959. The Postal Reorganization Act of 1971 gave the Board jurisdiction over unfair labor practice charges and representation elections affecting U.S. Postal Service employees. The Board has two principal functions: preventing and remedying unfair labor practices by employers and labor organizations, and conducting secret ballot elections among employees in appropriate collective-bargaining units to determine whether or not they desire to be represented by a labor organization. The Board consists of a chairman and four members.

Publications of NLRB include the *Weekly Summary of NLRB Cases* (LR 1.15/2), available from the issuing unit; the monthly *NLRB Election Report* series (LR 1.16); an irregularly issued *National Labor Relations Board Field Manual* (LR 1.6/3; Item 827-A), which contains instructions for the guidance of the agency staff in administering the National Labor Relations Act as amended; and *Decisions and Orders of the National Labor Relations Board* (LR 1.8; Item 826), for which an index and digests of the decisions are provided in cumulative supplements, which are issued separately. A bi-monthly *Digest of Decisions of the NLRB* (LR 1.8/5; Item 826-A) is available for sale from the Superintendent.

Civil Aeronautics Board

The Civil Aeronautics Act of 1938 created the Civil Aeronautics Authority as an independent agency. In 1940 the name was changed to Civil Aeronautics Board (CAB). Although independent of the Department of Commerce, the CAB administrator once performed his functions under the direction of the Secretary of Commerce. Thus publications issued by the Board were—and still are—classed in C 31.

The Board is composed of a chairman, vice-chairman, and three members. It has broad authority to promote and regulate the civil air transport industry within the United States and between the United States and foreign countries. Board decisions involving the domestic operations of air carriers are not subject to review or approval by the President or by any department or agency of government, but adverse decisions may be referred to the United States Courts of Appeal. Like the other "Big Seven" establishments, the CAB enjoys quasi-executive, -legislative, and -judicial powers: members set forth policies, promulgate rules, and adjudicate. CAB licenses domestic air carriers; issues permits to foreign air carriers landing in the United States; sets passenger, freight, and mail rates; and controls mergers and other arrangements between carriers.[3]

Regulations of the Civil Aeronautics Board (C 31.206/7; Item 186), a looseleaf subscription service available from SUDOCS, includes the basic volume plus supplements that are issued irregularly. The annual *Handbook of Airline Statistics* (C 31.249; Item 183-A) is a useful reference source for commercial air transportation in the United States. Data show trends in passenger, freight, express, and mail revenues and traffic; flying operation expenses; aircraft maintenance and depreciation; capital gains; and the like. The annual information can be updated by the quarterly *Air Carrier Financial Statistics* (C 31.240) and the monthly *Air Carrier Traffic Statistics* (C 31.241), both of which are available from CAB's Publications Service Section for a fee.

CODIFICATION

As we noted in the preceding chapter, the publications of departments and agencies are not confined to classed Items available to depositories or otherwise sold and distributed by the issuing unit. Administrative regulations, rules, opinions, hearings, investigations, cease and desist orders, notices, etc., are published in the *Federal Register* and later codified by Title and Chapter in the *Code of Federal Regulations*.

Duplication permits the user a choice based on the needs of recency. Thus, for instance, CAB regulations may be found under Item 186 (C 31.206/7) or in the *Federal Register* and the CFR. And this duplication exists throughout the issuing structure of the executive branch. Administrative edicts for the "Big Seven" may be found in the appropriate Title and Chapter of the *Code of Federal Regulations*, as follows on page 218.

Agency	CFR Title/Chapter
Interstate Commerce Commission	49, X
Federal Trade Commission	16, I
Federal Power Commission	18, I
Federal Communications Commission	47, I
Securities and Exchange Commission	17, II
National Labor Relations Board	29, I
Civil Aeronautics Board	14, II

* * *

All the agencies in the executive branch that have regulatory powers derive them from acts of Congress. Functions that have become too complex for Congress to handle by means of ordinary legislation are delegated to the numerous administrative units; hence their authority to write regulations that have the force of law and that reach into virtually every aspect of our individual and institutional lives.

The so-called "independent agencies," including the "Big Seven" regulatory establishments, are ideally as free as possible from both White House and congressional political influence. In order to insure this independence, regulatory agencies usually have commissioners with long, staggered terms. Appointments are presidential, but the Senate must advise and consent. A President's power to remove the officers is limited, and no political party may have more than a one-member majority on any of the "Big Seven" bodies. In this way, free from undue political interference by the executive branch and Congress, the agencies can theoretically discharge their duties honorably in the public interest.

One problem in translating theory into practice stems from the notion that the regulatory bodies are "arms of Congress." Thus they are susceptible to the influence of a Representative or Senator as well as to that of the President or his assistants. But the greater question is suggested by Juvenal's famous apothegm: *Quis custodiet ipsos custodes?* For the most intense pressures brought to bear on the independent regulatory commissions are likely to come, not from the three branches of government, but from the very interests being regulated.

Thus the railroads, the telecommunications industry, and the airlines are anxious to see the agency rule favorably in their interests, which may not be the same as the best public interest. Who, then, shall regulate the regulators?[4]

OTHER INDEPENDENT AGENCIES

ACTION

Created as an independent agency in 1971, ACTION has absorbed the functions, powers, and responsibilities of the Peace Corps (created in 1961); it includes agencies like VISTA (Volunteers in Service to America), SCORE (Service Corps of Retired Executives), and the Foster Grandparent Program. Its purpose is to strengthen and develop citizen participation in voluntary programs providing personalized services to people in need, both in the United States and abroad.

Periodicals issued by ACTION include *Transition* (AA 1.10; Item 74-C-1), a monthly for VISTA and Peace Corps members whose tours of duty are nearing completion; tips for the adjustment to "civilian" life are proffered. *Synergist* (AA 3.9; Item 74-D-1) is issued three times a year and features articles on all aspects of the National Student Volunteer Program. The *VISTA Fact Book* (AA 1.9; Item 857-H-13), a monthly, was issued prior to July 1971 by the Office of Economic Opportunity and classed in PrEx 10.21; it includes lists of active projects undertaken by VISTA, with a directory of names of project contracts and local sponsors.

Arms Control and Disarmament Agency

Established by act of Congress in 1961, the United States Arms Control and Disarmament Agency is responsible for the conduct of studies and the provision of advice relating to arms control and disarmament policy formulation. Much of the Agency's effort goes into preparing for and participating in discussions and negotiations with the Soviet Union and with other countries on matters such as strategic arms limitations. The act creating the Agency permits the establishment of a General Advisory Committee not to exceed 15 members and to be appointed by the President with the advice and consent of the Senate.

An important annual issued by the Agency is *Documents on Disarmament* (AC 1.11/2; Item 865-B), which was issued by the State Department prior to 1961. In it basic official documents regarding disarmament and arms control, including texts of speeches and papers presented in forums like the United Nations General Assembly, are printed. A bibliography is included.[5]

World Military Expenditures and Related Data (AC 1.16; Item 125-A-8) annually surveys the size of the world's military expenditures for over 100 countries; the data represent approximate orders of magnitude.

Atomic Energy Commission

Although not considered one of the "Big Seven," the Atomic Energy Commission (AEC) has powerful regulatory functions; the Commission is responsible for assuring that the civilian uses of nuclear materials and facilities are accomplished without endangering public health and safety, environmental quality, or national security.

AEC was established by the Atomic Energy Act of 1946 as amended. Its governing board consists of a chairman and four commissioners, and its licensing and regulatory functions are administered by a Director of Regulation and nine assistants. Statutory oversight is exercised by the congressional Joint Committee on Atomic Energy.

Atomic Energy Commission publications may be obtained through the Superintendent, NTIS, or from the Commission's Technical Information Center in Oak Ridge, Tennessee. They range from popular information booklets for the general public to esoteric, highly technical documents. Publications of more than routine interest include *AEC Research Reports*, unclassified studies considered by the AEC to "have a high public interest." These are made available through NTIS in 26 subject categories. *Nuclear Safety*, which is a bimonthly technical progress review, is sold by SUDOCS (Y 3.At7; Item 1051-H) and consists of concise and authoritative evaluations of scientific and technological developments relating to nuclear safety as they emerge from atomic research and development programs.

Best known of AEC's publications is *Nuclear Science Abstracts* (Y 3.At 7:16; Item 1051-A), a semi-monthly abstracting service for the literature of nuclear science and engineering. Indexes (Y 3.At 7:16-5) are issued quarterly under the same Item and include a cumulative *Report Number Index* (Y 3.At 7:16-2). Quinquennial cumulative indexes were published by GPO and made available to depositories from 1948 to 1973; at that time the AEC commissioned Xerox University Microfilms, Ann Arbor, Michigan, to publish future quinquennial cumulations.

AEC's Technical Information Center in Oak Ridge, in addition to its information booklets, offers to the general public films, posters, and pamphlets useful to school and public libraries. Over 200 16mm films are available for free loan and are listed in the Commission's *Combined Film Catalogue*.

Environmental Protection Agency

The Environmental Protection Agency (EPA) was established in the executive branch as an independent agency pursuant to Reorganization Plan 3 of 1970, effective December 2, 1970. It was created to permit coordinated government action on behalf of the environment, to serve as the public's advocate for environmental quality. Its regulatory functions endeavor to abate and control pollution systematically, by integration of a variety of research, monitoring, standard setting, and enforcement activities.

Series include *Water Pollution Control Research* reports (EP 1.16; Item 473-A-1), which describe the pollution abatement results and progress with respect to our nation's waters. Some are sold by SUDOCS, many are available through NTIS. A *Grants Administration Manual* (EP 1.8/2; Item 431-I-10) is issued irregularly; subscription includes the basic manual plus supplemental material for an indefinite period. *Air Pollution Abstracts* (EP 4.11; Item 483-E-3) includes approximately 1,000 articles monthly, taken from over 1,000 domestic and foreign serial publications, patents, government reports, technical society papers, and proceedings.

Federal Reserve System

Established pursuant to authority contained in the Federal Reserve Act of 1913, the Federal Reserve System (Fed) is comprised of a Board of Governors, a Federal Open Market Committee, twelve Federal Reserve Banks and their twenty-four branches situated throughout the United States, a Federal Advisory Council, and member banks (which include all national banks in the fifty states). The Board of Governors is composed of seven members appointed by the President with the advice and consent of the Senate. The body has broad supervisory powers; it determines general monetary policy and exerts powerful influence over credit conditions in the United States.

The monthly *Federal Reserve Bulletin* (FR 1.3) is sold by the issuing unit and presents articles of general and special interest, policy statements issued by the Board, and statistical data relating to domestic and international financial business developments. The weekly *Deposits, Reserves and Borrowings of Member Banks* (FR 1.11/4) publishes data on gross and net demand deposits, time deposits, demand balance due from domestic banks, and the like. The monthly statistical release, *Business Indexes* (FR 1.19), contains tables on industrial production, consumer durable goods, utility output, employment and payrolls, etc. *Consumer Credit* (FR 1.36) gives monthly data on consumer installment credit, personal loans, and related information in this area.

General Services Administration

The General Services Administration (GSA) was established by Section 101 of the Federal Property and Administrative Services Act of 1949. GSA establishes policy and provides for the government an economical and efficient system for the management of its property and records. It is organized much like a large corporation, with many diverse activities including construction and operation of buildings; procurement and distribution of supplies; disposal of property; transportation, traffic, and communications management; and stockpiling of strategic materials.

In addition to the publications discussed in Chapters 6 and 7, which are issued from GSA's Office of the Federal Register, other bureaus within the Administration produce important series.

Federal Supply Service

This unit is responsible for maintaining a government-wide supply system including emergency defense supplies. *Federal Specifications* (GS 2.8; Item 563), issued irregularly, are representations of the technical requirements for materials, products, or services. They are in the form of written descriptions, drawings, prints, commercial designations, and other descriptive references. Specifications are designated by a number that has three components: 1) a single, double, or triple combination of the *same letter*, which indicates the procurement group; 2) a single letter, which designates the first letter of the name of the item covered by the specification; and 3) a serial number, which represents the item's numerical location within the procurement group. Any revision to a specification is identified by the addition of a letter to the serial number. Specifications are issued in looseleaf form and punched for ring binder.

Federal Standards (GS 2.8/3; Item 563), issued in the same way, establish engineering or technical limitations and applications for materials, processes, and designs. Both issuances are bibliographically controlled by an *Index of Federal Specifications and Standards* (GS 2.8/2; Item 565), which affords access alphabetically and numerically by procurement groupings. A complete listing of procurement groupings and identifying letter symbols is contained in the front portion of the *Index*, which is issued in monthly cumulative supplements. The *Index* also includes an appendix, which contains a complete list of cancelled and superseded documents.[6]

National Archives and Records Service

A *Guide to the Ford Film Collection in the National Archives* describes the 1.5 million feet of motion pictures in the Henry Ford Historical Film Collection, which was presented to the Archives in 1963 by the Ford Motor Company. The *Guide* describes the collection by general subject headings. All of the film may be used freely, and reproductions may be purchased. The *Guide* is available from the Publications Sales Branch, NARS-GSA, Washington, D.C. 20408.

National Aeronautics and Space Administration

The Administration (NASA) was established by the National Aeronautics and Space Act of 1958, as amended. The principal statutory functions of NASA are to conduct research for the solution of flight problems within and outside the earth's atmosphere, and to develop, test, and operate aeronautical and space vehicles.

Scientific and Technical Aerospace Reports (NAS 1.9/4; Item 830-K), known as STAR, is a semi-monthly that announces, abstracts, and indexes reports issued by NASA and by other government agencies, universities, and industry and research associations doing work in this field. Cumulative indexes are issued (NAS 1.9/5); subscription through SUDOCS includes three quarterly indexes and an annual cumulation, printed in four volumes.

NASA Activities (NAS 1.46; Item 830-H-1) informs personnel employed by the Administration of important developments in the space program, but it also contains useful information for all persons not connected with NASA who are interested in the program. *NASA Tech Briefs* (NAS 1.29) are issued irregularly and made available through NTIS. They are prepared by NASA to acquaint the public with innovations resulting from the Administration's research and development program, including NASA/AEC interchange efforts. *Aerospace Medicine and Biology* (NAS 1.21:7011) is a continuing bibliography compiled and published through the joint efforts of NASA, the Library of Congress, and the American Institute of Aeronautics and Astronautics. The bibliography assembles within the covers of a single publication references that were formerly announced in separate journals, and it emphasizes applied research studies. It is available monthly on an annual subscription basis from NTIS.

National Science Foundation

The National Science Foundation (NSF) was established by the National Science Foundation Act of 1950, as amended, and was given additional authority by the National Defense Education Act of 1958. Its purposes are to increase the nation's base of scientific knowledge and to develop science education programs that will prepare the country for challenges in the decades ahead. NSF awards grants and contracts to universities and to non-profit and other research organizations to support fundamental and applied research in all the scientific disciplines.

Grants and Awards for [Fiscal Year] (NS 1.10/4; Item 834-E), an annual, includes a list of grants with name of individual and institution, and amount of grant. The publication also contains a list of fellowship recipients and institutions they have chosen.

Scientific Information Activities of Federal Agencies (NS 1.16; Item 834-J), issued irregularly, describes the policies and practices of the several agencies with regard to their scientific and technical information activities.

Current Research and Development in Scientific Documentation (NS 2.10; Item 834-K) reports semi-annually all pertinent activities in the field of scientific documentation in the United States, as well as foreign projects that have come to the Foundation's attention. Categories include information needs and uses, information storage and retrieval, mechanical translation, and equipment.

Mosaic (NS 1.29; Item 834-F-1) is a quarterly sold by SUDOCS. It serves as a medium of communication to and among individuals and groups directly affected by the Foundation, as well as interested parties—federal agencies, science writers, etc.—who share a concern for the progress of science.

Antarctic Journal of the United States (NS 1.26; Item 834-Y) is a bi-monthly prepared by the Foundation's Office of Polar Programs with the assistance of DoD. It provides a common outlet for all information on the United States Antarctic Program and is intended for a broad audience of interested observers.

Postal Service

The United States Postal Service was created as an independent establishment in 1970. The existence of this venerable institution dates back to 1775; Benjamin Franklin was the first Postmaster General. By act of 1872 the Post Office achieved departmental rank, although the Postmaster General had been a member of the President's Cabinet since 1829. The act of 1970 abolished the Department and reorganized mail services as an independent agency.

The Postal Service commenced operations on July 1, 1971. It has a Postmaster General and Deputy, the principal officers of the Service, who report to a board of nine governors appointed by the President with the advice and consent of the Senate for overlapping nine-year terms. Its major purpose, as always, is to provide prompt, reliable, and efficient postal services to individuals and institutions.

The weekly *Postal Bulletin* (P 1.3; Item 837-C) contains orders, instructions, and information relating to the Service, including changes in airmail, money orders, stamps, etc. It is sold by SUDOCS. The *Directory of Post Offices* (P 1.10/4; Item 839), an annual, lists all post offices, branches, and stations arranged alphabetically by states, including Army and Air Force postal installations. Zip code numbers are included for each post office as well as a numerical list of offices by zip code. Changes are updated by the weekly *Postal Bulletin*. A *National Zip Code Directory* (P 1.10/8; Item 839) identifies each postal delivery unit alphabetically by state.

Of outstanding reference value is *Postage Stamps of the United States* (P 4.10; Item 840). It was formerly revised biennially, but now, in response to many suggestions from the public, updated editions are issued in looseleaf form. *Postage Stamps* presents a comprehensive review of all United States issues, from the first adhesive stamp of 1847. Provided are black and white illustrations of the stamps, with detailed information as to why each stamp was issued, its dimensions and color, what or whom it pictures, when and where it was first placed on sale, and any other pertinent information that might serve to identify the stamp. Also included are data on many other points of interest about stamps and other postal materials—postal cards, stamped envelopes, and the like. Information is given concerning the number of stamps printed for each of the commemorative issues and the number of plates used in printing them, a list of the designer and engravers of each stamp issued since 1933, and special information on first-day covers.

Small Business Administration

The Small Business Administration (SBA) was created by the Small Business Act of 1953, as amended. Its purposes are to aid, counsel, assist and protect the interests of small business, to make loans to small business concerns, to license, regulate, and make loans to small business investment companies, to improve the management skills of small business owners, and to conduct studies of the economic environment.

Small Business Bibliographies (SBA 1.3; Item 901-K) are issued irregularly and cover specific types of small businesses such as handicrafts, home products, and mail order selling. The Management Aids for Small Manufacturers (SBA 1.10/2; Item 901-E) are annual compilations of an irregular series of publications written by specialists on functional management problems in such fields as financing, maintenance, personnel, and business-government relations.

The Small Business Management series (SBA 1.12; Item 901-C) issues booklets, ranging widely in number of pages, that discuss general management problems associated with small businesses. Small Marketers Aids (SBA 1.14; Item 901-J), also issued irregularly, presents articles for owners and managers in retail, wholesale, and service enterprises; advice on management problems encompasses such fields as accounting and record keeping, human relations, selling, and office management.

The Starting and Managing series (SBA 1.15; Item 901-L) likewise consists of booklets recommending helpful ways to start and operate various small businesses, such as a print shop or a bookkeeping and accounting service. SBA's Bibliographies and Lists of Publications (SBA 1.18/2; Item 901-N) provide bibliographic coverage for these very useful aids. Both small and large libraries can hardly do without these fine series.

Smithsonian Institution

The Smithsonian Institution was created by act of Congress approved August 10, 1846, under the terms of the will of James Smithson of London, who in 1829 bequeathed his fortune to the United States to found an establishment for the "increase and diffusion of knowledge among men." It is governed by a Board of Regents, whose members are appointed by joint resolution of Congress; the Institution itself is a federally chartered, non-profit corporation.

To carry out Smithson's mandate, the Institution performs fundamental research; publishes the results of studies, explorations, and investigations; preserves for study over 60 million items of scientific, cultural, and historical interest; maintains exhibits representative of the arts, American history, technology, aeronautics and space exploration, and natural history; and engages in programs of education and national and international cooperative research and training. Its several units issue a number of publications of interest, some of which are indicated below.

Office of the Secretary

Smithsonian Contributions to Astrophysics (SI 1.12/2; Item 909-B) is a series of technical papers that communicates the results of research conducted at the Astrophysical Observatory of the Institution. Smithsonian Contributions to the Earth Sciences (SI 1.26; Item 910-B) is an irregular series which provides reports of original research in such fields as meteoritics, mineralogy, physical oceanography, and geology. Other specialized series include Smithsonian Contributions to Zoology (SI 1.27; Item 910-D), Botany (SI 1.29; Item 910-E), and Anthropology (SI 1.33; Item 921-A). *Smithsonian*, a monthly magazine handsomely illustrated, contains articles on such diverse subjects as Ceylon's vanishing elephants, the cleaning up of London and the Thames, satellite colonies in space, and the like. The magazine also features opulent art reproductions. Subscribers are entitled to the magazine when they become a national associate member of the Institution.

National Museum

A Bulletins series (SI 3.3; Item 919) makes available monographs of a technical nature, including treatises on fauna, reports of expeditions, and the like. Contributions from the U.S. National Herbarium (SI 3.8; Item 920) is likewise a series of scholarly treatises on floral groups relating to the Herbarium's botanical collections.

American Historical Association

The *Annual Report* of the American Historical Association (SI 4.1; Item 915) is issued in two volumes. Volume 1 contains the proceedings; Volume 2 is titled *Writings on American History, [Year]*. This is a classified list of books and articles on United States history that were published during the reported year, a splendid bibliography for student and scholar. Both volumes are also issued in the House *documents* series.

Veterans Administration

The Veterans Administration (VA) is a large independent agency that administers laws covering a wide range of benefits for veterans, their dependents, and beneficiaries of deceased former members of the armed forces. Veterans' benefits include hospital care, education and rehabilitation, life insurance, and loans for home and farm purchases. Established by executive order in 1930 in accordance with the act of July 3, 1930, the VA, through its Board of Veterans Appeals, has statutory jurisdiction to decide appeals to the Administrator under laws administered by the agency.

Of reference value are the VA Pamphlets and Fact Sheets series. The former (VA 1.19; Item 988) contains individual titles such as *Benefits for Veterans and Servicemen with Service Since January 31, 1955, and Their Dependents* (VA Pam 20-67-1) and *Summary of Benefits for Veterans with Military Service Before February 1, 1955, and Their Dependents* (VA Pam 20-72-2). VA Pam 1-1 contains the *Rules of Practice, Board of Veterans Appeals*. The non-depository library may obtain all of these by writing the VA in Washington, D.C.

VA Fact Sheet IS-1, *Federal Benefits for Veterans and Dependents* (VA 1.34; Item 989-B), is revised appropriately and sold through the Superintendent.

CONCLUDING OBSERVATIONS

Including departments and their agencies, there are over one hundred offices within the executive branch to which Congress has delegated the authority to promulgage regulations that have the force of law. These regulations, standards, and other administrative decisions are, as already noted, published in the *Federal Register* and codified in the appropriate Title of the CFR.

The task of developing improvements in the legal procedures by which the several departmental and independent agencies administer regulatory programs is the charge of a body called the Administrative Conference of the United States. Itself an independent establishment, the unit was brought into being by act of 1964 to conduct studies of procedures that fix the rights and obligations of private persons and business interests through agency adjudication, rulemaking, and investigative proceedings. Its membership includes heads of agencies, other federal officials, private lawyers, university professors, and others qualified in administrative law and government.

Although the Administrative Conference has authority only to recommend changes in administrative procedures, the prestige of the agency has resulted in substantial change upon recommendations by its several study groups. The Conference issues an *Annual Report* (Y 3.Ad 6:1, Item 1049-G) and interim *Recommendations and Reports* (Y 3.Ad 6:9; Item 1049-H) on its activities.

As we discussed, the role of the independent establishments is never wholly free from the larger political process. As Justice Jackson averred uneasily, these "seemingly necessary bodies" pose difficult constitutional problems.[7] The regulatory bodies are assigned the almost impossible task of remaining independent of the Congress, the executive, the courts, and—most vexing of all—of the influence of the institutions they regulate.

Sometimes the cast of characters engaged in watching one another becomes confusing. The Federal Communications Commission attempts to regulate the mighty broadcasting industry. Meanwhile the Office of Telecommunications Policy in the Executive Office of the President declares itself responsible for overall supervision of national communications matters, including desirable regulatory policies for broadcasting services. Radio and television feel the political pressure of the not-so-independent Office of Telecommunications Policy, which in turn watches the FCC. No ultimate resolution of the role of these establishments within the framework of the constitutional trinity is possible because the problem is philosophically antinomic. We are thus inescapably brought back to Juvenal's unanswered question: *Quis custodiet ipsos custodes?*

REFERENCES

1. J. M. Burns and J. W. Peltason, *Government By the People* (5th rev. ed.; Englewood Cliffs, N.J.: Prentice-Hall, 1963), p. 464.

2. Richard L. Worsnop, "Federal Regulatory Agencies: Fourth Branch of Government," *Editorial Research Reports*, February 5, 1969, p. 90.

3. Although the Federal Aviation Administration's regulatory jurisdiction is different from that of CAB, the latter enjoys in theory a greater degree of "independence."

4. "People lobbies" like Common Cause and the several activities loosely supervised by Ralph Nader suggest one answer that merits cautious optimism.

5. An excellent quarterly bibliography, *Arms Control and Disarmament* (formerly LC 2.10; Item 806-H), was issued by the Library of Congress but, unfortunately, was discontinued with v. 9, no. 2 (Spring 1973).

6.   A useful schema, "How to Identify Federal Specifications," is reproduced in John Andriot's *Guide to U.S. Government Publications* (1973 edition), vol. 1, p. (GS 2) 3, September 1973.

7.   *FTC v. Ruberoid*, 343 *U.S.* 470 (1952).

10

REPORTS OF ADVISORY COMMITTEES AND COMMISSIONS

Upon the testimony of these facts [the Whiskey Insurrection] an associate justice of the Supreme Court of the United States notified to me that "in the counties of Washington and Allegheny, in Pennsylvania, laws of the United States were opposed, and the execution thereof obstructed, by combinations too powerful to be suppressed by the ordinary course of judicial proceedings or by the powers vested in the marshal of that district."

My proclamation of the 7th of August last was accordingly issued, and accompanied by the appointment of commissioners, who were charged to repair to the scene of insurrection. They were authorized to confer with any bodies of men or individuals. . . .

Although the report of the commissioners marks their firmness and abilities, and must unite all virtuous men, by showing that the means of conciliation have been exhausted, all of those who had committed or abetted the tumults did not subscribe the mild form which was proposed as the atonement, and the indications of a peaceable temper were neither sufficiently general nor conclusive to recommend or warrant the further suspension of the march of the militia.

Thus the painful alternative could not be discarded. I ordered the militia to march, after once more admonishing the insurgents in my proclamation of the 25th of September last.

–George Washington, *Sixth Annual Address*,
November 19, 1794

INTRODUCTION

Groups created to provide advice and support to the federal government have existed since the days of Washington's administration. The quotation from his *Sixth Annual Address* that serves as a preface to this chapter alludes to the first appointed advisory committee. That the commissioners failed in negotiating with the rebel farmers did not negate the value of their appointment. It was important at the time, and continues to be important today, that government receive advice from private citizens to aid in the making of policy.

Government probably came into being through the effort of committees. After Washington's precedent, advisory bodies were commonly established to assist the President, the departments and agencies, and the Congress on matters of greater or lesser moment. Indeed, there appears to be an overwhelming tendency to appoint a committee or commission whenever a problem or an emergency occurs which at the time seems difficult to resolve. Ideally, the advisory body effects a significant contribution by the governed to the government; it provides a means by which the best brains and experience available in business, labor, and the professions can be made accessible. Understandably, as government has increased in size and responsibilities, the number of advisory committees has grown.

While growth of advisory units has been substantial, their functions and management have been haphazard. Many statutes exist that either have created specific committees or have granted the President and the agencies broad authority to create advisory groups. The vast majority of committees and commissions come into being in the latter way. During calendar year 1972, for example, 211 new advisory commissions were created, of which 19 were specified by statute. Of the 1,439 advisory bodies extant as of December 31, 1972, 251 (or 18 percent) were created by act of Congress.[1]

Presidents and other officers within the executive branch often fail to make use of a committee's findings. In fact, creation of a committee can be used to delay, stall, or thwart solution or resolution of a problem. When a controversy erupts, the announcement of a committee to study the problem may be a ploy to mollify public outrage. Incidents that create headlines often result in the creation of a presidential commission to study the problem; when the report is finally issued, a President is frequently obliged, for political or other reasons, to ignore, pigeonhole, or even denounce the findings. Richard Nixon, for example, repudiated the recommendations of the Commissions on Obscenity and Pornography and Marijuana and Drug Abuse *before* their publication.[2]

From time to time Congresses and administrations have engaged in housecleaning of committees that have become obsolete. But this process, known as "committee-killing" or "committee-flushing," has been effectively countered by the penchant of administrations to create large numbers of new or reconstituted advisory groups. The runaway nature of committee growth led President Kennedy, in 1962, to issue Executive Order 11007, which attempted to impose upon the advisory bodies throughout the government uniform standards for their formation and regulations prescribing their activities. Section 2(a) of EO 11007 defined the term "advisory committee" to mean any committee, board, commission, council, conference, panel, task force, or other similar group, or any subcommittee or other subgroup thereof, that is formed by a department or agency of the Government in the interest of obtaining advice or recommendations, or for any other purpose, and that is not composed wholly of officers or employees of the Government. The term also includes any committee, board, commission, council, conference, panel, task force, or other similar group, or any subcommittee or other subgroup thereof, that is not formed by a department or agency, but only during any period when it is being utilized by a department or agency in the same manner as a Government-formed advisory committee.

The Executive Order further signified an "industry advisory committee" to be one composed predominately of "members or representatives of a single industry or group of related industries, or of any subdivision of a single industry made on a geographic, service or product basis."

While EO 11007 prescribed regulations for the formation and use of advisory committees in the executive branch, it did not provide for executive overseeing of the formation, management, and use of those bodies. Moreover, it did not suggest guidelines for funding the advisory units, was not inclusive enough, and contained only vague provisions for reporting and records access. In short, the Executive Order provided minimum basic management control over only a small portion of the advisory committee mechanism.

In December 1970, the House Committee on Government Operations issued a report based upon a study of advisory bodies by its Special Studies Subcommittee. Entitled *The Role and Effectiveness of Federal Advisory Committees* (91-2: H.rp. 1731), the study attempted to review the operations and effectiveness of committees advising the government, to assess the possibility of abuse and over-use of the committee device, and to make recommendations for improving the machinery. Findings and recommendations led to EO 11671 in June 1972, which rescinded earlier advisory committee regulations and established a centralized management system. Finally, Congress passed the Federal Advisory Committee Act (PL 92-463) which was approved and signed on October 6, 1972.[3]

The Federal Advisory Committee Act mandates a Committee Management Secretariat within the Office of Management and Budget to review each advisory committee in order to determine whether it is carrying out its purpose, and whether its responsibilities should be revised, merged, or abolished. The President is required to submit an annual report to the Congress on advisory committees. Section 11 of the Act requires that agencies with advisory committees make available to the public copies of transcripts of proceedings of their meetings. Section 13 designates the Library of Congress as a depository for "at least eight copies of each report made by every advisory committee and, where appropriate, background papers prepared by consultants"; these documents "shall be available to public inspection and use."

In 1973 the Senate Committee on Government Operations issued a massive five-part report submitted to the Committee by the Office of Management and Budget as required by Section 6(c) of the Federal Advisory Committee Act. Parts 1 through 4 of the report entitled *Federal Advisory Committees*, contain detailed information on every advisory committee within the executive branch—name, date of and authority for its creation, termination date or reporting date, functions, publications, meeting dates, members (including affiliations and addresses), and the total estimated annual cost of funding and maintaining the committee. Part 5, which was not issued until January 1974, was the index volume, a 995-page listing of the almost 25,000 persons who serve on federal advisory bodies.[4]

Interested parties who want to be apprised of the creation of new federal advisory committees between annual listings may consult the *Federal Register*, which is required to make their establishment a matter of formal record. Moreover, the *Federal Register* must publish "timely notice" of each meeting of an advisory body except those that are closed to the public for reasons of national security.[5]

The 1972 Act appears to provide systematic management and to increase public access to the activities of the government advisory boards. Libraries should attempt to secure the five-volume committee print issued by the Senate Government Operations Committee as well as the annual report, *Federal Advisory Committees, First Annual Report of the President*, which was issued in the "departmental edition" (Pr 37.12; Item 848-C). The latter document, although weakened by lack of an index, contains a list of all advisory committees—arranged alphabetically by title—within the White House, Executive Office of the President, the departments, the independent establishments, and those within selected committees, commissions, and councils.

The importance of securing bibliographic control of and a measure of access to the activities and publications of these committees and commissions cannot be overemphasized. In its report, the House Committee on Government Operations suggested something of their consequence in our governmental structure:

> Advisory groups are present throughout the legislative, executive, and judicial branches of Government and are created to advise either the officer or the agency in the performance of its responsibility, or as a communication aid in coordinating functions. There are, even, committees to advise advisory committees. Their functional use and growth have led to the description, "Government by Committee." The number, scope and use of the advisory committees appear to entitle committees to be termed the "fifth arm of the Federal establishment"—along with the constitutionally created legislative, executive, and judicial arms as the first three branches of Government, and the regulatory boards, possessing administrative, judicial, and executive functions as the fourth arm.[6]

PROVENANCE

In the May 1973 revised *Explanation of the Superintendent of Documents Classification System* (GP 3.2:C 56/8/year; Item 551) the following information is given under the heading *Boards, Commissions, and Committees*:

> Those agencies established by act of Congress or under authority of act of Congress, not specifically designated in the Executive Branch of the Government nor as completely independent agencies, are grouped under one of the agency symbols assigned to Congressional publications—namely, Y 3. This place in the scheme is reserved for all such agencies.

When a President appoints an advisory committee or commission by executive order, the report that eventually issues from that body is properly to be classed in Pr (President of the United States). However, committees listed in the *First Annual Report of the President on Federal Advisory Committees* (Pr 37.12:973) under the heading "Presidential Advisory Committees" have had their publications classed in either Y 3 or Pr; the distinction is a subtle one because executive orders, as we noted in Chapter 7, may be published by a President in virtue of his office or pursuant to legislation.

Accordingly, presidential advisory committees such as the Advisory Council on Historic Preservation (Y 3.H 62), Committee for the Preservation of the White House (Y 3.W 58/10), National Advisory Council on the Oceans and Atmosphere (Y 3.Oc 2), and Joint Commission on the Coinage (Y 3.C 66/1) have issued publications under one class, whereas reports of committees to advise the President such as the Citizen's Advisory Commission on Environmental Quality (Pr 37.8:En 8) and the President's Council on Physical Fitness and Sports (Pr 37.8:P 56/2) have been issued under the Office of the President. Furthermore, as the *First Annual Report* shows, some committees advise a department or agency and also serve as "Presidential Advisory Committees."[7]

BIBLIOGRAPHIC CONTROL

As long as the reports of advisory bodies can be acquired and are indexed properly, punctilios of classification do not greatly matter. Of importance, however, is the inclusion of the popular name—usually taken eponymously from the chairman of the commission—as part of the bibliographic information. The news media use this sobriquet to refer to a report that has gained notoriety and, indeed, studies that are merely newsworthy (rather than controversial) become known by the name of the individual most closely identified with the report. This phenomenon occurs in enacted legislation, where the *United States Code* features a separate index of acts cited by popular names; one can also use the well-known *Shepard's Acts and Cases by Popular Names, Federal and State*. When this important piece of information is absent, problems arise in bibliographic control.

Monthly Catalog

The *Monthly Catalog* has not attempted to index advisory commission studies by popular name. Indexing is accomplished by reference to key word, title, and subject, but consistency has not always reigned supreme.

Andriot

Andriot's *Guide to U.S. Government Publications* includes the name of the commission in its agency index, but not always by key word. Nor is the title index very helpful in this respect. There is no popular name approach.

Gale Research Company

Gale Research is publishing a quarterly entitled *Encyclopedia of Governmental Advisory Organizations*; the first issue was dated July 1973. The subtitle reads *A Reference Guide to Federal Agency, Interagency, and Government-Related Boards, Committees, Councils, Conferences, and Other Similar Units Serving in an Advisory, Consultative, or Investigative Capacity*. Emphasis is on currently active advisory committees, but the *Encyclopedia* also includes some defunct bodies of historical interest.

Anyone familiar with Gale Research Company's *Encyclopedia of Associations* will recognize the arrangement of this work. Information on each committee includes name, address, telephone number, name of the senior staff member, history and authority, a description of the committee's activities, membership and affiliation, names of subcommittees, frequency and location of meetings, and publications and reports. The index affords a keyword title approach.

Popular Name Catalog

The Serial Division of the Library of Congress has issued a publication entitled *Popular Names of U.S. Government Reports: A Catalog* (LC 6.2:G 74/year; Item 818-F). The bibliography, now in its third (1974) edition, first appeared in 1966 and was revised in 1970. Entries are photographic reproductions of Library of Congress printed catalog cards arranged alphabetically by popular name. Some cross-references are included; for example, in the 1970 edition under the heading "Riot Report" the user is referred to "Kerner Report."

The editors of the 1974 edition called upon documents librarians to serve as informers in identifying reports that were overlooked in the earlier editions. It must be emphasized that this is a *selective* bibliography. Reports included in the *Catalog* were published as early as 1821 and each edition since the first has been enlarged as it was revised. However, as long as the *Monthly Catalog* does not index by popular name, there is no one tool that reliably lists *all* reports of advisory bodies with *all* the bibliographic information.[8]

Popular Names is available from the Superintendent of Documents. When the 1970 edition was issued, it sold for $0.55; by April 1974, before the third edition was released, the 1970 edition was priced at $1.10.

SOME COMMISSION STUDIES OF RECENT YEARS

The most controversial report of the 1960s was unquestionably the "Warren Report" on the assassination of John F. Kennedy; it is noted in Chapter 7. Other commission reports that have enjoyed exposure in the media are noted below. All of the following were placed on sale by the Superintendent.

Eisenhower Report

Milton Eisenhower, the brother of the President, headed a National Commission on the Causes and Prevention of Violence, which was created by EO 11412 (33 *Federal Register* 8583). The Commission issued a *Progress Report to President Lyndon B. Johnson* in 1969 (Pr 36.8:V 81/R29/969; Item 851-J). It was indexed in the *Monthly Catalog* under title, subject ("Campus Unrest"), and "President's Commission on. . . ."

Katzenbach Report

Former Attorney General Nicholas de B. Katzenbach chaired a President's Commission on Law Enforcement and Administration of Justice, which was established by EO 11236 (3 *CFR* 329, 1964-65 comp.). In 1967 this Commission issued task force reports including *The Challenge of Crime in a Free Society* (Pr 36.8:L 41/C 86; Item 851-J). The publication was indexed in the *Monthly Catalog* under the subject ("Crime and Criminals"), title, and name of commission.[9]

Kerner Report

Otto Kerner, former governor of Illinois and federal judge who in 1971 was convicted of conspiracy, bribery, perjury, mail fraud, and income tax evasion, chaired the prestigious National Advisory Commission on Civil Disorders, which was formed by EO 11365 (3 *CFR* 674, 1966-70 comp.). It issued its *Report* in 1968 (Pr 36.8:C 49/R 29; Item 851-J). In addition, a number of *Supplemental Studies for the . . . Commission* were conducted independently of the Commission and of one another by research groups at the University of Michigan, Johns Hopkins, and Columbia. The *Report* was indexed in the *Monthly Catalog* under the heading "Civil Disorders" and "Riots" and under the Commission's name.

Lockhart Report

Chairman William B. Lockhart, Dean of the School of Law at the University of Minnesota, headed the Commission on Obscenity and Pornography, which was brought into being by PL 90-100 (84 *Stat.* 1237) in 1967. The Commission's *Report* (Y 3.Ob 7:1/970; Item 1089) did not appear until 1970. When it was issued, the Nixon administration was quick to disassociate itself from the findings of the majority. According to news reports, Vice-President Agnew stated administration sentiment when he promised that "as long as Richard Nixon is President, Main Street is not going to turn into Smut Alley." Also issued under Item 1089 was a nine-volume *Technical Report*; prepared by the Commission's staff, it was neither reviewed nor approved by the full Commission. *Monthly Catalog* indexing included subject ("Obscene Matter") and title of commission.

Rockefeller Report

Impeccable Republican John D. Rockefeller III headed the Commission on Population Growth and the American Future. Created by PL 91-213 (84 *Stat.* 67), the Commission in 1972 issued several Research Reports with individual titles (for example, *Aspects of Population Growth Policy*); the series was classed in Y 3.P 81:9/nos. (Item 1089). Indexing in the *Monthly Catalog* followed the usual subject, title, and name of commission format. The Commission urged the liberalization of state abortion laws, from which the Nixon administration dissented.

Scranton Report

William Scranton, former governor of Pennsylvania, chaired the President's Commission on Campus Unrest, established by EO 11536 (35 *Federal Register* 9911). The *Report* issued in 1970 was classed in Pr 37.8:C 15/R 29 (Item 851-J) and indexed in the *Monthly Catalog* with a "see" reference from the subject, "Campus Unrest" to the title and name of commission. Agnew voiced the administration's reaction to the Commission's recommendations as "pablum for permissiveness."

Shafer Report

Raymond Shafer, another former governor of Pennsylvania, headed a Commission on Marihuana and Drug Abuse. Created by PL 91-513 (84 *Stat.* 1237), the Commission issued a widely heralded study entitled *Marihuana, Signal of Misunderstanding* (Y 3.M 33/2:2 M 33; Item 1089) as well as *Technical Papers* in two volumes. Published in 1972, the study urged the decriminalization of smoking "pot," a position that was rejected by the administration. The *Monthly Catalog* indexed the study under subject, title, and name of commission.

OTHER ADVISORY BODIES

Issues of the *United States Government Manual* include a section entitled "Guide to Selected Boards, Committees and Commissions," which contains brief descriptions of bodies that have enjoyed a degree of permanence. The purpose of each unit is given, with a citation to the statutory or executive authority for creation. What follow are examples of selected advisory committees[10] that have issued publications of interest to libraries.

Table 5

LIST OF SELECTED ADVISORY COMMITTEES

Title	Class Number	Item Number
Advisory Commission on Intergovern-mental Relations	Y 3.Ad 9/8	1049-D
Advisory Council on Historic Preservation	Y 3.H 62	1064-A
American Revolution Bicentennial Administration[11]	Y 3.Am 3/6	non-depository
Board of Foreign Scholarships	Y 3.F 76/4	1063-F
Cabinet Committee on Opportunities for Spanish-Speaking People	Y 3.Sp 2/7	1067-K
Citizens Advisory Committee on Environmental Quality	Pr 37.8:En 8	851-J
Federal Council for Science and Technology	Y 3.F 31/16	1061-B
Federal Library Committee[12]	LC 1.32	non-depository
Interdepartmental Committee on the Status of Women	Y 3.In 8/21	1067-I
National Advisory Council on Inter-national Monetary and Financial Policies	Y 3.N 21/16	non-depository
National Council on Indian Opportunity	Y 3.In 2/9	non-depository
United States Advisory Commission on Information	Y 3.Ad 9/7	1049-B
United States Advisory Commission on International Educational and Cultural Affairs[13]	Y 3.Ad 9/9	1049-F
Water Resources Council	Y 3.W 29	1090

This list represents but a few of the advisory groups. Other bodies that advise departments or that are interagency in nature are found in other sections of the *Manual*. For example, the National Industrial Pollution Control Council, an advisory board to the Commerce Department, is listed in the *Manual* as a "Constituent Operating Unit" under Commerce. In the *First Annual Report of the President* all the sub-councils are mentioned by name.

SUMMARY

The accountability of advisory bodies to the Congress and public seems to be reasonably assured under the provisions of PL 92-463 (86 *Stat.* 770). The Congress must determine, before considering the creation of an advisory commission, whether that body will perform a necessary function not already being rendered by an existing board. The President must make an annual report to the Congress on the activities, status, and changes in the composition of advisory bodies in existence during the preceding calendar year. Each agency must maintain systematic information on the nature, functions, and operations of every advisory committee within its jurisdiction. Newly created advisory councils must furnish a copy of their charter to the Library of Congress. Committee meetings must be open to the public, except when national security is involved; notices of meetings are to be published in the *Federal Register*. Moreover, advisory groups are required to make available to the public copies of transcripts of their proceedings, at the actual cost of duplication.

In 1970 no one in government knew exactly how many advisory bodies were in existence. The House Committee on Government Operations had to determine the number of committees by means of a detailed questionnaire and numerous personal interviews. Consequently, the investigators discovered many "inactive, meaningless, obsolete, and redundant" committees. Section 14 of PL 92-463 establishes systematic procedures for the termination of committees after their usefulness has ended.

REFERENCES

1.   *Federal Advisory Committees, First Annual Report of the President* (Washington: U.S. Govt. Print. Off., 1973), p. 2.

2.   An interesting account of the frustrations of working on special presidential commissions to study major national problems is given by William Chapman in *The Washington Post*, August 29, 1973, p. A2.

3.   EO 11671 was an interim executive order designed to create the administrative machinery in anticipation of the new act. Accordingly, when the President signed PL 92-463 into law, he revoked EO 11671 and issued EO 11686 (October 7, 1972), directing compliance with the provisions of the act by all executive agencies.

4.   Issued as a committee print with the same title as the annual report (reference 1 above), Parts 1 through 4 were dated May 2, 1973. The volumes (Y 4.G 74/6:Ad 9/4/973/pts.) were abstracted in *CIS/Index*, July 1973, which

did not indicate that they were available on deposit but did indicate a sales price through SUDOCS.

5. This and other provisions of the act are discussed in a usefully explicative manner in the *Congressional Record* (daily edition), July 16, 1973, S 13566-69.

6. 91-2: H.rp. 1731, p. 5.

7. For example, one finds the President's Committee on Mental Retardation listed on page 1 under "Presidential Advisory Committees" and on page 41 as a committee to advise HEW. The summary tables on pages 4-6 of the *Annual Report* indicate that certain so-called presidential advisory committees are assigned to the appropriate federal agency for jurisdiction.

8. The Government Publications Division of the University of Minnesota Libraries issued in 1973 *A Bibliography of Presidential Commissions, Committees, Councils, Panels, and Task Forces, 1961-1972* (A. M. Tollefson and H. C. Chang, eds.), which sold for $1.50. Selective in scope, the bibliography lists 243 publications alphabetically by main entry, with indexes for personal name, title, and subject-keyword. Bibliographic data include SUDOCS class number.

9. Other titles issued by the Katzenbach Commission include *The Courts* (Pr 36.8: L 41/C 83), *Juvenile Delinquency and Youth Crime* (Pr 36.8:L 41/J 98), *The Police* (Pr 36.8: L 41/P 75), and *Narcotics and Drug Abuse* (Pr 36.8: L 41/N 16).

10. As cited in the 1973/74 edition of the *U.S. Government Manual*.

11. The Administration issues a monthly called *Bicentennial Times* (Y 3.Am 3/6:10); the periodical is available from the issuing unit.

12. The Committee issues *FLC Newsletter* (LC 1.32:nos.) irregularly; it includes a library vacancy roster and a roster of prospective federal librarians. This Committee is not to be confused with the more recently created National Commission on Libraries and Information Science (84 *Stat.* 440).

13. This advisory body issues a quarterly, *International Educational and Cultural Exchange* (Y 3.Ad 9/9:9), which is sold by SUDOCS.

11

PUBLICATIONS OF THE JUDICIARY

The result of these observations to an intelligent mind must be clearly this, that if it be possible at any rate to construct a federal government capable of regulating the common concerns and preserving the general tranquillity, it must be founded, as to the objects committed to its care, upon the reverse of the principle contended for by the opponents of the proposed Constitution. It must carry its agency to the persons of the citizens. It must stand in need of no intermediate legislations; but must itself be empowered to employ the arm of the ordinary magistrate to execute its own resolutions. The majesty of the national authority must be manifested through the medium of the courts of justice.

—*The Federalist*, XVI (Hamilton)

Regarding the due administration of Justice as the strongest cement of good government, I have considered the first organization of the Judicial Department as essential to the happiness of our Citizens, and to the stability of our political system. Under this impression it has been an invariable object of anxious solicitude with me to select the fittest Characters to expound the laws and dispense justice.

—George Washington, *Letter to John Rutledge*,
September 29, 1789

INTRODUCTION

The judicial branch of the federal establishment forms a pyramid. At the bottom of the pyramid stand the United States District Courts. On the next level stand the United States Courts of Appeals. At the pyramid's apex stands the Supreme Court, the highest tribunal in the land. Because our government is a dual one—federal and state—the powers of the United States courts are limited in that they can exercise only that authority granted by the Constitution. They are also limited in judicial function in that they cannot exercise authority belonging to the legislative or executive branches of the government.

State judicial systems have general, unlimited power to decide almost every type of case, subject only to the limitations of state law. They are comprised of a state supreme court, or state court of appeals, and a group of lower bodies, such as municipal, police, and justice-of-the-peace courts. These are the tribunals with which citizens most often have contact. The great bulk of legal business concerning divorce, the probate of estates, and all other matters except those assigned to the United States courts, is handled by state courts.[1]

The independence of the judicial branch is assured by the Constitution, even though federal judges are appointed by the President with the advice and consent of the Senate. Under the Constitution federal courts can be called upon to perform only judicial work, the application and interpretation of the law in the decision of real differences: that is, in the language of the Constitution, the decision of "Cases" and "Controversies." The courts cannot be called upon to make laws, which is the function of the legislative branch, nor to enforce and execute laws, the function of the executive. Federal judges hold their positions "during good behavior" and can be removed from office against their will only by impeachment. Independence is further insured by compensation that "shall not be diminished" during a judge's tenure in office; neither the President nor the Congress can reduce the salary of a federal magistrate.

Provision for a federal judiciary was stated with utmost simplicity in Article III, Section 1 of the Constitution: "The judicial Power of the United States shall be vested in one supreme Court, and in such inferior Courts as the Congress may from time to time ordain and establish." In accordance with this constitutional provision and by authority of the Judiciary Act of September 24, 1789, a Supreme Court, three circuit courts, and thirteen district courts were created. In 1974 there were eleven circuit courts of appeals, 97 district courts, and four territorial courts (Canal Zone, Guam, Puerto Rico, and Virgin Islands). The "Cases" and "Controversies" that can be decided in these courts are set forth in Article III, Section 2 of the Constitution.

Although independence and the concommitant ideal of integrity theoretically characterize the base of the federal judiciary, selection is largely a political process. Tradition has awarded to Senators of the President's party the prerogative of naming persons for federal judgeships within their states. If the Senators are not of the President's party, the White House looks to its party organization within that state for suggested nominees.

Judicial appointment is a powerful patronage lever for an incumbent President. Two sections of the Constitution govern appointment. Article II, Section 2 empowers a President to nominate, with the advice and consent of the

Senate, "judges of the Supreme Court, and all other officers of the United States"; and Article II, Section 3 provides that a President "shall commission all the Officers of the United States." From these constitutional provisions evolved the stages in the selection process: nomination, appointment, commission.

Nomination involves considering many factors, not the least of them being political compatibility; but advice is also proffered by national, state, and local bar associations. Appointment is often a highly political act, involving as it does the consent of the Senate. Commission is a technicality in which the President gives the appointee the authority to carry out the duties of his office. In the selection of men and women to serve as judges and justices, ideological considerations loom significant if not paramount.[2]

In addition to the jurisdiction exercised as constitutional courts under Article III of the Constitution, the Court of Appeals and the District Court in the District of Columbia have, in the past, exercised jurisdiction with respect to local matters normally exercised by state courts. This jurisdiction was conferred upon these courts by the Congress in the exercise of the exclusive sovereignty over the District of Columbia delegated to it under Article I, Section 8 of the Constitution. However, pursuant to 84 *Stat.* 473, local jurisdiction is being transferred to the Superior Court and the D.C. Court of Appeals.[3]

Congress has from time to time created special courts to deal with particular kinds of cases. The Court of Claims, for example, is a constitutional court and has nationwide jurisdiction. It renders judgment upon any claim against the United States founded upon the Constitution, upon any act of Congress, and upon any regulation of an executive department. Other special courts include the Court of Customs and Patent Appeals, Customs Court, Tax Court, and Court of Military Appeals. Moreover, as was noted in Chapter 9, a number of administrative agencies hear and decide cases; they exercise quasi-judicial power even though they rank as neither constitutional nor legislative courts.

A few important decisions of the district courts may be appealed directly to the Supreme Court, but the appellate process generally rises hierarchically from district court to court of appeals and then to the final tier of the tri-level pyramid, if the Supreme Court has jurisdiction. The courts of appeals review decisions of the district courts within their circuit and also some of the actions of the independent regulatory agencies. One Supreme Court justice is assigned to each circuit, but his duties as circuit justice are nominal.

Lower court judges are required to follow the precedents established by the Supreme Court, but the system is not a monolithic unit in which, like the military chain of command, orders flow from the top. District and circuit judges have wide latitude in determining the lineaments of Supreme Court decisions. Those at the lower levels often take a different point of view toward legal disputes than do the members of the high court. And, since few of the thousands of cases reach the Supreme Court, the magistrates of the lower federal courts are important policy-makers. The federal judiciary, like the executive and legislative branches, reflects in its judgments the shifting and variegated interests of the body politic.

REFERENCE AND RESEARCH AIDS

The scope of legal reference and bibliography is vast and complex. Indeed, as Cohen points out, "Legal sources have been more fully described and cataloged than perhaps any other literature. The bibliographic approaches of legal research are the most highly developed and sophisticated in pre-computer documentation."[4] Because mastery of these sources requires some familiarity with the law, special training is usually needed for law librarianship. The account that follows is intended merely to introduce the reader to some of the salient secondary materials supportive of federal case law. The nature of materials in this area is such that a host of commercial publications surround and amplify a relatively small number of official government documents.

Basic Texts

For the beginner, Morris L. Cohen's *Legal Research in a Nutshell* (St. Paul, Minnesota: West Publishing Co., 1971) affords a concise though limited introduction to legal bibliography. As the author notes in his "Preface," the narrative "for best effect should be followed by some form of bibliographic exposure in a library setting."

Perhaps the best text in the field is Miles O. Price and Harry Bitner's *Effective Legal Research* (3d ed.; Boston: Little, Brown, 1969). Consisting of 26 chapters and containing many specimen pages, it covers thoroughly the basic legal sources and will answer most questions in a general library situation. Other texts include Ervin Pollack's *Fundamentals of Legal Research* (3d ed.; Mineola, New York: Foundation Press, 1967) and William Roalfe's *How to Find the Law* (6th ed.; St. Paul, Minnesota: West Publishing Co., 1965). Beyond these basic sources, there are numerous specialized casebooks and textbooks on the many subdisciplines within the law.[5]

Encyclopedias

Two general legal encyclopedias dominate the field and provide topical coverage of the law in narrative form; they are *American Jurisprudence Second* (Am. Jur. 2d) and *Corpus Juris Secundum* (C.J.S.). The former is published by Lawyers Co-operative Publishing Company, the latter is issued by West Publishing Company. As will become evident, these two publishers are responsible for producing most of the tools of legal bibliography.

Both encyclopedias are multi-volume works arranged alphabetically by topic with a general index to supplement the index in each volume. Both have scope notes and definitions and are supplemented annually by pocket parts. Each cites decisions found in its own sister publications. Neither encyclopedia has a table of cases.

Legal scholars warn that encyclopedias are "often slow to reflect subtle changes in the law" and "lack the careful analysis and fine distinctions of a good treatise." Nevertheless, they are useful as a starting point in a legal search and, although not binding on courts, are sometimes cited in judicial opinions.[6]

Dictionaries

Unfortunately, the renowned Bouvier's *Law Dictionary and Concise Encyclopedia* (Kansas City, Mo.: Vernon Law Book Company, 1914) is dated. *Black's Law Dictionary* (West Publishing Co., 1968) is as satisfactory as any of the standard legal dictionaries. It includes legal terms and words as defined by the courts in actual cases, citations to court decisions supporting the definitions, legal maxims, and a guide to legal abbreviations. West Publishing Company also issues a multi-volume *Words and Phrases* covering definitions used in reported cases from earliest times to the present. The terms are arranged alphabetically with a table of contents for each word or phrase and cross references to related terms; the work is kept current by annual pocket supplements. Most legal dictionaries and encyclopedias define maxims, and, of course, the dictionary function of legal encyclopedias must not be overlooked.

Directories

The superior entry in this form is the annual, five-volume *Martindale-Hubbell Law Directory* (Summit, N.J.: Martindale-Hubbell, Inc.). Subdivided by states, it lists the names of attorneys and firms alphabetically by city and town. *Martindale-Hubbell* contains a section on federal law that includes digests of United States copyright, patent, tax, and trademark law. The directory also includes a list of key personnel, jurisdiction, terms and calendars of federal, District of Columbia, Canal Zone, and state courts.

Digests

Because judicial decisions are published in chronological order, a digest is necessary as a guide to legal precedent. The several digests are not to be used in lieu of the case itself, for they lack primary authority. But they are of significant utility as subject approaches to case law. As such, their value may be compared to the *Digest of Public General Bills and Resolutions*, an abstracting-indexing service for legislation. Cohen's definition of these case-finding aids is clear and succinct:

> A digest to judicial decisions superimposes a subject classification upon chronologically published cases. The classification consists of an alphabetically arranged scheme of legal topics and subtopics which can be approached through a detailed index. Brief abstracts of the points of law in decided cases are classified by subject and set out in the digests under appropriate topical headings. They are then located and retrieved by the researcher through the index to the digest.[7]

One distinctive feature of digests is the absence of editorial comment or synthesis of rules relating disparate cases to jurisdiction or historical development. "The digest thus leaves to the reader the task of determining for himself for each statement its present place within the hierarchy of decisions on the point, and its applicability to his own specific problem. This presupposes possession by him of all the skills and techniques necessary for the digest's proper use; that is why the digest is peculiarly the lawyer's tool."[8]

West Publishing Company's American Digest System is the most comprehensive of case digests for this country. It consists of the *Century Edition* and the several *Decennial Digests*, and purports to cover all standard law reports of the appellate decisions handed down in the United States.

The *Century Edition of the American Digest* is subtitled *A Complete Digest of All Reported American Cases from the Earliest Times to 1896* and includes cases from 1658. It was issued in 50 volumes, the final volume of which was a *Descriptive-Word Index*. The *First Decennial Digest*, subtitled *A Complete Digest of All Reported Cases from 1897 to 1906*, appeared in 20 volumes with a five-volume *Table of Cases* covering both it and the *Century Edition*. A *Second Decennial Digest* (1907-1916) has been followed by others covering ten-year periods, the *Seventh* (1956-1966) being currently updated by bound volumes and monthly pamphlet issues of the *General Digest, Fourth Series*.

In 1924 West published in one volume a *Descriptive-Word Index* to the first and second *Decennial Digests* as "a means of finding the authorities in point through the words descriptive of the legal principles or of the facts in the case"; in 1940 the publisher issued in two volumes a *Descriptive-Word Index* covering the third and fourth *Decennial Digests*.

Thus the American Digest System is the master index to United States case law. The digest paragraphs are arranged by subject under West's Key Number classification, and under each Key Number the paragraphs are arranged by jurisdiction and further by date of decision. Accordingly, United States Supreme Court cases appear first, followed by courts of appeals cases, federal district courts, and state court cases in descending order of court rank. A variety of tables and indexes follows the voluminous digests and provides the several access approaches to the abstracts.[9]

Although virtually all reported cases are covered in the American Digest System, West Publishing Company issues digests covering federal courts, in order to save time for the researcher interested only in federal cases.

Federal Digest, 1754-1938 brings together under one standard classification digests of all federal constitutional and legislative courts of record. Volume 1 of this *Digest* is a complete *Descriptive-Word Index* listing alphabetically thousands of cross-references or descriptive words, many of which are peculiar to federal practice. References point to the Digest Topic and Key Number where the material has been digested. Volumes 66 through 68 provide a list of all cases by name of plaintiff, showing the title of the case, the Digest Topic and Key Number under which each point is digested, and the volume and page of the standard sets of reports where each case is reported. Moreover, there is a defendant-plaintiff table arrangement, a complete numerical listing of patents adjudicated by the courts covered by this *Digest*, a table of trade marks and trade names, a tabulation of cases construing federal court rules, a popular name table, and a section on words and phrases judicially defined.

Modern Federal Practice Digest continues the coverage of *Federal Digest* for cases after 1938. Supplementation is quarterly with annual pocket parts. Tables and indexes follow the pattern of the predecessor *Digest* above. Federal practice was changed so radically "because of the federal rules governing district courts in civil and criminal matters promulgated in 1938 . . . that the publishers . . . felt that there should be a clean break between the older digested cases and the newer ones, and consequently inaugurated the publication of the *Modern Federal Practice Digest*."[10]

Digests of special courts include West's *Court of Claims Digest* and a *Tax Court Digest* issued commercially by Bobbs-Merrill (Indianapolis, Indiana: 1952 to date). Although Supreme Court cases are digested both in the American Digest System and in *Federal Digest* and *Modern Federal Practice Digest*, the high court enjoys two digests for its cases alone. *United States Supreme Court Digest* is a standard West Key Number digest that has the several features of such digests. Lawyers Co-operative Publishing Company (Rochester, N.Y.) also issues a *Digest of United States Supreme Court Reports, Lawyers' Edition*. It is a typical case digest, but it contains some distinctive features; it is generally considered excellent by the legal community.

The *Lawyers' Edition* purports to offer something more than the conventional digest. The publishers call their technique an "annotated" digest, by which they mean that certain features in the body of the digest amplify and explain the digest paragraphs in the light of other decisions, and that the collateral references go far beyond the classification of the material itself.

The features include scope notes, which define the precise scope of the topic with respect to what is covered and what is considered elsewhere in the *Digest*. References to annotations include those in the *United States Supreme Court Reports, Lawyers' Edition* (L.Ed.) and in the *American Law Reports* (A.L.R.). If either the L.Ed. or A.L.R. annotation is appended to a Supreme Court case, this fact is noted as part of the citation of the case on the appropriate digest paragraphs. Cross references are internal and external, the former referencing collateral material under the same topic, the latter referencing related material on a different topic. Case annotations afford the researcher an automatic check on the reliability of the case as authority. Whenever a point contained in a paragraph has been expressly overruled, distinguished, limited, or questioned by the Supreme Court in any of its decisions, that fact is noted in small type under the paragraph at the place where it appears in the *Digest*. Moreover, the precise holding of the later case is given, enabling the user to determine its exact relationship to the principal case.

Auxiliary aids to research in the *Lawyers' Edition* include a table of cases digested; every Supreme Court decision, whether by full opinion or memorandum only, is listed in every way by which the case may be known. There is a table of statutes cited and construed, a table by popular name, rules of the various federal courts, text of the Constitution, a Word Index to all *Digest* material, and an index to annotations in a separate volume. Annual pocket-part supplements are used to keep the *Digest* current.[11]

Citators

Because the law is a dynamic process, the lawyer must know what cases or acts are valid and may properly be cited as authority. Case citators provide a record for tracing the judicial history of a case, establishing whether it is still effective law, and finding later cases that have cited the principal case. In addition, the citator process permits one to develop research leads to periodical articles, opinions of the Attorney General, law review comments, and annotated reports system comments on cases.

The most complete and well-known citator system is Shepard's Citations. Indeed, the word "Shepardizing" is used in legal parlance to describe the operations in determining the applicability of statutes and cases as authority. Shepard's Citations cover all federal statutes and cases, labor law, administrative decisions, District of Columbia reports and statutes, regional and state law.

Supreme Court coverage is found in Shepard's *United States Citations* (Colorado Springs, Colo.: Shepard's Citations, Inc.). The work is divided into two parts, the Case Edition and the Statute Edition.

Case Edition

Citations shown are found for opinions reported in 1) *United States Reports* (Ju 6.8; Item 741), the official GPO edition; 2) West Publishing Company's *The Supreme Court Reporter*; and 3) *United States Supreme Court Reports, Lawyers' Edition*, published by Lawyers Co-operative Publishing Company. Both official and unofficial reports are citable in courts. To save space, Shepardizing information is given under the official *United States Reports*, with parenthetical reference to the case in the *Supreme Court Reporter* and *Lawyers' Edition*.

Statute Edition

Shepardizing legislation is complicated because, as noted in Chapter 6, session laws published chronologically in the *Statutes at Large* and statutes in force published in topical order in the *United States Code* are both official sources, although usually only one of these forms is the authoritative text. Moreover, the U.S. Constitution is amended, codes are amended and repealed and at intervals revised, and there are jurisdictional problems of statutory coverage in our federal system. Accordingly, the process involves tracing subsequent action on a given law and subsequent judicial action construing the legislation.

The Statute Edition of *United States Citations* includes citations to the Constitution, the *United States Code*, official edition (Y 4.J 89/1:Un 3/3; Item 991), the *United States Code Annotated* (West Publishing Co.), the *Federal Code Annotated* and *United States Code Service* (Lawyers Co-operative Publishing Co.), *U.S. Statutes at Large* (GS 4.111; Item 576),[12] *U.S. Treaties and Other International Agreements* (S 9.12; Item 899-A), and various rules of court.

United States Citations appears in an "Advance Sheet Edition" with two parts—"Cases" and "Statutes and Court Rules." Cumulative supplements are issued quarterly. Because each issue of the cumulative supplement shows all citations since the publication date of the last bound volume, only one paper supplement need be retained. From time to time, a cumulative supplement is permanently bound.

Federal reporter citations cover the courts of appeals and the district courts, except local rules for district courts, which are covered in the Statute Edition of *United States Citations*. Court rules include rules of the Supreme Court, Courts of Appeals, Court of Claims, Court of Customs and Patent Appeals, and Tax Court. Shepard's *Federal Circuit Table* identifies the circuit or district of any reference shown in any edition of Shepard's Citations by volume and page of *Federal Reporter* or *Federal Supplement* since 1960. A bound volume of this service covers the years 1960-1971 and is updated by a paperbound annual volume.[13]

Annotations

Annotated reports comprise a selective system in which a relatively small number of cases of widespread, seminal interest are remarked upon with an editorial discussion of the law of that case. Annotated cases offer a gloss for the development and impact of a case upon the law. The annotation system often provides faster access to significant cases than do digests, which are inclusive rather than selective.[14]

American Law Reports Annotated (A.L.R.), a service of Lawyers Co-operative Publishing Company, is the only current system in this approach to case reporting. Earlier competing annotation services were merged in 1918 to form *American Law Reports Annotated, First Series*. Now in its *Third Series*, A.L.R. is classified in the Digest Service to digest topics and sections, and is fully indexed in the complete *Word Index*. Annotations vary from a one-page to a 300-page treatment of a case. *Second* and *Third Series* annotations are updated by a *Later Case Service* series; these should be examined for reference to additional cases in point reported since the publication of the annotation, and for further development in the text of the annotation, either within its original framework or by the addition of new sections.

The *Word Index* is designed as a quick reference tool to lead the user to all the points of law discussed in the annotations. Arrangement is by key words descriptive of the topics involved. Entries will also be found for well-known legal titles, rules, or doctrines, such as Evidence, Limitations of Actions, etc.

The editorial selection for A.L.R. includes all American jurisdictions, but very few Supreme Court cases are annotated. For high court cases, one should consult the annotations provided in the *United States Supreme Court Reports, Lawyers' Edition*, as noted above.

Periodical Indexes

The Wilson Company's *Index to Legal Periodicals* indexes articles under subject and author. Coverage includes legal periodicals published in the United States, Canada, Great Britain, Australia, and New Zealand. Annual surveys of the law of a jurisdiction or a court are indexed under the name of the jurisdiction. *Index to Legal Periodicals* also includes a Table of Cases alphabetically by name of plaintiff; case notes of insufficient length to be indexed as articles are cited at the end of each subject under the subheading "Cases." The Book Review Section lists reviews under the name of the author, or under the title of the work if the author is unknown. Published monthly except September, *Index to Legal Periodicals* cumulates annually and triennially.

A *Current Index to Legal Periodicals* is issued jointly by the University of Washington (Seattle) Law Library and the Washington Law Review on a weekly basis. Articles indexed are arranged in a broad subject format—e.g., Bankruptcy, Civil Rights, Contracts, etc. The service is mimeographed and supplements material found in *Index to Legal Periodicals*.[15]

Some legal periodicals can be Shepardized. Shepard's *Law Review Citations*, which began in 1968, shows where articles in legal periodicals have been cited in other law review articles or court decisions. Over 140 law reviews and legal periodicals are covered. *Law Review Citations* permits the user to locate articles written since 1947 that have been cited either in later articles from 1957 to the present, or in state or federal decisions.

The 1968 bound volume of *Law Review Citations* is updated by paperbound cumulative supplements, a standard feature of Shepard's. The law reviews and legal periodicals to which citations are shown are arranged in alphabetical order; in most instances citations to a particular law review or periodical may be located by reference to the name of the publication, which appears at the top of each page of citations. When the desired citations have been obtained, the user can track down the relevant citations in the appropriate Shepard publications that cover the jurisdictions in which the citations occurred. Jurisdictions include law reviews and legal periodicals as cited by the United States Supreme Court in cases reported in the official and unofficial series, by the lower federal courts in any case reported in *Federal Reporter, Second Series*, *Federal Supplement*, or *Federal Rules Decisions*, and by state courts in any case reported in any series of state reports or any unit of West's National Reporter System.

FEDERAL COURT REPORTS

The magisterial bibliographic apparatus created and maintained by commercial publishers like West and Lawyers Co-operative is necessary in large measure because of the doctrine of *stare decisis*, which holds that principles of law established by judicial decision be accepted as authoritative in cases similar to those from which such principles were derived.[16]

From this principle, it follows that an attorney must have access to the latest cases in order to advise his client correctly. Case law is geared to speed; prompt reporting—not only of the opinions and decisions of courts but of the indexes and other finding aids—is crucial to effective legal deliberation.

Decisions relied upon as precedent are usually those of appellate courts. Consequently, availability of published decisions and opinions increases in ascending order of the federal court hierarchy. Whereas only selected decisions of district courts are readily available to those with a need to know, almost all written and *per curiam* (literally, "by the court") decisions of the appellate courts, special courts, and Supreme Court are reported either officially or unofficially. Nevertheless, total bibliographic control does not exist; Price and Bitner state that "not all decisions of any federal court, even of the Supreme Court, are reported."[17]

District and Appellate Courts

During most of the nineteenth century, decisions of United States District Courts and U.S. Circuit Courts of Appeals were published in a number of separate series cited by the names of their official reporters. This "nominative" reporting, which caused bibliographic confusion, was rectified by the publication of a thirty-volume series known as *Federal Cases* (West Publishing Co.); the series was arranged by title and arbitrary case number, with a table translating the nominative report series to *Federal Cases* notation. The new series incorporated selected lower court decisions of importance from 1789 to 1880.

For the years 1880 to the present three units of West's National Reporter System are consulted for the reports of the lower federal courts.

Federal Reporter

From 1880 through 1931, West's *Federal Reporter* covered district court and Circuit Court of Appeals cases, as well as selected cases, primarily on tax matters, of the U.S. Court of Claims.

Federal Supplement

This West venture covers the district courts beginning with the October Term, 1932. At this time the *Federal Reporter* ceased its district courts coverage and reported only cases of the intermediate courts of appeals, including the special courts. From October 1932 to March 1960 *Federal Supplement* reported Court of Claims cases; because its hierarchical status changed, they are once more reported in the *Federal Reporter* as of 1960.

Federal Rules Decisions

Another West publication, *Federal Rules Decisions*, began publication in 1940 and covers selectively decisions of the lower courts—primarily at the district court level—relating to civil and criminal procedural matters. The series also includes speeches and articles dealing with federal practice. Rules are annotated to the cases published in all standard report series.[18]

Special Courts

As noted, the so-called special courts occupy the second tier of the federal court hierarchy; they have been created by the Congress to deal with particular types of cases, and their decisions may be appealed to the Supreme Court. Although some reports of special courts are published in the West system, decisions of the bodies are also issued in the official edition.

Court of Claims

Decisions of the Court of Claims, including abstracts of the decisions of the Supreme Court in Court of Claims cases, are issued in *Cases Decided in the Court of Claims of the United States* (Ju 3.9; Item 730). Other Court of Claims publications received by depository libraries include *Rules* (Ju 3.10; Item 732), *Regulations and Instructions* (Ju 3.10/3; Item 731-B), and the Handbooks, Manuals and Guides series (Ju 3.10/4; Item 731-B).

Court of Customs and Patent Appeals

Volumes 1 through 6 of this series were issued by the Court of Customs Appeals. In 1929 the name of this court was changed to its present designation, and beginning with Volume 17 reports have been issued in two separate parts, one called *Customs Cases Adjudged*, the other titled *Patent Cases Adjudged* (both of these are Ju 7.5; Item 733).

Customs Court

Whereas the above court decides certain questions arising under the customs laws and reviews certain patent and trademark cases, the Customs Court has exclusive jurisdiction over civil actions arising under the tariff laws. United States Customs Court Reports (Ju 9.5; Item 736) are issued semi-annually under the title *Cases Adjudged in the United States Customs Court*. A weekly *Customs Bulletin* (T 1.11/3), issued by the Customs Bureau of the Treasury Department, contains regulations, rulings, decisions, and notices concerning customs and related matters, and decisions of the Court of Customs and Patent Appeals and of the Customs Court.

Tax Court

Considered a "quasi-judicial tribunal" rather than a "true court," the Tax Court tries and adjudicates controversies involving deficiencies or overpayments in income, estate, gift, and personal holding company surtaxes in cases where irregularities have been determined by the Commissioner of Internal Revenue. *Tax Court of the United States Reports* (Ju 11.7/a2) are issued monthly in consolidated pamphlets; the final issue of each volume includes a Table of Cases reported in the volume. The bound volumes, called *Reports of the Tax Court* (Ju 11.7; Item 742), are issued semi-annually. To complement the official reports, Commerce Clearing House (CCH) of Chicago publishes *Tax Court Reporter*, which consists of memorandum decisions of the Tax Court reported on a current basis. CCH then issues *Tax Court Memorandum Decisions* annually, in which the full texts of all decisions of the Court on the subject of federal taxation are presented in permanent bound volumes.

Court of Military Appeals

Another "quasi-judicial tribunal," the Court of Military Appeals is located administratively in the Department of Defense and is the final appellate tribunal in court-martial convictions. Although assigned a SUDOCS class number (D 1.29), *Court-Martial Reports, Holdings and Decisions of the Judge Advocates General, Boards of Review, and United States Court of Military Appeals* is published annually by Lawyers Co-operative Publishing Company.

THE SUPREME COURT

Background

Article III, Section 2 of the Constitution sets forth the areas of original and appellate jurisdiction of the Supreme Court. While the Congress has no authority to change or amend the original jurisdiction of this Court, appellate jurisdiction has been conferred by various statutes under the authority given Congress by the Constitution. Furthermore, Congress has from time to time conferred upon the Supreme Court power to prescribe rules of procedure to be followed by the lower courts of the United States. Pursuant to these statutes are rules governing civil and criminal cases in the district courts, bankruptcy proceedings, admiralty and copyright cases, appellate proceedings, and minor criminal offense proceedings before United States magistrates.

After the appointment of John Jay as the first Chief Justice, the Supreme Court opened its first session at New York on February 2, 1790. The judges wore gowns of black and scarlet, but honored Jefferson's appeal to "discard the monstrous wig which makes the English judges look like rats peeping through bunches of oakum."[19] Today the Supreme Court comprises the Chief Justice and "such number of Associate Justices as may be fixed by Congress." Under that authority and by virtue of the act of June 25, 1948 (62 *Stat.* 869), the number of associate justices is eight. Nominated by the President and appointed by and with the advice and consent of the Senate, justices serve life terms.

Curiously, there are no specific qualifications for the office of Supreme Court justice. However, the Senate's role in the process of advisement and consent is designed to insure that only the highly qualified attain the position. Indeed, from 1789 to 1973, twenty-seven Supreme Court nominations failed to receive Senate confirmation. Although most justices have retired in advanced age and several have died in office, some have resigned to accept other positions or have quit for other reasons. Abe Fortas was the first justice to resign, in 1969, under charges of extra-judicial misconduct. Samuel Chase was the only Supreme Court justice to be impeached. In 1804 the House of Representatives charged him with "harsh and partisan conduct on the bench and with unfairness to litigants"; however, he was acquitted by the Senate.[20]

Popular civics holds that the Supreme Court is an ultimate court of appeals for all, a bulwark of freedom to which every citizen can press his claim under federal law or the Constitution. That concept has long since ceased to be a physical possibility. In addition to the jurisdictional limitations prescribed by the Constitution, the high court over the years has been further restricted in its range of judicial authority by the Congress. Yet the number of cases has grown. In 1945 the docket showed 1,448 cases; in 1971 the Court heard 4,533 cases, an increase which some justices found alarming. A committee appointed by the Chief Justice in 1972 to review the workload recommended the creation of a National Court of Appeals, whose chief function would involve the preliminary winnowing of cases for Supreme Court review. The suggestion aroused considerable opposition from judges, lawyers, and a few justices themselves, on the grounds that the rights of litigants to appeal to the Court would be severely abridged.[21]

With its power of judicial review—the authority of the Court to strike down acts it deems unconstitutional—the decisions of this tribunal are both legally and politically of momentous consequence. Lawyers are accustomed to say that the truth is in the Supreme Court record; that is, it is not unusual for the passage of time to show that some dissenting justice saw the case more clearly than did the majority. Justice Jackson's epigram voices precisely the Court's power and influence in the structure of the federal establishment: "We are not final because we are infallible, but we are infallible because we are final."[22]

Services

United States Law Week

A weekly looseleaf service published by the Bureau of National Affairs (Washington, D.C.), *United States Law Week*'s section on the Supreme Court contains a number of useful features. There are articles summarizing the opinions and work of the Supreme Court during its recent term, a list of cases filed on the appellate docket of the Supreme Court for the preceding week, a summary of cases recently docketed arranged by subject matter referencing the docket number, and other features including arguments before the Court, a summary of orders, hearings scheduled, and cases awaiting decision. The valuable subject, case, and docket number indexes cumulate irregularly during the term with a final cumulated issue at the end of the term.

Journal [of the Supreme Court of the United States] (Ju 6.5)

Issued daily when the Court is in session, the official *Journal* reports the proceedings of the Court; the text of the decisions and orders is presented, but not the opinions. Lacking an index, the *Journal* is, fortunately, reprinted in *United States Law Week*.

United States Supreme Court Bulletin

Another useful Commerce Clearing House looseleaf service, the *Bulletin* contains facsimile reprints of decisions and orders, a statement of official Court actions for the preceding week, Court rules, a Table of Cases on the docket, and highlights of recently docketed cases including cases awaiting decision.

Case Reporting

Slip Opinions

As the individual opinions are announced, the official *Slip Opinions* are issued by the government (Ju 6.8/b; Item 740-A) and sold through the Superintendent of Documents. Where it is feasible, a syllabus (headnote) precedes the body of the slip opinion. The text includes the docket number, title, how it came to the Court (e.g., on Writ of Certiorari, etc.), date of decision, and the text of the opinion and of the decision. *Slip Opinions* are subject to formal revision before publication in "preliminary print" form. Facsimile editions of the slip opinions are published in both *United States Law Week* and the *United States Supreme Court Bulletin*, described above.

Preliminary Prints

The official edition in its next form is called *Official Reports of the Supreme Court: Preliminary Print* (Ju 6.8/a). Issued in paperbound form irregularly, each part combines a number of slip opinions; headnotes are always supplied and the pagination of the *Prints* is the same as that which will appear in the bound volumes, thereby making early citations possible. However, the *Prints* are still subject to revision; users are requested to notify the Reporter of

Decisions of any typographical or other formal errors, in order that corrections may be made before the bound volume goes to press. In the unofficial editions, *Prints* are usually known as *Advance Sheets* and are issued by Lawyers Co-operative and West. In all editions, access to the opinions is through a subject index and Table of Cases reported. The commercial editions are, of course, classed and keyed to their respective sister publications.

United States Reports

The full title of the final bound volumes issued by the government is *United States Reports, Cases Adjudged in [the] Supreme Court at [the] October Term [date]* (Ju 6.8; Item 741); it is cited as *U.S.* In addition to the full text of the opinions and of the decisions, plus the other editorial matter, the bound volumes contain tables of cases reported and cited, arranged alphabetically; a table of statutes cited, arranged by date (year and month); and a subject index.

The footnote, or citation, form includes bound volume number and page. Thus, in our example, Port of Portland v. United States is cited as 408 *U.S.* 811 (1972); the year in which the decision was rendered (1972) is usually but not always cited (Figures 47 and 48). Like the material included in the *Preliminary Prints*, the *United States Reports* contain decisions *per curiam* and miscellaneous orders.

United States Supreme Court Reports, Lawyers' Edition

The so-called "unofficial" edition published by Lawyers Co-operative Publishing Company is now in its Second Series. In this edition a full summary of each case precedes the report. Headnotes are keyed to the excellent *Digest of United States Supreme Court Reports, Lawyers' Edition*, described in the section on digests. The subject index has a degree of specificity lacking in the official *United States Reports*. Following our example, the form of the citation for this edition would read 33 L.Ed. 2d 723 (see Figure 49, page 258).

Supreme Court Reporter

The other "unofficial" reporter is a service of West Publishing Company. Typical of West's system is the key-numbering of headnote paragraphs. The proper citation if one is using this reporter is 92 S.Ct. 2513 (1972). Note in the example that West, like Lawyers Co-operative, cites all three editions. A table called "Cumulative Statutes Construed" is useful for its citation of state court decisions interpreting federal statutes. *Supreme Court Reporter* is keyed to West's American Digest System (see Figure 50, page 259).[23]

Figure 47

UNITED STATES REPORTS (OFFICIAL EDITION)

PORT OF PORTLAND ET AL. *v.* UNITED STATES
ET AL.

**APPEAL FROM THE UNITED STATES DISTRICT COURT FOR THE
DISTRICT OF OREGON**

No. 70–31.   Argued October 20, 1971—Decided June 29, 1972

The Spokane, Portland & Seattle Railway Co. (SP&S), a subsidiary
of Burlington Northern, and the Union Pacific (UP), sought Interstate Commerce Commission (ICC) approval under § 5 (2) of the
Interstate Commerce Act of a joint acquisition of control of the
Peninsula Terminal Co. (Peninsula), whose tracks provide an access route to Rivergate, an industrial complex being developed by
the Port of Portland, Oregon.   Peninsula would continue to operate as a separate carrier.   The Milwaukee and the Southern Pacific
(SP), the two other line-haul carriers serving Portland, sought
inclusion as joint purchasers of Peninsula, and trackage rights
linking their lines with Peninsula, under §§ 5 (2)(b), (c), and (d)
of the Act.   SP, by a separate proceeding, also sought trackage
linking its lines with Peninsula, under § 3 (5).   The ICC (subject
to conditions to protect the traffic of the other railroads) approved
the purchase of Peninsula by Burlington Northern and UP, but
denied the Milwaukee and SP petitions.   It concluded that the
adverse effects on SP&S and UP of the proposed four-railroad
ownership of Peninsula and accompanying trackage rights would
outweigh the advantages to SP, Milwaukee, and the Rivergate industries.   Milwaukee contends that Condition 24 (a) to the Northern Lines merger, which gave Milwaukee access to the Portland
area over the Burlington Northern-SP&S tracks, required that
Milwaukee be included in the purchase of Peninsula.   *Held:*

1. On the record in this case (which is ambiguous with regard
to many factual and procedural issues) it has not been shown that
the ICC's order authorizing UP and Burlington Northern alone to
acquire Peninsula met the "public interest" standard of § 5 (2).
Pp. 834–842.

(a) In stressing the small share in Peninsula's traffic that
Milwaukee had before the Northern Lines merger, the ICC ignored
any possible increase in that share after Condition 24 (a) took
effect.   Pp. 839–840.

Figure 48

UNITED STATES REPORTS: SUBJECT INDEX

INDEX 967

JUDICIAL REVIEW—Continued.

3. *Line-haul carriers petitioning for inclusion in control of switching railroad—ICC decision—Applicable legal principles.*—In view of uncertainties about the northern access to Portland's Rivergate industrial complex—given the physical limitations of the present facilities of Peninsula Terminal Co.—and the apparent fact that physical operation over Peninsula into Rivergate was not at issue here, approval of the ICC order, with its protective conditions, may still be in the public interest, but the announced grounds for the ICC decision do not comport with the applicable legal principles. Port of Portland v. United States, p. 811.

4. *Line-haul carriers petitioning for inclusion in joint purchase of switching railroad—Market shares and existing traffic.*—In stressing the small share in Peninsula Terminal Co.'s traffic that Milwaukee Railroad had before the Northern Lines Merger, the ICC ignored any possible increase in that share after Condition 24 (a) of the merger took effect. In announcing a principle of preserving the market shares of the two railroads currently connecting with Peninsula, the ICC failed to explain why it was not taking into account the potentially enormous traffic over Peninsula, should Peninsula become the northern route into Portland's Rivergate industrial complex. Port of Portland v. United States, p. 811.

5. *Line-haul carriers seeking joint acquisition of switching railroad—Petitions of inclusion denied by ICC.*—On the record in this case (which is ambiguous with regard to many factual and procedural issues) it has not been shown that the ICC's order authorizing Union Pacific and Burlington Northern alone to acquire control of the Peninsula Terminal Co. met the "public interest" standard of § 5 (2) of the Interstate Commerce Act. Port of Portland v. United States, p. 811.

6. *Petitions for inclusion—Shifting market shares—Anticompetitive effects.*—The ICC's denial of inclusion of the Southern Pacific Transportation Co. and the Milwaukee Railroad because their gain would work a corresponding loss to Burlington Northern and Union Pacific is not a proper approach under § 5 (2) of the Interstate Commerce Act, given the principle that the anticompetitive effects of any § 5 (2) transaction must be explicitly considered. Port of Portland v. United States, p. 811.

JUNIOR COLLEGE PROFESSORS. See **Constitutional Law,** III, 9; **Procedure,** 2.

Figure 49

UNITED STATES SUPREME COURT REPORTS,
LAWYERS' EDITION, 2d SERIES

[408 US 811]
PORT OF PORTLAND et al., Appellants,

v

UNITED STATES et al.

408 US 811, 33 L Ed 2d 723, 92 S Ct 2513

[No. 70–31]

Argued October 20, 1971. Decided June 29, 1972.

SUMMARY

The Interstate Commerce Commission authorized the joint acquisition of a Portland, Oregon, switching railroad by two of the four line-haul railroads serving Portland, and denied petitions by the other two line-haul railroads serving Portland, for inclusion as joint purchasers of the switching railroad, on the ground that to the extent that the latter two railroads might gain by the four-railroad ownership of the switching railroad, the first two railroads would lose (334 ICC 419). A three-judge United States District Court for the District of Oregon affirmed without opinion.

On direct appeal, the United States Supreme Court reversed and remanded with instructions to return the case to the ICC. In an opinion by BLACKMUN, J., expressing the unanimous views of the court, it was held that the ICC's approach failed to consider the anticompetitive aspects of the acquisition, and that the ICC should have explicitly considered the latter two railroads' economic positions as compared with those of the first two railroads, or at least clearly stated why such an inquiry was inappropriate.

POWELL and REHNQUIST, JJ., did not participate.

Briefs of Counsel, p 982, infra.

Figure 50

SUPREME COURT REPORTER

PORT OF PORTLAND v. UNITED STATES   **2513**
Cite as 92 S.Ct. 2513 (1972)

408 U.S. 811, 33 L.Ed.2d 723

PORT OF PORTLAND et al., Appellants,

v.

UNITED STATES et al.

No. 70–31.

Argued Oct. 20, 1971.

Decided June 29, 1972.

Proceeding to review ICC order authorizing joint acquisition of an independent switching railroad at Portland, Oregon, providing entrance route to a modern industrial and port complex by two of four line-haul railroads serving that city and denying petition of other two line-haul railroads to be included as joint purchasers. A three-judge District Court for the District of Oregon affirmed the order without opinion and appeals were taken. The Supreme Court, Mr. Justice Blackmun, held that view of "public interest" taken by ICC, which concluded that adverse effects on former two railroads of proposed four-railroad ownership and accompanying trackage rights would outweigh advantages to latter two railroads, was too narrow and was not consistent with the "public interest" standard found in Interstate Commerce Act.

Reversed and remanded with instructions.

Mr. Justice Powell and Mr. Justice Rehnquist took no part in consideration or decision of the case.

1. Commerce ⚖️85.7

View of "public interest" taken by ICC, which authorized joint acquisition of an independent switching railroad that provided entrance route to a modern industrial and port complex by two of four line-haul railroads serving city and denied petition of two other railroads to be included as joint purchasers on basis that adverse effects on former

two railroads of proposed four-railroad ownership and accompanying trackage rights would outweigh advantages to latter two railroads, was too narrow and was not consistent with the "public interest" standard found in Interstate Commerce Act. Interstate Commerce Act, § 5(2), 49 U.S.C.A. § 5(2).

2. Commerce ⚖️85.7

ICC is obligated to consider anti-competitive effects of any railroad unifications, mergers, and acquisitions of control. Interstate Commerce Act, § 5(2), 49 U.S.C.A. § 5(2).

3. Commerce ⚖️85.7, 120

Line-haul railroads, which sought to be included with other line-haul railroads as joint purchasers of independent switching railroad, were entitled to explicit consideration of their economic positions as compared with that of other line-haul railroads or, at least, a clear statement why such an inquiry was not appropriate. Interstate Commerce Act, § 5(2), 49 U.S.C.A. § 5(2).

4. Commerce ⚖️183

It is not role of the Supreme Court, in reviewing order of ICC, to arrive at its own determination of public interest on facts of the case, but rather the court's appellate function is limited to considering whether the announced grounds for the agency decision comport with applicable legal principles.

Syllabus *

The Spokane, Portland & Seattle Railway Co. (SP&S), a subsidiary of Burlington Northern, and the Union Pacific (UP), sought Interstate Commerce Commission (ICC) approval under § 5(2) of the Interstate Commerce Act of a joint acquisition of control of the Peninsula Terminal Co. (Peninsula), whose tracks provide an access route to Rivergate, an industrial complex being developed by the Port of Portland, Oregon. Peninsula would continue to operate as a

---

* The syllabus constitutes no part of the opinion of the Court but has been prepared by the Reporter of Decisions for the convenience of the reader.

See United States v. Detroit Timber & Lumber Co., 200 U.S. 321, 337, 26 S.Ct. 282, 287, 50 L.Ed. 499.

Records and Briefs

Microcard Editions, an information service based in Washington, D.C., has made available to subscribers *Supreme Court Records and Briefs* on microfiche. Current term subscriptions include full opinion, *per curiam*, and certiorari denied cases.[24] *Briefs*—the arguments presented by opposing attorneys before the Court—include a concise statement of the case, the statement of questions presented for review, the citation of any constitutional provisions, treaties, statutes, ordinances or regulations that are involved, a statement of the grounds on which jurisdiction is invoked, the argument showing the points of fact and of law being presented, and the conclusion. *Records*—the various printed documents related to a case—include relevant docket entries, relevant pleadings, charges, findings or opinions, the judgment, order or decision in question, and any other parts of the record to which the parties wish to direct the Court's attention.

The index in *United States Reports* serves as the index to the microfiche collection. Orders may be placed for previous terms for full opinion, or for *per curiam* and certiorari denied materials as separates, and an *1832-1896 Records and Briefs* series is also being reprinted. A list of cases filmed is included with each shipment, and for potential subscribers a sample fiche is available upon request.

ADMINISTRATION OF THE FEDERAL JUDICIARY

The federal judiciary, like all government agencies and institutions, carries an administrative burden and seeks to improve the business of the courts. To this end, two units of the judicial system have been created to review operational tasks.

Administrative Office of the United States Courts

Created by act of Congress in 1939, the Office has a director and deputy director who are appointed by the Supreme Court. The director, as administrative officer of the United States courts (except the Supreme Court), is required to supervise administrative matters relating to the clerical personnel of the courts, disburse monies appropriated for the operation of the courts, and perform generally a host of duties relating to the courts' processes and activities.

Pursuant to 28 *U.S.C.* 331, a Judicial Conference of the United States is held annually. The director is required to submit to this annual meeting a report on the activities of the Administrative Office. His report, along with the proceedings of the Conference, is issued as the *Annual Report of the Proceedings of the Judicial Conference of the United States [and] Annual Report of the Director of the Administrative Office of the United States Courts* (Ju 10.1; Item 728).[25] A substantial portion of the director's report is devoted to statistical data on various aspects of the lower federal courts and their workloads.

Federal Judicial Center

The Federal Judicial Center was created by act of Congress in 1967. It is required to conduct research and study of the operation of the courts, develop and present for consideration by the Judicial Conference recommendations for improvement of the management of the federal courts, conduct programs of continuing education and training for judges and personnel of the judicial branch, and provide staff, research, and planning assistance to the Judicial Conference and its committees.

Publications of the Center include an *Annual Report* (Ju 13.1) and a General Publications series (Ju 13.2). The Center issues jointly with the Administrative Office a monthly called *Third Branch, A Bulletin of the Federal Courts* (Ju 10.3/2; Item 728-B). Non-depository libraries may secure this periodical from the Federal Judicial Center in Washington, D.C.

REFERENCES

1.   A concise account of the legal distinction among cases that may be tried in state or federal courts is found in a House Judiciary committee print, *The United States Courts: Their Jurisdiction and Work* (Washington: Govt. Print. Off., 1971), p. 11.

2.   See *The Supreme Court: Justice and the Law* (Washington: Congressional Quarterly, Inc., 1973), pp. 6-7, 65-68.

3.   *United States Government Manual*, 1973/74, p. 67.

4.   M. L. Cohen, *Legal Research in a Nutshell* (St. Paul, Minnesota: West Publishing Co., 1971), p. 8.

5.   A useful survey of official publications and secondary sources for public libraries was published in *American Libraries* 4: 360-63 (June 1973).

6.   Cohen (p. 190) is more critical of their utility than are Price and Bitner. The latter analyze the two in depth in Chapter 17 of *Effective Legal Research* (1969 ed.).

7.   Cohen, pp. 40-41.

8.   Price and Bitner, p. 187.

9.   *West's Law Finder: A Research Manual for Lawyers* (St. Paul, Minnesota: West Publishing Co., 1967) provides an explanation of the company's National Reporter System and the way it is related, through the "Key Number" concept, to the American Digest System. See also Price and Bitner, pp. 186-215.

10.   Price and Bitner, p. 209.

11.   Volume 14 of this *Digest* lists Supreme Court decisions citing and construing treaties (see Chapter 7).

12.   If the session law has not been codified, *United States Citations* will note it by date of enactment referencing all subsequent legislative and judicial action.

13.   Looseleaf services, such as Commerce Clearing House's *Standard Federal Tax Reporter*, perform a citator function, especially in the fields of tax and labor cases and statutes.

14.   See Price and Bitner, pp. 146-56; Cohen, pp. 31-33.

15.   Subscribers to *Current Index* were advised to discard issues prior to the January 11, 1974, number because material covered in earlier issues was now indexed in the February 1974 issue of *Index to Legal Periodicals*.

16.   Literally, *stare decisis et non quieta movere* ("to adhere to precedent and not to unsettle things which are settled"); Price and Bitner, pp. 120ff, contains a useful analysis of the doctrine.

17.   Ibid., p. 128. *Per curiam* (literally, "by the court") refers to an unsigned opinion of the court, or an opinion written by the whole court.

18.   Lawyers Co-operative Publishing Company began in 1969 issuing *American Law Reports–Federal: Cases and Annotations*. The service reports the leading decisions of the federal courts as they are handed down, with an analytic annotation following each decision. Annotations are kept current by pocket part supplements, and a *Federal Quick Index* is keyed to, among other ALR tools, *United States Supreme Court Reports, Lawyers' Edition*.

19.   Samuel Eliot Morison, *The Oxford History of the American People* (New York: Oxford University Press, 1965), pp. 321-22.

20.   Congressional Quarterly, Inc., *Guide to the Congress of the United States* (Washington, 1971), p. 270.

21.   In 1973 a joint congressional commission, appointed ad hoc to study the structure of the lower courts system, recommended the creation of two new circuits for the Courts of Appeals in order to lessen the workload.

22.   *Brown v. Allen*, 344 *U.S.* 433 (1953).

23.   For a fuller discussion of federal law reports adumbrated here, the reader should consult Price and Bitner, pp. 127-38.

24.   "Certiorari denied" refers to cases that the Court, after evaluating a preliminary petition, refuses to hear, having determined that no further action is required from it.

25.   The *Report of the Proceedings of the Judicial Conference of the United States* (Ju 10.10; Item 729) can be secured as a separate publication.

ACRONYMS, ABBREVIATIONS, AND CITATIONS

ACRL	Association of College and Research Libraries
AEC	Atomic Energy Commission
AID	Agency for International Development
Am. Jur. 2d	*American Jurisprudence Second*
ALA	American Library Association
A.L.R.	*American Law Reports Annotated*
ASI	*American Statistics Index*
BLS	Bureau of Labor Statistics
BNDD	Bureau of Narcotics and Dangerous Drugs
CAB	Civil Aeronautics Board
CCH	Commerce Clearing House
CCM	Crowell Collier and Macmillan, Inc.
CFR	*Code of Federal Regulations*
CIA	Central Intelligence Agency
CIJE	*Current Index to Journals in Education*
CIP	Cataloging-in-Publication
CIS	Congressional Information Service
C.J.S.	*Corpus Juris Secundum*
Cong. News	*United States Code Congressional and Administrative News*
COSATI	Committee on Scientific and Technical Information
CPI	*Consumer Price Index*
CQ	Congressional Quarterly
CRS	Congressional Research Service

DA	Department of the Army
DA Pam	Department of the Army Pamphlets
DDC	Defense Documentation Center
DocEx	Documents Expediting Project
DoD	Department of Defense
DSA	Defense Supply Agency
EO	Executive Order
EPA	Environmental Protection Agency
ERIC	Educational Resources Informational Center
ERIC/CLIS	ERIC Clearinghouse on Library and Information Science
ERIC/IR	ERIC Clearinghouse on Information Resources
ERS	Economic Research Service
ESSA	Environmental Science Services Administration
FAA	Federal Aviation Administration
FBI	Federal Bureau of Investigation
FBIS	Foreign Broadcast Information Service
F.C.A.	*Federal Code Annotated*
FCC	Federal Communications Commission
FDA	Food and Drug Administration
Fed	Federal Reserve System
FLC	Federal Library Committee
FPC	Federal Power Commission
FR	*Federal Register*
FTC	Federal Trade Commission
GAO	General Accounting Office
GODORT	Government Documents Round Table
GPO	Government Printing Office
GRA	*Government Report Announcements*
GRI	*Government Reports Index*
GSA	General Services Administration
H. Con. Res.	House Concurrent Resolution
H. doc.	House Document
HEW	Department of Health, Education, and Welfare
H.J. Res.	House Joint Resolution
H.R.	House Bill
H. Res.	House Resolution
H. rp.	House Report
HUD	Department of Housing and Urban Development
I & N	Immigration and Naturalization
ICC	Interstate Commerce Commission
IRS	Internal Revenue Service
JAG	Judge Advocate General
JCP	Joint Committee on Printing
LC	Library of Congress
L. Ed.	*United States Supreme Court Reports, Lawyers' Edition*

LRTS	Library Resources and Technical Services
MA	Manpower Administration
MC	*Monthly Catalog of United States Government Publications*
NARS	National Archives and Records Service
NASA	National Aeronautics and Space Administration
NBS	National Bureau of Standards
NGUS	National Guard of the United States
NLRB	National Labor Relations Board
NOAA	National Oceanic and Atmospheric Administration
NSF	National Science Foundation
NTIS	National Technical Information Service
NUC/GP	*National Union Catalog of U.S. Government Publications Received by Depository Libraries*
OBR	*Overseas Business Reports*
OE	Office of Education
OMB	Office of Management and Budget
PAIS	*Public Affairs Information Service. Bulletin*
PL	*Price List*
PL	Public Law
RIE	Research in Education
S.	Senate Bill
SBA	Small Business Administration
SCIM	Selected Categories in Microfiche
S. Con. Res.	Senate Concurrent Resolution
SCORE	Service Corps of Retired Executives
S. Ct.	*Supreme Court Reporter*
S. doc.	Senate Document
SEC	Securities and Exchange Commission
SESA	Social and Economic Statistics Administration
S. J. Res.	Senate Joint Resolution
SMSA	Standard Metropolitan Statistical Area
S. Res.	Senate Resolution
S. rp.	Senate Report
SSA	Social Security Administration
STAR	*Scientific and Technical Aerospace Reports*
Stat.	*Statutes At Large*
SUDOCS	Superintendent of Documents
TAB	*Technical Abstract Bulletin*
TIAS	*Treaties and Other International Acts*
U.S.	*United States Reports*
USAR	United States Army Reserve
U.S.C.	*United States Code*
U.S.C.A.	*United States Code Annotated*
UST	*United States Treaties and Other International Agreements*
VA	Veterans Administration
VISTA	Volunteers in Service to America

NAME/SUBJECT INDEX

TITLE/SERIES INDEX